Praise for *Cerridwen*

Hughes retrieves gems of wisdom to form a well-researched portrait of Cerridwen and one that is rich in mythology, language, and landscape. What is offered here is a sophisticated exploration of Cerridwen that seamlessly bridges the gap between scholarly inquiry and experiential gnosis.

—Olivia Church, author of *Isis: Great of Magic*

As a first-language Welsh speaker, Hughes's intimacy with this original Middle Welsh source material has enabled him to speak with authenticity and authority about a goddess who has been both misunderstood and misrepresented for a millennium.

—Liz Riley Jones, author of the Hiraeth Trilogy

A thrilling and deep immersion into the mysteries of Cerridwen and the Bardic tradition that has the power to transform the reader with its inspiration and its scholarship.

—Philip Carr-Gomm, author of *Druid Mysteries*

By offering so much of his personal experience, research, and knowledge, Kristoffer opens a doorway to that sacred place where the worlds of humankind and deep mystery meet.

—Lisa & Anton Stewart, authors of *Simply Wicca*

This book will help you to discover a sacred relationship with the keeper of the cauldron, a story as relevant to us today as it was in the past.

—Adrienne Piggott, lead singer of Spiral Dance

An extraordinary, breathtaking experience channeling Cerridwen's solicitous energy—a journey for the mind and soul.

—Caryl Bryn, award-winning author
of *Hwn ydy'r Llais, Tybad?*

Kristoffer brings Cerridwen into the present, where she touches not only the world around her, but also those who reach out to her.

—Jean (Drum) Pagano, Archdruid ADF

While taking care to present the historical sources, Kristoffer Hughes has also conveyed his own deep insight into this ancient, yet perpetually new, mythology. Read it, learn from it, and enjoy it.

—Dr. Gwilym Morus-Baird, Celtic scholar

Kristoffer has given us all the elements we need in order to enter into a meaningful relationship with Cerridwen, inviting the Awen which that relationship brings.

—Tiffany Lazic, author of *The Great Work*

As a first-language Welsh speaker, a native of Anglesey, and a practicing Druid with over twenty years of involvement with Taliesinic mysteries, Hughes offers a unique perspective and a vision that is simultaneously profound and accessible.

—Will Parker, author of *The Four Branches of the Mabinogi*

If you want to meet Cerridwen, drink from her cauldron, and be inspired by the Awen, this is the book for you.

—John Beckett, author of *The Path of Paganism*

Kristoffer Hughes dives deep, both into the academic and the mystical aspects of Cerridwen.

—Cerri Lee, Pagan artist

With every page you will walk in the footsteps of the bards who knew her, and know her still. Then, seated before the great cauldron, you will meet with Cerridwen herself—muse, goddess, keeper of the cauldron, inspirer of bards and mother of Awen.

—Damh the Bard, Pagan musician and pendragon of the Order of Bards, Ovates and Druids

Kristoffer Hughes breathes new life into the ever-evolving story of Cerridwen, bringing her lessons and gifts into the twenty-first century and reinstating her as the preeminent deity of Wales and the Isles of the Mighty.

—Gwion Raven, author of *The Magick of Food*

An incredible and groundbreaking dive into the mythology and practice surrounding the Welsh goddess Cerridwen.

—Laura Tempest Zakroff, author of *Sigil Witchery*

Destined to become a classic among Celtic scholars and spiritual practitioners alike.

—Jhenah Telyndru, author of *The Mythic Moons of Avalon*

CERRIDWEN

© Bob Jones

About the Author

Kristoffer Hughes (Wales) is chief of the Anglesey Druid Order, a Mount Haemus scholar, and a member of the Order of Bards, Ovates and Druids. He is a teacher, writer, workshop leader, and guest speaker at Pagan conferences, camps, and festivals throughout the United Kingdom, United States, and Europe. Hughes has also contributed to Welsh and English television and radio. Videos, soundbytes, and contact information for the author can be found here:

WWW.ANGLESEYDRUIDORDER.CO.UK

Celtic
Goddess
of
Inspiration

CERRIDWEN

KRISTOFFER HUGHES

Llewellyn Publications
WOODBURY, MINNESOTA

FIRST EDITION
Third Printing, 2021
Book design by Rebecca Zins
Cover design by Shira Atakpu
Cover illustration by Fletcher Sibthorp/Debut Art Ltd.
Interior illustrations by Llewellyn Art Department
Llewellyn Publications is a registered trademark of Llewellyn Worldwide Ltd.

Library of Congress Cataloging-in-Publication Data
Names: Hughes, Kristoffer, author.
Title: Cerridwen : Celtic goddess of inspiration / Kristoffer Hughes.
Description: FIRST EDITION. | Woodbury, Minnesota : Llewellyn Publications,
2021. | Includes bibliographical references and index. | Summary: "The
witch goddess Cerridwen is the focus of devotion and reverence among
witches and Pagans around the world. This book traces Cerridwen's roots
through layers of history and myth, and it provides hands-on exercises
and visionary rites to help you realize her power in your own magical
practice. Welsh Druid Kristoffer Hughes shows you how to evoke the magic
of ecstatic poetry and song as you join the lineage of magical bards who
have explored the secrets of Awen and Cerridwen's cauldron of
inspiration"—Provided by publisher.
Identifiers: LCCN 2020053588 (print) | LCCN 2020053589 (ebook) | ISBN
9780738763828 (paperback) | ISBN 9780738764238 (ebook)
Subjects: LCSH: Mythology, Welsh. | Ceridwen (Welsh mythology) | Goddesses,
Celtic—Wales. | Witches—Wales.
Classification: LCC BL980.G7 H8355 2021 (print) | LCC BL980.G7 (ebook) |
DDC 299/.1612114—dc23
LC record available at https://lccn.loc.gov/2020053588
LC ebook record available at https://lccn.loc.gov/2020053589

Llewellyn Publications
A Division of Llewellyn Worldwide Ltd.
2143 Wooddale Drive
Woodbury, MN 55125-2989

www.llewellyn.com

Printed in the United States of America

Contents

CONTENTS

Stirring the Cauldron:
Ritual & Practise 259

◆ ◆ ◆

I Cerridwen—Mam yr Awen

Prologue

The flicker of moonlight on water appeared like molten silver; the brilliance of each wave crest stirred my heart and imagination, for they appeared like creatures. Unknown and alien, they would rise from the fathoms of the lake and sip at the glistening rays of our nearest satellite. Their eventual lapping on the shores would sing another song as two worlds collided, and yet there upon the lake's inky surface stood the epitome of an even deeper world.

Her face was obscured by the fluid fabric of her immense cloak that moved about her form sensuously, making love to her bodily contours and each molecule of water that caressed her. Tendrils of black fabric stretched out in all directions about her, seemingly unaffected by the constant pull of land to water. The trees whispered about me, their chitter-chatter telling of other mysteries unknown to me, and yet we shared something within this moment: they understood what I was seeing, and I, in a language alien to me, could understand their connection to this being that stood impossibly upon the lake—not within it but upon its surface.

The figure on the lake moved her right arm, long, slender, and black as night, and held aloft a staff of darkened wood, which twisted up from the lake's surface. Her presence felt as ancient as the valley that surrounded me. Clouds passed over the moon, and the silver crests became jet-black and almost solid, to the extent that even their lapping changed its tune. A sigh—audible, loud even—seemed to rise from somewhere...the lake? The being? The trees? Who could tell, but something stirred, something changed. A sudden flash to my right and a burst of yellow appeared in the curtain of night that hung adorned with stars in the deep blue Welsh sky. It was accompanied by a delayed boom as something unknown sucked the sound from the moment, only to expand it back into being a second later. Three bodies of light streaked across the sky towards the sharp peaks of Aran Benllyn. Mouths gaped in awe at the sight. From the depths of space, meteor lights burst into our world, bringing with them stories of unknown places a million light-years away. Before us stood someone from another world, and yet at this juncture they expressed themselves here, on the shores of Lake Bala. The world of humankind, the world of origins, and the world of deep mystery collided.

The figure lifted both arms—had she seen the meteor crash to the mountains behind her or had she sensed it, did she call it? What magic was this? In awe, I fell to my knees before the figure on the lake and whispered:

> *O Cerridwen,*
> *Duwies yr Awen,*
> *Ceidwad y Pair,*
> *Rho dy Awenyddiaeth*
> *A'r fy siwrne*
> *Ac ar fy ngwaith.*[1]

> *O Cerridwen,*
> *Goddess of Awen,*
> *Keeper of the Cauldron,*
> *Bless me with the light of Awen*
> *On my journey*
> *And on my work.*

---

1 Search YouTube for my channel—Kristoffer Hughes—for sound files of all Welsh entries in this book.

The hard pebbles dug into my knees, and I winced in discomfort, momentarily breaking the illusion of solitude that I had felt to this point. I became intensely aware of other figures around me, calling, singing, whispering, and crying. The sploshing sound of cold water as others entered the lake momentarily obscured my vision of she who stood upon the inky surface. I pulled myself back into focus, and there she was again: Cerridwen, keeper of the cauldron, goddess of inspiration, testing, and transformation. Slowly I arose to my knees and entered the cold waters of her lake to stand before her, and there to ask my question, which was related to what you now hold in your hands. Should I write it? Should I expand on what I had previously penned?

Her answer was as clear as day, unexpected and momentarily disarming: "If not you, then who? If not now, when?"

Before I realised what was slipping from my lips, I heard myself say, "Oh, come on, that was Hillel—he was the Jewish scholar who said that!"

To which she replied, "Even he drank from my cauldron, albeit he called it something else."

So I guess I had my answer. It made me giggle. I bowed to the lady on the lake and walked steadily backwards out of the frigid waters as others walked past me to seek her counsel. The clouds parted yet again, and the creatures of the crests returned to play along the lake's choppy surface.

◆ ◆ ◆

You might wonder that the above account may appear fantastical or even purely fictional, but I can assure you that it was not. This was yet another year where over seventy people descended to the shores of Lake Bala (Llyn Tegid) in North Wales, the legendary home of Cerridwen and her family, the location for the saga of the tale of the birth of Taliesin, to immerse in ritual and vision. Cerridwen really did stand on the lake's surface, although beneath the fabric stood an actual human being, a person who gave up their identity to allow for something else to take her shape and form temporarily. This was an act of magic and devotion to a deity that has long been a part of my life.

Since I first stepped foot onto the path of Paganism in the early 1990s, Cerridwen has been there. As a child and a teenager, Cerridwen was there. In the pen-and-ink drawings of Margaret Jones and the dancing words of Gwyn Thomas in their illustrated history of Taliesin and Cerridwen, she was there.[2] In this book, my hope is to explore the nature of Cerridwen in the hope that how I was inspired may in turn inspire you. Together we will explore where she came from, who she is, what the past can teach us about her, and, perhaps most appropriately, how she is perceived and worked with in the present day.

This book contains a lot of history and scholarship necessary to delve into the cauldron of Cerridwen's making, for her evolution is as colourful and varied as the history of the land that gave rise to her name. Whilst the historical and scholarly component is important, this is also a book that is indicative of the power of relationship. In essence, this is not Cerridwen's story alone. It is the story of Cerridwen, the people and traditions of Wales, and me, and my hope is that this will also become a part of your story.

---

2   Gwyn Thomas, *Chwedl Taliesin*, darluniwyd gan Margaret Jones (Caerdydd: Gwasg Prifysgol Cymru, 1992).

Introduction

Eight years ago I wrote a book called *From the Cauldron Born: Exploring the Magic of Welsh Legend and Lore*, and in it I explored a single tale from Wales that tells the story of the birth of Taliesin. Within it the reader encounters what has become a goddess of the New Age, Cerridwen; alas, the space that I had within that book was limited and my exploration of Cerridwen condensed to a single chapter, albeit threads of her were stretched through the entire book. I felt that I did not do her great justice, and I have wanted to expand on that ever since. To those familiar with my previous works, there is much in this tome that will feel familiar and much that will be new. I have written this book to expand on *From the Cauldron Born*; to some extent it is its sequel.

So, who am I and why exactly am I writing this book? My own spiritual practise follows a Welsh Druid path. I am the current chief of the Anglesey Druid Order in North Wales, the ancestral seat of the ancient British Druids. We are a mytho-centric order, where we glean spiritual teachings and practises from the mythologies of Britain preserved by the Welsh. We are an order immersed in a living mythological landscape, where the spirits, beings, and gods of the old legends feel very much present and alive. We utilise scholarly and visionary tools to explore the function of mythology and the beings that inhabit that landscape, and we do so in a way that makes them relevant to twenty-first-century practitioners of Druidry and Celtic-inspired Paganism. The aim of this book is to provide you with an in-depth exploration of Cerridwen: where she came from, the landscape and peoples that perpetuated her, and who she is today.

The book will commence with the physicality and material evidence for Cerridwen's existence through various guises and over vast periods of time. Here I will delve into the mythologies that refer to her, medieval bardic poetry, and the landscape that she is connected to. We will also look at the relationships she had with other Welsh mythological figures. This section will focus on the scholarly, where I explore the material aspect of Cerridwen's evolution. Here, location is also of great importance, for Cerridwen did not arise and develop in a vacuum, but rather from the moist green mythological and rugged landscape of Wales; this in itself tells us much of the deity that she has become. There is a lot of information in the early chapters of this book and a lot to take in, but I offer it to honour the enormous span of time and the people who recorded Cerridwen's name and function. It is important to me as a Welsh person that these systems are honoured as the spirit of preservation that guarded and maintained this material.

Eventually I will move steadily away from the scholarly, albeit I shall not entirely abandon it, and look at Cerridwen in relation to deep mystery, profundity, and what she can teach us about what lies within the cauldron's belly. In this part we look deeper into the mysteries of origin and of the power that Cerridwen arises from. I will also be exploring the progression of Cerridwen from muse to witch to goddess. Here I will focus on the expression of mystery and explore the nature of the breath of Awen, the spirit of inspiration—this is the place of deep initiation and the precursor to transformation. In this realm we will explore Cerridwen's function within modern witchcraft.

The closing chapters will be focused entirely on devotional practises, prayers, inner journeys, and invocations. This will be the nuts and bolts of modern daily practise and how we integrate Cerridwen and her function into our everyday spirituality.

The Function of Magic

Whilst a significant chunk of this book is an exploration of where Cerridwen came from and the systems that gave rise to the creation of the name itself and her function, it is also a book of magic and practise. There are times within this book where I will ask you to stop and consider the information that you have read and journey inwardly to discover the magic within those concepts. I will primarily do this through the power of sigils. Truth be told, I am a terrible and horrible meditator. I have struggled with meditation since I first started this path—my mind will wander, I get bored, and I have tried every technique and method one can find, but to no avail. I hasten to add that I do not believe I am alone in this.

So, with that, I will not ask you to meditate as such but rather to contemplate, using sigils that capture the essence and spirit of what is being considered. Combined with imagined scenes and the power of your imagination, the sigils will come to life and capture the essence of what I am describing to you. I find this technique suits my fickle brain far more effectively than trying to meditate on a subject. The sigil contains all the details of the written description preceding it, so all you need do is gaze at the image and contemplate.

The Dilemma of Deity

Within my spiritual practise Cerridwen is perceived as a goddess, but what exactly is a goddess and do they in fact even exist? This book does not expect you to conform to the manner by which I work with and perceive deity. There are a number of ways that people may develop relationship with what some may refer to as a god or goddess, and neither is right or wrong. In that spirit, I do not expect you, the reader, to even be a theist, or an individual that works with deity. Cerridwen is flexible enough to be a psychological component to those who may be atheistic or nontheists. The rise of a figure to the status of deity is a process referred to as apotheosis, and this is important, for often the main complaint and criticism of modern-day Pagan practitioners is that they connect to and are often devoted to deities that may not ever have been identified as such in the past. I shall delve deeper into the function of apotheosis in the coming chapters.

From my perspective, I am a polytheist, and the deities of Celtic Britain are very much a living part of my spiritual expression. All of this will be explored in this book in direct relation to Cerridwen.

Language and the Celts

There is a lot of Welsh in this book, but I ask that you do not despair nor lose heart, for Welsh is not as difficult as people are often led to believe. The Welsh language has the benefit of being phonetic, meaning every single letter is pronounced, unlike many in English. English is my second language, and as such I can tell you from first-hand experience how difficult learning English was; whilst the structure of the English language has rules, there are also numerous exceptions to those rules, which is not the case in the Welsh language.

To not include the Welsh language would do the material and Cerridwen a disservice, for it is the primary language that served to preserve, protect, and disseminate the tales, legends, and poetry that refer to her and her family. But before I commence with the main body of work, it is important to provide you with a brief introduction to what constitutes the term Celtic and what the Welsh language actually is.

Modern Welsh is a widely spoken language for 875,600 people, with at least 100,000 first-language Welsh speakers residing in other parts of the world.[3] The language itself evolved from what linguists refer to as the Indo-European family of languages. It is believed that Proto-Indo-European came into being around six thousand years ago and evolved into the cultural melting pot of Europe and parts of Asia. As the people moved steadily across the European landscape, language differentiated into several dialects influenced by the people and their connection to the various lands they settled upon. Indo-European is commonly asserted to have nine branches with various offspring. Celtic is one of those branches, which in turn splits common Celtic

---

3   See https://gov.wales/welsh-language-data-annual-population-survey-2019.

and further into two family groups of related but distinct Celtic tongues, insular Celtic (of the British and Irish isles) and continental Celtic, e.g., Celto-Iberian. The insular Celtic languages in turn are categorised as Brittonic or P Celtic, consisting of Breton, Cornish, and Welsh, and the other member being Goidelic or Q Celtic, consisting of Irish Gaelic, Manx Gaelic, and Scots Gaelic.

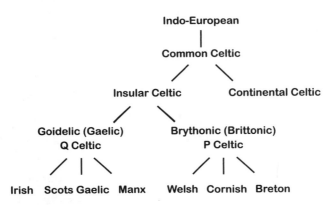

Whilst biological archaeology can express much about the movement and origins of people, there is another avenue of human exploration: that of culture. The term Celtic does not wholly apply to the archaeology of blood and genetics alone but refers to a cultural continuum that reaches back to the distant past whilst simultaneously being firmly rooted and given expression in the present. All too frequently the term Celtic is utilised in a past-tense manner, and often this is to the expense of the realisation that the Celts are also a people of the now, of today. I am a Celt and my first language is Welsh, which in turn is defined as a Celtic language and as such is connected to the subtle streams of cultural expression that reach back almost three thousand years. Many of the symbols, myths, legends, traditions, and subtle regional artistic expressions of my culture are inherently Celtic; they voice the sum totality of that line of consistency and quiddity.

It is doubtful that any of the perceived ancient Celtic cultures would have identified as Celtic, but there are strong idiosyncrasies that connect these people to each other, such as the use of torcs, the veneration of the head, commonality of artistic style, depositions of precious objects into water, and the style and décor of coins. Particularly telling is the fact that many of these styles of expression remained even after the disruptive Romanisation of the ancient European world. All of this gives credence to a commonality of culture.[4]

Language is a living thing, it is not a relic, and cultures are primarily identified by their use of language. Whilst the Welsh language has evolved and developed over centuries, it still is at its heart a Celtic language similar to that spoken on these lands during the time of the Iron Age Druids, around 2,100 years ago. In fact, the Welsh language is an example, and a rare one at that, of an indigenous language that continues to be widely spoken today. The islands of Britain have many languages that decorate it and add flavour and diversity to our glorious landscape, but it is the Welsh language that has the oldest roots reaching deep into the soil of Britain—a language that J. R. R. Tolkein described as "the senior language of the men of Britain."[5] It is something that was birthed on mainland Europe and then given expression and colour, vibrancy, and vitality by the connection that early Britons had to these islands. In this way it is organic, and the current regional dialects and subtle variations give further credence to a tongue that was very much influenced by the land itself.

However fickle and complicated the term Celtic may appear in its historical countenance, in the twenty-first century it is a term that millions of people who occupy the western flanks of Europe—from Galicia in Spain across Brittany, Cornwall, Wales, the Isle of Man, Ireland, and Scotland (particularly the western Scottish islands)—connect with as a functionality of their identity.[6] This identity, whilst sociopolitical for many, is a cauldron of bubbling influences that speaks of a deep, ancient connection to the land. For a people that were often displaced and forced into the western regions of the islands, slaughtered and subjugated to shame and humiliation, we are still here. Even as recently as the nineteenth century, people were humiliated for speaking Welsh in the classrooms, owing to the pecuniary interests of

---

4   Aldhouse-Green and Howell, *Celtic Wales*, 1–12.
5   Davies, *The Welsh Language*, 1–13.
6   Aldhouse-Green and Howell, *Celtic Wales*, 13.

educational institutions to boycott the Welsh language for economic reasons. Simply for speaking their native tongue, Welsh children were often forced to wear a large wooden plaque about their necks called the Welsh Not.[7]

Fundamental to this sense of survival is our identity as peoples who shelter beneath the Celtic umbrella, which in and of itself is an important and deeply healing component of our centuries-long search for rootedness and meaning.[8] Today music, art, language, and literature unite a people connected by something deeper than blood alone: the spirit of Celtica. Whilst there continues to be much heated argument in academia as to the use and validity of the term Celtic, to an extent the ship of Celticism has sailed, and a new Celtic dawn has risen high into the skies of Western Europe.

With all this in mind, whenever you come across the term Celtic within the pages that follow, I am referring to Celtic as it is used and understood by millions of Celts today, myself included, not to a romantic and idealised version of the past but something that is present right now, in this time. In a manner, the term Celtic is similar in nature to the term Pagan: it is an umbrella. In that spirit, "Pagan" can shelter and give meaning to those that walk beneath it—Wiccan, Asatru, Druid, etc. "Celtic" has a similar function: it gives shelter and meaning to the living languages and cultures of Celtica today.

As such, Cerridwen is a living aspect of this cultural continuum, which stretches deep into the distant past. She has developed and evolved, changing her shape and form to suit and fit the needs and wonderings of the people. She has developed in the same manner that the Welsh language has evolved over so many centuries. There is an element of her that transcends location, and her spirit is truly universal, but it is also important and honourable to be mindful of the cultural keys that gave her function and form, and this has been preserved for everyone to enjoy by the Welsh.

As a Welsh person, I can say that we do not own this material nor the keys that provide access to Cerridwen's mysteries. We are simply custodians of it, caretakers and guardians, not in a possessive sense, for no inspiration could

---

7 Davies, *The Welsh Language*, 75–76.
8 Collis, "The Origin and Spread of the Celts," 25.

be gleaned from that. Rather, our function as a people is to assist others who are thus moved to discover the beauty, magic, and transformative qualities of the Celtic heart and its deities and spirits whilst honouring our foundations. It is also vitally important to develop nonappropriative practises whilst keeping the source, development, and locality-specific idiosyncrasies of the material in mind. This will lead to a sincere and honourable way to simultaneously respect and work with the material. The often-contentious subject of cultural appropriation and the development of nonappropriative practises will be explored later in this book.

A pronunciation guide is offered to you at the back of this book. In itself this can be a little two-dimensional, therefore, in addition, online videos of the poems, words, terms, and phrases are available for you to watch and listen; please see the resources section at the conclusion of this book for details. These will offer you a deeper insight into the beauty of the language. I also ask that where Welsh versions of devotional practises and prayers are given, you give it your best shot and have a go—nobody is going to judge you, and in my experience the gods certainly like a trier. When using the Welsh language, use the resources I offer and listen deeply to the sounds and the patterns within the sounds, for these are what you will be imitating.

My hope and wish to inspire you is infused into every word of dry ink on paper that follows—every single one of them is written with the intent that maybe, just maybe, you will be moved to develop your own relationship with Cerridwen. When I tell you with utmost conviction that it has totally transformed my life, I do not jest nor say it lightly. For when I sipped from her cauldron, I was destined to never be the same again, and ever since my life has been a rollercoaster of magical experiences. Are you willing to take a similar journey?

Kristoffer Hughes
Isle of Anglesey, Wales
SPRING 2020

At the Chair of the Bard

In the days of Arthur, a nobleman lived in the land called today Penllyn. His name was Tegid Foel, and his homestead, according to the story, was a body of water, known today as Llyn Tegid. And the story says that he also had a wife and to her was given the name Cerridwen, and she was learned in the three crafts, which are known as magic, witchcraft, and divination. Also, the tale says that Tegid and Cerridwen had a son, whose looks, shape, and form were terribly ugly. They named him Morfran, meaning sea crow, but owing to his ugliness they eventually called him Afagddu, or utter darkness.

Because of their son's wretchedness, his mother became very sad in her heart, for there was no obvious means by which her son would win acceptance amongst the learned men of the day unless he beheld qualities markedly different from his looks. And so to deal with this matter, she turned her thoughts towards her craft to see how best she could make him in possession of the prophetic spirit and a great storyteller of the world to come.

After much labouring, she discovered that there was a way of bestowing upon him such knowledge by using the powers of the herbs of the earth and the effort of a human. This was what she must do: gather certain herbs and plants upon certain days and hours, and cast them all into a cauldron of water, then arrange the cauldron upon a fire. This had to be warmed continuously in order to boil the cauldron night and day for as long as a year and a day. Within this allotted time, she would see that three drops, of all the multitude of herbs, would spring forth, and upon whichever man they would fall, she would see that he would be all-knowing in all arts and full of the prophetic spirit. She would also see that the remaining liquid of the herbs, except for the three drops which came before, shall be the most powerful poison there could be in the world, and this shall cause the cauldron to shatter and spill its poison upon the earth.

The body of the story tells how she did collect great numbers of herbs of the earth; these she put into the cauldron of water and placed upon a fire. The story says that she took in an old blind man to stir the cauldron and tend it. The name of the boy who led the old man was Gwion Bach; to him Cerridwen set the task of stoking the fire beneath the cauldron. In this manner, each kept to his task, tending the fire and stirring the cauldron, whilst Cerridwen kept it full of water and herbs until the end of a year and a day.

At that time Cerridwen took her son Morfran and placed him close to the cauldron to receive the drops when their hour of readiness arrived for them to leap out of the cauldron. In that time Cerridwen set her haunches down to rest; in that time she happened to sleep, and during that time the three amazing drops leapt from the cauldron and fell on Gwion Bach, who had pushed Morfran out of the way. And at that the cauldron let out a scream and, owing to the poison, it shattered. At that Cerridwen awoke from her slumber and was enraged to see Gwion, who was filled with knowledge. Gwion in his wisdom sensed her temper was poisonous and that she intended to destroy him totally as soon as she discovered how he had deprived her son of the remarkable drops. At this he took to his feet and fled. Cerridwen, upon recovering from her madness, discovered by enquiring of her son the long account of how Gwion had driven him away from the place she had stationed him.

Cerridwen in her fury ran from the house, her heart pounding in anger that her son, her only son, had been cheated by the young one who had done nothing worthy of the gifts of the cauldron. The skies darkened beneath her anger as clouds billowed and blackened above her with peels of thunder followed by streaks of white-hot light. She lifted her skirts and took to pursuing the young one, who fled for the foothills of the Berwyn Mountains.

A scream rose in Cerridwen's chest as the sight before her laid claim to Gwion's possession of the three blessed drops. His arms fell forward with palms striking the ground, and he appeared to run with haste on all four of his limbs. His clothing wisped about him as grey mist and rose almost as smoke into the cooling damp air. A stub of a tail appeared at his rump and his legs buckled and changed their form; his skin morphed from pink and beige into the rusty brown of the soil. With an otherworldly crack his form collapsed in on itself and became smaller. Long, sharp ears sprouted from the head, and with that Gwion Bach had vanished, and in his place ran a hare.

Gwion did not foresee the power of Cerridwen, for the scream that rose from her lungs punched the air about him, a scream like no other and a scream only a mother could invoke. The clap of thunder above the running hare startled the creature to momentarily cower near the ground, and in that moment it turned its head to observe its hunter. With her hands raised she summoned the mighty one of the skies, Taranis, the god of thunder. An eight-spoked wheel appeared in the clouds above and spun furiously. The ensuing lightning blinded the hare, who cowered further as if seeking to become one with the wet grass. The burst of light and simultaneous crack blasted through the crown of Cerridwen's head. She screamed as her clothing vaporised, her teeth elongated, and her form descended nearer and closer to the ground. Her mouth in a frozen scream lengthened into a snout, and without breaking her pace for a mere second, Cerridwen's form became that of a slim greyhound. The hare took to its feet and ran with every strength of its being, but the breath of the greyhound was nearing; she would catch him and she would tear him apart, limb from limb—she would have her vengeance. Her heart threatened to tear the ribs of her chest apart, the hills steepened, but she would feel her teeth sink into the hare's hot flesh. The hare turned on its hind legs and headed downhill towards a river that flowed back into the depths of the lake. In hot pursuit she ran.

The River Ayrwen loomed into sight, her still waters reflecting the blue of the sky and offering sanctuary to the spirit that now inhabited the hare. The hare turned sharply to reach the river. Its heart pounded dreadfully against its ribs; it could feel the rabid spittle and dank breath from the greyhound. But somehow it knew what must be done, and what could be done, and as it neared the very edge of the river bank, the hare leaped into the air.

The greyhound growled a deep, guttural sound in surprise and shock. Gwion, on the other hand, felt something stir within him—a light from a depth within him that he had never felt or had awareness of previously. He saw the image of a salmon in his mind and expanded that image outwards. He felt a shift in his shape and form and felt the soft hair shuffle off his nimble frame. Bones cracked and his focus changed, arms and legs vanished within themselves and still he occupied the air. But the air was of no benefit to him. He felt his lungs gasp in desperation for air that he could not grasp. The water—dive for the water!

As he felt the first wetness of the river about him, his transformation was complete. Within a single moment he knew what his new body could do: his lungs opened to receive vital breath from a source that was all at once familiar and yet oddly alien. The muscles in his new tail swooped from side to side, causing him to speed through the river. But she was in pursuit—he could sense her, and yet he took advantage of the brief moment of confusion he had caused her.

Cerridwen pursued him. As he leaped into the air, she barked angrily as his fur sloughed off his back, revealing scales beneath. Lights dazzled about the form as it transformed into a sleek salmon. Her powerful hind legs pushed her from the ground in one leap, she was in the air, words spilled from her mind to utter as growls from the throat of the greyhound, and yet they were words of magic and power. She pushed against herself and in a sudden flash of blinding light she had transformed. It was an otter that crashed through the surface of the water.

She saw him immediately, there before her, his tail flapping madly against the currents. He was no match to her power, no match to a creature designed to pursue and hunt down its prey. She would consume him. Her anger boiled within her, sending violent shock waves through the water. Other creatures of the river were propelled away from her course.

Every sense in his sleek body told him that he was losing the chase, and yet the fear in his body was replaced with a deep knowing. He sensed the other beings about him, small and large; he felt the presence of something greater than the river itself, and yet it was a part of the very fabric of the water. It was Ayrwen, the goddess of the river. A sudden glint above him caught his eye, and as he turned slightly he saw her coming for him. A terror rose in his chest as her mouth opened to reveal long sharp teeth that would surely shred his flesh apart. He knew what must be done. He reached down into the depths of his being and pushed against himself. In one swift motion he shot upwards through the water towards the surface, bursting forth into the bright sunlight, gasping at the intrusion of atmosphere.

Gills snapped shut, dissolving into new flesh that was neither meat nor fish. The sense of pure air blew in a space within the creature that ascended into the sky. A shattering pain coursed through its body as scales were shed and the sharp quill of feathers exploded in an instant from soft flesh. As the salmon's snout atrophied, a beak broke forth and opened to allow a scream to rise from the newly formed lungs within its body. Scales and bones and flesh fell from the sky, and from the falling carnage a tiny wren flew up into the great blue yonder. As the new shape took hold, Gwion opened his mouth to sing the song of the wren. He heard his kin beneath him sing in unison. He knew the smallest of places, the hidden spaces in hedgerow and undergrowth. He felt the reverence of the Druids, who called him the King of Birds. The song in his chest was as pure as the light of the sun and carried within it an ancient knowing.

But his joy at this newfound form was short-lived. A piercing squawk rang out beneath him. He dared a glance towards the river below to see brown fur and bones falling like a dark cloud from a winged creature fifty times his size. Piercing yellow eyes filled with rage soared towards him, the outstretched wings a perilous sight that held beneath them the deadliest of talons. Unable to gain significant height, Gwion flitted between low-lying branches and hedgerows, confounding the hawk, who cried in anger and loathing. The sound of her beating wings invoked a terror in Gwion that compelled him deeper into the hedgerows and into the darker places. Yet the hawk kept at him. Her talons tore at the foliage in her determination to destroy him, pushing him in and out of safety.

Exhausted, Gwion rose as high as his tiny wings could propel him and saw beneath him a sanctuary. The farmer's yard below held a large mound of freshly winnowed wheat. Gwion knew what he must do. As the hawk approached him at tremendous speed, Gwion pushed his mind into another form. The wren vanished in a second, just as the talons reached him. Cerridwen screamed as a single grain of wheat fell from the sky. She could barely keep her eye upon it as it descended into the great pile beneath her.

Undeterred, Cerridwen as the hawk descended through the blue sky, and as she did so, she changed her form into the shape of another feathered creature. The feet of a hen touched the farmyard ground as black feathers erupted from the newly formed body. She approached the mount of wheat with no clue as to the location of her foe.

And steadily she began to peck.

The hen's beak scraped sharply against the edges of the seed. Gwion flinched, knowing his fate as the hen took him into herself. Immense pain erupted through his being as the inner heat of the hen began to break him down, to tear him molecule by molecule, transforming him into something other, and yet, through all this, Gwion was aware. The pain was replaced by an all-consuming silence and a sense that all his parts were in all places and no place all at the same time. It was the screaming that roused him into a sense of being held by warm liquid, a tunnel of light appeared before him. The pressure was immense, the light blinding, his vision occluded by tears that ran down newly formed cheeks. Fear enveloped the tiny figure until something else, more powerful, more abiding, pushed the terror aside. The hands that held him and the soft skin he felt against his own radiated with an intense love. He could make no sense of where he was, where he had come from, memories eluded him, and yet none of that mattered. The love he felt was all that he needed.

It was that same love that caused Cerridwen's heart to melt, and in turn she placed the child in a skin belly and entrusted him to the mystical waters that flow between the worlds. Upon those currents the child floated for eight decades until fate would have it that the vessel was caught in the salmon weir of Gwyddno Garanhir. His loyal servent, Elffin, caught the skin belly, but instead of salmon, within it lay a small child with a gleaming brow. Taliesin was born.

1

The Quest for Cerridwen

The eminent Celtic scholar John Morris-Jones wrote in the early twentieth century:

> I think enough has been said to show that these poems, which were mist and mystery to those who looked at them though glass, become clear when we focus at them from a distance, and the mist, with most of the mystery, vanishes.[9]

This is a pretty bold statement, but one which has revolutionised future immersive experience of the Celtic mysteries, for in it, and together with the work of other scholars and visionaries, one is offered a starting point, a stage from which to perceive and engage with the jigsaw of Celtic mysteries.

The current New Age trend of spiritual commercialism has dissected the mysteries to their component parts, where each aspect of the mysteries can be focused upon with a magnifying glass. This has profoundly affected our relationship with the mysteries. From this exploration, it is tempting to direct one's attention to the individuation of the archetypes/deities that swim within the mysteries, and from this we attempt to place meaning and

---

9   Morris-Jones, "Taliesin," 253.

attributes upon them as individuals. However, the paradox of this analysis is that we may fail to see the bigger picture and in turn damage the internal organs of the material as we strive to examine it, making its piecing back together again a frightfully difficult task, if not impossible. Good scholarship is an honourable and worthy quality, yet in the desire for authentication and substantiation there is the danger of damaging the component that we explore through overanalysis. It is equally as important and valuable to take pause and appreciate the subtle quality of the material and the inherent fact that we are also dealing with spiritual matters. Finding moderation as opposed to balance is essential to ensure the least possible damage is caused to the vitality of the archetypes, spirits, or concepts that swim within the sea of myth.

The above paragraph may at face value appear to contradict the function of a book whose focus is one deity. Whilst this is primarily a book that focuses mostly on Cerridwen, it is vitally important that you understand she does not exist in a vacuum; she is an aspect of a much larger mythological landscape. To fully understand and develop a relationship with Cerridwen, we must also understand the landscape that she is inherently an aspect of. The permanent individuation of the gods to the exclusion of the landscape in which they exist does them a disservice, for the landscape inspires and breathes life into the divine as we perceive and connect with them. This is not limited to the mythological landscape alone, but to the sociopolitical and cultural landscape and the physicality that they are an inexorable aspect of.

The magic that we find in our connection to Cerridwen is made so much complete and more extraordinary when we rise above the individual archetype / deity and perceive them as an intrinsic component of the wider mysteries. Removing an element of the mysteries from its landscape shatters it into ever smaller pieces that become increasingly difficult to stick back together again. So rather than looking at Cerridwen through glass, as Morris-Jones expressed, one must rise above the landscape of myth and magic and climb ever higher into the blue sky that shines light upon their countenance. At this distance, the mists that lie at the edge of fragmentation vanish and the mysteries swim into focus.

THE QUEST FOR CERRIDWEN

With that in mind, in this book, whilst Cerridwen herself swims at the heart of the discourse, you will also find other beings, spirits, enigmatic human individuals, and archetypes that circumambulate the story, and whilst some may at first appear quite arbitrary, they are of equal importance to our exploration.

A RITUAL FOR MEETING CERRIDWEN

Lighting the Fire Beneath the Cauldron

What follows is a deeply personal journey to initiate a meeting between yourself and Cerridwen. It is the method that I first used to meet Cerridwen at Lake Tegid in Snowdonia, and it continues to be the tool that I use to maintain my connection with her. As I mentioned previously, I am a horrible meditator and prefer the term "imagine"—and whilst this may well be just the fickleness of semantics, my little brain copes with the task of imagining. I have shared elements of this process in a previous compendium, but it is worthy of repetition here.[10] I will ask you to kindly memorise the verse that is included, and the reasons for this will become more apparent through the course of this book. In addition, I suggest that you secure a cauldron that can be used for this and all subsequent rituals, ceremonies, and magical practises that I offer to you. This cauldron will become your primary vessel during this exploration. Ideally it will be iron or metal and watertight, with an opening of at least four inches wide. Whilst statuary and expensive paraphernalia are all well and good, they are not a requirement, as Cerridwen's primary symbol—a cauldron—is perhaps all that one really needs.

The Ritual

Create a space that can be made sacred in a way that you are accustomed to doing so, and try to ensure that you will not be disturbed for at least an hour. If you are able to do so, perform this short ritual late at night, where only candlelight will be utilised to offer any illumination. If you have any incense that is heavy on the resin side of the scent spectrum, all the better.

---

10 Edited version from "Cerridwen: Meeting the Witch Goddess" in *Llewellyn's 2016 Witches' Companion*.

In the centre of your space, place a cauldron or other similar vessel, and sit yourself down comfortably before it. Around the central cauldron arrange three smaller vessels, or three smaller cauldrons if you have them, to represent the powers of land, sea, and sky. Now position the vessel you will designate for the land aspect to the left of the central cauldron, and place within it an item that represents your physical life, i.e., a photograph of yourself, a lock of your own hair, or a poppet made in your own semblance. Position the vessel that represents the sky to the right of the central cauldron and within it deposit an item that represents your magical persona. This may be a necklace or pendant, a sacred object, tool, or talisman, a poem or a song written on a piece of paper—anything that adequately represents your creative aspect. Finally, position the third vessel directly behind the central cauldron and place within it a stone that has come from a beach or riverbed or has been submerged or spent some of its time in natural water. This will represent the powers of sea/water. By all means place some actual water in the vessel if you so wish.

Ensure that you are quite comfortable, then close your eyes and take a deep breath with the land that you currently occupy. See the land around you in your imagination—what does it look like, what shapes and forms does it express?—and with that breath, honour the land beneath you. Now tilt your chin slightly skywards and imagine the skies far above you, the winged beings that take to flight, the dance of clouds and sunlight, the silver glow of the moon. Whilst the sky covers us all, our little patch of sky can be quite different: some have limited views of the sky, others have a big, gigantic expanse of sky. Breathe with the sky. Now imagine an ember of light, somewhere around your solar plexus, and give it a lovely colour; using your imagination, now extend that light like the flash of a camera to the edges of your land where the ocean waves crash onto the beaches, extend that light—now! And take a deep breath with the seas that surround your sacred shores.

Before you open your eyes, imagine what it would be like if the ground beneath you were to dissolve away—carpets, tiles, or boards vanish and you find yourself floating in the heavy mists. What would that feel like, do you

4

think, to be held by nothing but air and mist? Imagine a breeze that chases the mists away from beneath you, and you look down to see an ancient moonlit landscape carved by the power of ice. A long narrow lake edged by mountains and woodlands greets your inner visions: this is Lake Bala in the mountains of Wales, Cerridwen's home.

Breathe deeply and imagine yourself descending—don't worry about trying to visualise, just imagine, make believe. Imagine that as you descend you see a wooden pontoon formed of rough plants, and it floats in the centre of the long lake. Upon it sits a cauldron, and it is surrounded by three vessels, just like the ones that occupy your sacred space in the physical world. As you imagine your feet touching the rough wood, the pontoon wobbles slightly and the waves lapping gently at its side sing the song of water. Imagine that as you look upwards into the night sky where you floated down from, a sickle-sharp moon hangs in the starlit sky, like a lamp at the head of the valley, and a long silver corridor of light glows towards your point in the centre of the lake. Stretch out your arms in the physical world and imagine your otherworldly counterpart doing the same, arms out, hands open in a greeting gesture, as these words tremble from your lips:

Cerridwen divine, your Awen be mine!
Awaken, arise, your wisdom to shine.
Cerridwen, wise one, keeper of seeds,
Arise, I beseech thee, witness my deeds!
Cerridwen sublime, by Awen divine,
Awaken, arise, your magic be mine!

The silver corridor swells just ahead of you, and the form of Cerridwen rises slowly from the glistening water. In your imagination, what would she look like? Imagine her features; perhaps she wears a gown as fluid as the lake itself. Under the lamp of moonlight, imagine her rising from the lake and sweeping across its surface towards you. Imagine her gently rising and her naked wet feet slapping against the pontoon as she stands before you. Separated only by the cauldron, you are confronted by Cerridwen herself. Imagine.

Once more your lips tremble with the words of the sacred verse:

Cerridwen divine, your Awen be mine!
Awaken, arise, your wisdom to shine.
Cerridwen, wise one, keeper of seeds,
Arise, I beseech thee, witness my deeds!
Cerridwen sublime, by Awen divine,
Awaken, arise, your magic be mine!

Imagine that her hair is caught in the breeze, and it lifts in the wind to reveal her face. How would she appear to you? Bring her face to life in your imagination. Now cast your spirit towards her—the most effective way to do this is to breathe sharply into your solar plexus. Anyone who has felt the tinges of love, lust, and the pain of grief has felt the butterflies in their stomach. Invoke those butterflies now, and with each breath raise the emotional energy in your centre, hold it, and direct it towards your imaginary vision of Cerridwen.

And now, as you would with any new connection, introduce yourself. Tell her your name. Breathe sharply, summon the butterflies, and direct. Tell her who you are and what you are. Where you live. What you like, what you don't like. You are essentially on a first date with Cerridwen herself. You know a bit about her, so it is only fair and reasonable that she gets to know something about you—after all, you have just called her into your awareness.

Bask in this connection. Imagine all of it. Imagine the scene, embellish it, decorate it, imagine the interaction. Do not force it. Think of the entire exercise like a daydream, where you are building a story for a book. Just imagine, and enjoy the process of immersing yourself in your own imagination.

When it feels right, bid Cerridwen farewell, and tell her why you are parting company—for now at least. At this point, either let your own imagination dictate what happens next or imagine that she simply collapses in on herself and falls graciously back into the lake from where she arose. Take another series of sharp breaths, feel those butterflies, sweep your arms forward quickly with an outward breath, and see the mists occlude the entire scene.

Become aware of your physical space once more and, with eyes still closed, continue to imagine what it would feel like and look like to be surrounded by mists. Slowly open your eyes and be fully present in your physical space.

Breathe deeply with the land beneath you and reach out to your left, grasping whatever item you previously placed in the land vessel. Consider what it signifies, what it means to you, and then slowly position it, being fully present in the moment, in the central cauldron, and say:

> Cerridwen divine, your Awen be mine,
> To my human form let your wisdom shine.

Now reach to your right and take the item that you placed in the sky vessel. Consider its qualities and how they impart on your living, and slowly place them in the central cauldron. Say these words as you do so:

> Cerridwen, wise one, keeper of seeds,
> To my spirit arise, come witness my deeds.

Finally, reach forward and take the stone that you placed in the sea vessel. But as you do so, know the mystery: there is but one sea. All rivers, lakes, and streams lose their names and forms when they enter the sea, but their essence remains. This emulated the nature of the gods and goddesses; they are everywhere and nowhere simultaneously. Now place the stone in the central cauldron and say:

> Cerridwen sublime, by Awen divine,
> My soul does awaken, your magic be mine.

The central cauldron represents the mysteries of Cerridwen; she is its primary keeper and guardian. Hover both your hands above the central cauldron and sense your offerings being absorbed into the otherworld through her primary symbol and into the lap of Cerridwen. Sit quietly in peaceful contemplation for a while.

When the time feels right, return to your normal state of awareness and close your sacred space in the way that you are accustomed to doing so.[11]

◆ ◆ ◆

What you have inadvertently done is initiated a subtle landscape where you can meet Cerridwen at any time you wish. The cauldron begins the process of being a physical representation of you, held within the main symbol of Cerridwen. Each night before you fall to slumber, re-imagine the scene at Lake Tegid and keep playing it over and over in your imagination. Let what messages and connection she may have for you seep through into your dream-state during your sleeping hours.

Keep adding the things that happen to your life story to the cauldron. You may want to feature the cauldron as a central item on an altar or space dedicated to Cerridwen—this is precisely how I started my own special space to her. The important thing here is repetition, consistency, and continuation. It would be somewhat rude to call to a deity and then abandon them, so perpetuate the connection, keep talking, keep imagining. The human imagination is the most powerful tool we have; never underestimate the power of your own imagination.

---

11   Visit my YouTube channel for a sound file of this ritual journey.

2

Beginning the Chase

The mystery and magic of Cerridwen cannot be separated from the Taliesin material, which breathes life into our understanding of the Celtic mysteries.[12] If one was wont to condense the qualities of the complex relationship and inter-dynamics of Cerridwen and Taliesin into a few short sentences, it would in all probability and logic read along these lines…

Cerridwen is the divine conduit of transformative, creative, magical inspiration gleaned from the cauldron of Awen. Whilst the Awen is a complex subject in itself, and I delve into it in more detail a little later, for now it is sufficient that I articulate what the Awen is within a single sentence, just in case you are unfamiliar with the use of the term. I define the Awen as the creative, transformative force of divine inspiration that sings in praise of itself; it is an eternal song that sings all things into existence, and all things call to the Awen inwardly.

In turn, Taliesin is the physical embodiment of that process, the outward expression of the power, magic, and action of the Awen. They are indivisible. The result of the Cerridwen/Gwion Bach/Taliesin saga is the birth of the

---

12   Taliesin is a portmanteau of two separate Welsh words: *tal*, meaning forehead, and *iesin*, meaning radiant, bright, and gleaming.

enchanted, narrative, and prophetic spirit, and without exception, all references to Cerridwen come from the mouthpiece that is Taliesin or from the bards that held the Taliesin persona as their greatest ideal.

The Welsh scholar Ifor Williams made a rather bold statement in the first half of the twentieth century, one which was quite revolutionary at the time. And whilst he was to an extent mocked for such a revelation, he held fast and firm, and slowly transformed the way future scholars and visionaries alike connected to the mysteries. He said that the Taliesin material—i.e., all the mysterious and sometimes baffling poems—cannot be explained without reference to a folktale that he called Hanes Taliesin (The Story of the Birth of Taliesin), and it is within this body of work that we first encounter the popular tale of Cerridwen and the innocent boy she employed to tend to her cauldron of Awen, Gwion Bach. It is a tale of initiation and ultimately of deep transformation, where the seeker undergoes immense, cathartic processes that result in them becoming an expression of the Awen itself. The result is a profound catharsis resulting in deep change to the individual who connects with the subtle elements hid within the tale.

It is important to note at this point that the familiar tale of Cerridwen is a relative latecomer to the plethora of references to her. Compiled in the late medieval period, over two dozen manuscripts survive that contain some, if not all, of the prose, in addition to the poems attributed to be from the mouthpiece of Taliesin. Some of these manuscripts are fragmentary, with many elements either lost or never recorded in the first instance. The most complete of these manuscripts is recorded in Elis Gruffudd's *Chronicle of the History of the World*, written circa 1552. Whilst the latter manuscript presents a highly developed narrative, it is evident from the fragments contained in other manuscripts that the tale was widely known and popular among the ranks of Welsh bards for a number of centuries before it was developed to the extent that we see in Gruffudd's manuscript.[13] However, in current times, particularly in Neopagan explorations of the tale, its origins are rarely, if ever, explored or discussed. The aim of this book is to not only explore ele-

---

13   Ford, *Ystoria Taliesin*, 55–59.

ments of the popular late medieval tale, but to venture far from the glow of the fire that warmed the belly of Cerridwen's cauldron and into the shadows of the deep past.

The tale is best perceived as the culmination and the return of ancestral wisdom into a cohesive form that was relevant to that period in time. It is a process of distillation. For centuries prior to the tale being scribed onto parchment, it existed in a myriad of forms, with locality-specific idiosyncrasies within the oral storytelling tradition. As we further explore the relationship of the bards of Wales to Cerridwen, it will become apparent that all of this rises as bubbles in the vast cauldron of Welsh myth and poetry. Eventually thousands of these little bubbles reach the surface of the imagination and are collated into a story that captures the essence of all that came before it. In truth, what we see on the surface is merely a reflection of the depth of mystery and magic that gave rise to one of occulture's most enigmatic and well-loved goddesses.[14]

Williams's claim that the later tale acts as a key to understanding the mysteries held within it on the surface appears contradictory, for how can something that is a key come so late? In essence, the mysteries that Cerridwen embodies did not appear overnight, and it is vital that one appreciates the process of distillation that I explore. It took the best part of one thousand years for the mysteries of Cerridwen to become a cohesive body of work full of potential meaning. Once firmly rooted in the public and bardic consciousness, the mysteries gel to form a cohesive structure that can bring about further meaning and depth of exploration. However, any cohesion it achieves is short lived, for the glue that holds it together is the energy of the individuals who work with the material, and they are in a continuous state of flux. The distillation process of the early to late medieval period took centuries to arrive at the mysterious tale of Cerridwen, Gwion Bach, the cauldron of Awen, and the birth of Taliesin, and yet the tale captures the soul of the bardic mysteries that went into its making. But the process did

---

14 I use the term *occulture* to refer to the culture and communities of modern-day magical Pagan practises and traditions.

not stop there, for it continues to this day as the focus changes slightly and more and people beyond the reaches of Wales are moved into relationship with Cerridwen, the Awen, and the Taliesin mysteries.

It is important to stop for a moment and consider that we are the sum total of all things that went before us. The same truth can be applied to the processes of storytelling and myth-making; they are the culmination of a process that brought meaning, significance, and transcendence to groups of peoples and communities. They do not, however, exist in a vacuum. Each rendition contains seeds of the myth it expresses; each vocalisation and literation expresses the truth of sum totality.

Stop for a moment and imagine, if you will, a tall, clear drinking glass that is currently being filled with ice-cold tonic water. Bubbles suddenly appear as if by magic on the edge of the glass right near the bottom. Look at them closely: they appear to just manifest from nowhere and continue to do so. Further bubbles appear from the smallest bubbles, increasing in size as they either cling to the edge of the glass or climb up through the main body of liquid. Their aim is to break out in the expanse of air above the glass. And as each bubble journeys, they gather in numbers and in strength and volatility as they careen towards the top. But look again to the bottom and there are barely any bubbles at all—they just come into being as if by magic. As they crash to the surface, they explode into a life of froth and gas and sound. Spilling over the edge, the particles of gas leap into the air and travel beyond the confines of the glass. The tradition at hand is emulated in these metaphorical bubbles I'm describing. It arose as a mere hint of potential and gathered momentum and speed, power, tenacity, and volatility as each bubble of influence joined another. And this process of distillation, development, and evolution continues to this day. At times the process overfills the bardic glass and a profusion of creativity explodes into being; at other times, it is quiet and still.

Gaze at the sigil below and consider this process of magical distillation that was centuries in the making:

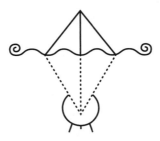

It is easy to remain focused and transfixed on the beauty of culmination alone, but to do this we miss out on the depth of inspiration and the magic hidden in continuity and survival. The realms of mystery are difficult to enter—to begin with, they are invisible to human eyes, they are hidden, as if obscured by the waves that prevent us from seeing into the depths of the ocean. You may find clues that allude to them, but they are elusive and enveloped in mists and secrets. To access them we must find the keys that unlock the appropriate doors, and the entire tale of Cerridwen and Taliesin is one of those. But even when we find the keys that match the mysteries, we must still find the locks into which they fit.

The material may at first seem compelling yet incredibly nonsensical, leaving one scratching the head in confusion and able to taste, if only on the tip of the tongue, the tantalising flavour of deep mystery. This is a typical symptom for the majority of folk who approach the doors of the Celtic mysteries. They may be confounded by the assumed complexities of language, regional variations and differences, and culturally specific adaptations and alterations. The promise of sweet mystery may well turn sour during one's exploration, particularly if one cannot make the content applicable in practise. But there is a significant key that allows all other keys to find their matching locks with ease.

It is the function of Cerridwen and her employment of Gwion Bach, who is subsequently transformed by means of successive initiations and a triple birth, which is the key to accessing the mysteries. The legendary and prophetic myths and poems of medieval Wales require this key to activate their power. When activated, the mysteries begin to glow with a light that shines to the furthest recesses of the spirit.

For the above to be effective, authentic, and cathartic, there must be an element of practise. The Pagan traditions work best when orthodoxy, something one believes in, is combined with orthopraxy, something that one does. This book will provide keys to effective and essential practise in order to transform the myths from static stories to elements of spiritual practise, illumination, and inspiration.

For the tale to be incorporated as experience, as something that one does and not simply a mental exercise, we must accept that the role of Gwion Bach is indicative of you, the hero on your own quest to inspiration and the divine receipt of Awen. This is achieved by seeing yourself in the role of Gwion Bach and accepting the tools that it provides along with its fellow archetypes to embark on the journey. This key is that of relationship, inspiration, innocence, initiation, and transformation. A journey and ritual to initiate this key can be found beginning on page 267.

3

The Power of Mythology

At the heart of this exploration is the power and magic of myth—but what is a myth, and why is it applicable to an exploration of Cerridwen and modern Pagan practise?

In the twenty-first century, we are accustomed to passive entertainment, yet we crave immersion. Our multimedia technologies are catching up with the need of humanity and its thirst for immersive and interactive experiences. Virtual reality technology along with augmented reality offer the traveller an experience that feels a little bit more visceral and real. We crave realness and the sense of truly being present within a world that is not wholly our own and yet to great extent is a product of the human imagination.

It is the power of imagination that enables the traveller to embark on increasingly intense and immersive experiences that break away from the passive observation of movies and TV shows. Our technological advances have skewed the manner by which we perceive a story; in essence, many no longer feel entirely satisfied by watching alone. We thirst for something more and yet invariably become reliant on the power of someone else's imagination to provide the intensity of experience that we crave. Mythology does not operate in the same manner, but owing to the fact that we perceive mythology as a story—as little novellas, if you like—our relationship to them is altered and influenced by the relationship we have to movies, TVs, theme parks, and immersive multimedia experiences. We live in a world that our ancestors, merely a hundred years ago, would not recognise. For the power of mythology to transform us, we must see them in a different light, not in 4K or High Definition but as internal processes that reflect the desire of humankind to learn about itself, move towards the deeper questions in life, and perhaps glean some of the mysteries that breathe life and meaning into our universe.

The difficulties that people face when attempting to move into relationship with mythologies, particularly those that they may be culturally removed from, is the perception that the very words on paper contain the mystery.

Modernity has preserved the words themselves whilst simultaneously causing many to consider that only the words themselves matter, and the eye is taken away from the vast space between the lines—wherein lies the magic. Moderation is required to balance the danger of extremes, where on one hand the power of vision could cause one to fall into the realm of unverified personal gnosis alone, with nothing else to moderate it. Unverified personal gnosis, or UPG, has its role, but we cannot solely rely on this function of occulture—something needs to moderate it, and that tool is scholarship. On the other hand, scholarship can and often falls into the realms of academic snobbery, which in itself is not useful; it needs the gifts of the visionary and UPG to moderate it. Therefore, finding that bridge between the two extremes is important and does the material and your experience of it justice.

We crave depth of experience, to feel and to be moved, and alas, the power of storytelling in its most basic form—around the hearth fire, with candles flickering and the wind howling at the windows—has waned. We want more! We have become distanced from the visceral, and our Western culture perpetuates a false myth that necessitates a belief that the public should be insulated from that which is bloody, gory, emotive, or distressing. The consequence of this insulating attitude has resulted in our thirst for entertainment that not only exposes us to what we do not see from day to day, but instils within us a sense of schadenfreude. We may be thrilled, hor-rified, scared, and to an extent terrified, whilst simultaneously knowing that we are safe.[15]

Safe: what a queer word, and one fraught with contradictions and per-plexities; we live in a world where safety is of paramount concern, and yet so many of us feel less safe than we have done in a frightfully long time. Mythology and its power is not safe; it never has been. Human society has always and will forever perpetuate mythology—we crave it and, on some level, we need it. Perpetuating and understanding mythology, however, are two very different things. Those who fail to understand the power and func-tion of myth are, by definition, doomed to be governed by it.

At its heart mythology expresses a simplicity that can often be overlooked. Mythology's primary function is service to the people. It organises the expe-rience of the people into a system of images and metaphors that express an essential wisdom. Myths do not exist in a vacuum, but they are indicative of a profound relationship between a people and their land, and they will reflect the values and traditions of culture. Myths cannot be categorised as merely stories alone, for they contain the seeds of wisdom necessary for the well-being of those yet to come.

Humankind will always look for meaning in the subtle, and yet the search for meaning, particularly in myth, can lead to fear responses in those on the other side of the coin to occulture, academia. So often academia has descended into a passive-aggressive attacking of mythological applications by modern enthusiasts. For decades the idea that myths may contain mean-ing and act locally to express ideas, wisdoms, and worldviews have been dismissed by many eminent scholars in Celtic academia. Comparisons have often been made between the scholarly and the unscholarly about how myths in the hands of the unscholarly become volatile and dangerous devic-es.[16] Myths may become commodities that only belong to the party that has the most to gain from their possession.

---

15   Taylor, *The Buried Soul*, 273–279.
16   Sullivan, footnote 25 to "Branwen," *The Mabinogi*, 116–117.

There has always existed a mostly benign, but at times malignant antagonism between the world of the academic and that of the visionary, with the function of myth being dragged into the boxing ring. Dr. Gwilym Morus-Baird in his article "The Magic of Meaning" is of the opinion that far too often the exploration of myth has served only to inflate the academic ego rather than to search for what meaning the myths may have had to the peoples who created them. Albeit the academic material is useful, worthy of praise and notice, and acts as an essential filter, he is of the opinion that the agenda of many in modern academic circles is the perpetuation of academic values as opposed to the search for meaning.[17]

How do we moderate this and find a way to effectively work with mythology that is honourable and well-intended? Primarily this must stem from the understanding of the function of mythology.

The mid-twentieth-century scholar W. J. Gruffydd elegantly articulated and differentiated the function of myth from legend when he said, "Mythology is the legend of the Gods, and legend is the mythology of man."[18]

So, what can we assume he meant by this statement? Essentially, myth and legend can be easily distinguished from each other. Mythology does not have its basis in fact or actual historical occurrences and figures, and it mostly deals with the trials and tales of gods, demigods, and other supernatural beings and characters. Legends, on the other hand, do have some basis in fact, albeit they are embellished and exaggerated over time. Examples of these can be exemplified by the myths of the Mabinogi in the Welsh tradition. Whilst rooted in location, with some later embellishments that hint at a potential point in time, they are primarily myths that do not contain historical facts, and they have an air of timelessness to them. An example of modern legend can be seen in the accounts of the Roswell incident of 1947 in New Mexico, where by embellishment and exaggeration the facts surrounding the actual crashing of a military device became a story of alien

---

17   Morris-Baird, www.whitedeer.earth/2016/07/04/the-magic-of-meaning/.

18   J. K. Bollard, "The Role of Myth and Tradition in the Four Branches of the Mabinogi," in Sullivan, *The Mabinogi*, 277.

contact. Robin Hood and King Arthur also fall into a similar category where a historical figure or situation gave rise to a legend.

Mythology makes assumptions that the gods and spirits are real, and it recounts their lives and acts in a manner that emulates legend. Eventually, legends can give rise to myths as the facts of their foundational attributes are lost to the mists of time. The peculiar quality inherent in myth is that they serve to inspire and imbibe the future with wisdom. In each generation there is a need for mythology, and the power of the inherent spirit of myth is seeded in those who step into its stream. These people dream the myths back into being in a manner that is conducive to transformation. This is the narrative spirit, the ethereal driving force of myth to seek out the dreamers in time and inspire them to plant the seeds of myth in the consciousness of the people. These myth makers do not create new myths, but rather they embellish existent myths with new meanings. Those who have been inspired in turn inspire others to reach for the subtle, see the magic hidden in a tale, and receive and transmit the power of wisdom returning.

Rupert Sheldrake in his *Science and Spiritual Practises* says:

> Myths are stories of origins. They concern the doings of gods, heroes and superhuman beings. They propose that the reason why things are as they are, is because they were as they were. The present repeats the past. This repetition goes back to the first time something happened.[19]

What I believe Sheldrake is alluding to is not a cycle of history repeating itself, which generally comes about when past lessons are not objectively assimilated, but rather the understanding that the seeds of myth repeat themselves through time. The sea will always be the sea and is given a culturally specific name and becomes a deity; the name might lose its impact in time, but eventually the seeds that gave rise to the relationship the people had with the sea returns. Love and war have the same quality today as they did 6,000 years ago; only the motives may differ, but their impact on the human condition remains the same. Mythology sings of this quality.

---

19   Sheldrake, *Science and Spiritual Practises*, 111.

In the Welsh tradition that I practise, the narrative spirit is the term given to the life force that is inexorably linked to mythology. We believe that myth has its own life, its own unique music, to which the people and landscape contribute the lyrics. The music is the same, but the words are always different. Like a river that flows through the landscape, the narrative spirit is alive and constantly moves through the pool of time. It is quite visible at times and at other times not, as it descends underground or through deep, inaccessible gorges. But the river always rises to the surface, at which point someone may step into its current where past, present, and future collide in relationship and awareness.

Consider the following statement. Every river began its life as a stream, and every stream had its origin in the minutest trickle. In turn, every trickle is the result of filtration through rock and sand and soil, and from this process a single drop of water arises. So often most of these single drops have not seen the sky or the light of the sun for hundreds, if not thousands, of years. The drops, drawn instinctively by mysterious forces, are drawn one to another, and they gather. Soon the trickles become rivulets of water, or they may bubble up as springs. Finding the course of least resistance, they gather together and traverse the land as small brooks, streams, and eventually rivers.

Their voices rise ever louder as more and more of them gather together, increasing in speed and depth and vitality. Creatures find their homes in them; humans seek sanctuary beside them. Eventually the rivers run into still lakes of deep community, where dozens of rivers contribute to the cauldron of water. In time the water exits, again finding the path of least resistance, and moves on towards the sea. At some unknown point in time, each molecule of water rises by heat to kiss the blue of the sky, to form clouds that rain back onto the mountains and hills, and thus the story begins again. There is no new water on earth. In turn, there is no new myth on earth but only the retelling of the same rivers of mythology, flavoured only by the passing of time.

Consider the above and contemplate the sigil below that captures the mystery of water and the origin of the river of myth:

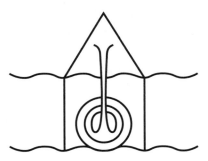

The mythology at hand, that which concerns Cerridwen, is different today than it was one hundred years ago. Its countenance of a hundred years ago differs again from that which was conveyed by the Welsh bards of the eleventh century. The river of Cerridwen's myth is travelling through a diverse and varied landscape, one formed by the effects of time and the relationships that people and places developed with the river in whose currents she swims. When we fall into the belief that myths are static and that they reflect only the values of a past peoples, we fail to seed them in the present and grow them into the future. Each generation is responsible for dreaming the myths of the past into the new age and, more importantly, into relevance. When we take the teachings of mythology and apply them in service to our communities, we cause ripples of transformation to echo out into the future. The function of this book is to dream the myth of Cerridwen into being in the here and now, to plant the seeds of Awen into you whilst simultaneously honouring their origins.

This book will focus on bodies of myth that may seem, on the surface, to not be connected to Cerridwen. However, she did not exist independently of mythology, but in a cauldron of ideas and philosophies, systems and teachings that informed and inspired one another. It is by exploring the adjacent mythologies and legends that we capture a glimpse of the entire jigsaw as opposed to a part of it. The Taliesin persona bleeds in and out of the various bodies of Welsh myths, and it is to this enigmatic being that we must look in our attempt to understand Cerridwen. The beauty of Welsh mythology is that they are intimately connected one to the other, like the intricate weaving of Celtic knotwork. The influence of Cerridwen's primary protégé—Taliesin—can be seen interwoven into the collection of Welsh myths. By examining the relationships expressed in mythology, we glean a better understanding of Cerridwen and the landscape that gave rise to her name and meaning.

4

The Quest for Meaning

Exploring ancient practises and principles and striving to make them relevant for the twenty-first century is seen by many, particularly in the world of academia, as foolhardy and a waste of time. So perhaps a reality check is needed—a brief discourse into the reasons why so many individuals are attracted to these constructs in the first place and what, if anything, it satisfies within them.

There is a lot of talk about gods and goddesses and the spirit of place or the ancestors, yet how comfortable are we in exploring what any of that means? How useful are they in today's world? I believe that the world of humankind has become increasingly disenchanted, and whilst enormous advances have been made in the fields of science, medicine, and technology, with people living longer and better quality of life today than they have in our entire history, we continue to thirst for the ethereal. We have a hunger for the magical.

Humanity has long searched for mystery and meaning, and without these I believe that we are the poorer for it. Whilst the issues of the present are far more pressing than those we perceive in the past, for the present is our primary point of reference, I do believe that every time and point in human history had its own set of crises. We face our own unique crisis in the here and now, with huge sociopolitical issues plaguing the public and causing vast swathes of the populace to feel utterly disempowered. As soon as this occurs, we find that our ability to glean meaning in the world may greatly diminish. We may feel increasingly insignificant by our inability to do anything proactive that brings about change. Overwhelmed by situations and circumstances beyond our control, we revert to social media to shout at those whom we perceive are doing less. We may fall into ever-increasing patterns of disenchantment and disempowerment. We can become increasingly vulnerable to other ulterior motives and agendas when we fall into believing that everything revolves around us.

The world needs enchantment; it always has done and always will. Every generation will carry its own enchanters, those who for reasons unknown even to themselves rise to a different calling—those who feel the pulsing heartbeat of magic flowing through the apparent world, coursing, rising, and falling. In our increasingly secular world, perhaps there has never been a more appropriate time for the old gods of the old world to make a comeback; it may very well be the reason why so many are turning their faces towards these ancient archetypes. But they do so not to connect to an antiquated concept, but to mysteries that are relevant in the twenty-first century. The world is as much in need of the function of Cerridwen today as it was a thousand years ago.

So, what is it that underlies these issues that blight humanity? In order for people to get up in the morning and live fully in the moment, they need to believe that their lives have meaning. We seek meaning in almost all of our actions; the more meaning that we can glean, the more fulfilling each task or connection feels. In a world that is wholly rationalised by scientific methodologies, I do not believe we will have spiritually fulfilled individuals because meaning is more than something explained or given credence by science—it is not easily quantified. The journey to find meaning is part of the big questions and the search for understanding the reason why we are here and what we are meant to do, if anything, whilst we are here. It is a soul quest, and this ties into matters of the spirit and existential issues. Knowing that the sun is a radiant sphere of nuclear fusion is one thing; it is another thing for that knowing to bring about meaning. Nuclear actions and comprehension are different to the awe-inspiring sense of deep wonder one feels when standing at the edge of the ocean watching a glorious sunset. For this brings about a sense of meaning on a soul level and informs the observer that there is more to the sun than just fusion.

There is an obvious side effect to the loss of meaning: depression. This is not to suggest that depression does not have chemical and neurological underpinnings, for it certainly does, but often the first stirrings of depression raise their heads when we lose the meaning of things. For meaning to profoundly move the spirit and the heart, the individual must have a sense of meaning that comes from feelings of significance. When we feel significant and that we are a part of something that is greater and makes us significant, we glean meaning from this.

Part of the reason why so many people are unhappy in their ordinary daily jobs is because they do not always feel significant and so often feel quite the opposite. When we do not feel significant, when we feel that our contribution is arbitrary, it all becomes rather meaningless. Our heart goes out of the task, and the entire process becomes mechanical. Keep your head down, keep on keeping on, just take the paycheck. Those who feel significant in their professions or within their communities not only glean meaning, but they will transcend. Transcendence is to feel a part of something that is greater than you, to have a deep sense that your contribution not only makes you feel significant, but brings significance and meaning to the lives of those around you or those whom you serve. Transcendence helps us feel that we are contributing to the greater good, to a collective idealism that transcends individuality and taps into a connectivity that serves to imbibe meaning and significance.

Myths serve to perpetuate this concept by expressing a sense of significance that has deep, profound meaning, which in turn causes one to transcend. They do this by placing the storyteller and listener centre stage; they are the story of you and your people in relationship with the land. They articulate the human condition in a manner that offers meaning.

The Spiral of Meaning

The Spiral of Transcendence   **The Spiral of Significance**

Consider the triskele above and the spiral of meaning, significance, and transcendence. Whilst I have briefly explored the function of this triplicity, in truth they all emanate from a central point. From the middle of the symbol of itself, this is the centre of your being, and the arms spiral out from and express the centre. Contemplate what brings to your life meaning, significance, and transcendence.

In this case, the sigil of the triskele itself is more than sufficient. Look at the image here for several minutes, then close your eyes and see the imprint of the triskele that is now burnt onto your retinas. The image exists there, in the darkness within your mind. It has potential to explore any aspect of your depth. Imagine that the centre of the triskele is moving slightly, shifting and pulsating with potential; now imagine one of its arms beginning to spin slowly: this is the spiral of meaning.

Consider what brings to your life the most meaning, and see it reflected within the spiral. Turn your imagination towards the next spiral, and watch as it begins to spin from the centre. Consider the things in your life that make you feel significant. What are they? How do they contribute to your being and well-being? Watch the spiral turn. Next, imagine the third and final spiral begin its turning, stretching out from the centre, and consider how the components that bring meaning and significance to your life also enable you to feel that you are a part of something greater than yourself. This triskele represents you and your living here in this world, in your life. All of your living can be seen captured in the essence of meaning, significance, and transcendence.

You may then wish to add those, in whatever manner you deem appropriate, to your cauldron from the ritual of meeting Cerridwen.

Whilst the academic critics may have espoused the dangers of finding meaning, I do not denigrate their fears that myth is not safe, for there is a grain of truth there. The journey into relationship with Cerridwen and her myth is not safe—how can it be? For in so doing, one potentially positions oneself at the edge of the cauldron of inspiration and transformation. Your life may never be the same again. This is a journey in the true sense of the word, for it involves a deep commitment to the study of mystery and immersion in the teachings of our ancestors, combined with the inspiration of modern teachers who have delved into Cerridwen's cauldron. The quest becomes a search for wisdom, our heartfelt attempt to access the blissful rapture of connection to the mysteries of the Celtic continuum, where we go on to plant the seeds of future wisdom. From this we are reborn as one with a radiant brow: Taliesin.

However, before we embark on working on our own radiant brows, who is Cerridwen? What does that name even mean, if it means anything at all, and what mechanisms have caused the survival of this enigmatic and ancient being?

5

Cerridwen and the Welsh Bardic Tradition

Cerridwen's history and evolution is as complex and varied as the numerous herbs and plants that went into making the cauldron's brew. Misinformation and poor translations have served to muddy the water of this complex archetype, and yet never before has she received so much attention. There is no doubt more people connected and devoted to Cerridwen today than at any other point in history; ironically, the majority of these adherents are not living in Wales. This is a pretty bold statement to make, but it is one that has some merit. Cerridwen was not always a goddess, not like the goddess that she is today—there was never a cult centre to her, no shrines have been found, no devotional prayers or invocations—and yet she was something of incredible importance to the bardic schools of Wales.

In her translation and notes on the *Legendary Poems from the Book of Taliesin*, Celtic scholar Marged Haycock makes a point that whilst Cerridwen has some abilities or powers that are directly related to the distilling of Awen and inspiration, she can hardly be called a goddess.[20] However, Haycock's

---

20 Haycock, *Legendary Poems from the Book of Taliesin*, 314.

criticism looks only to Cerridwen's position in the past and does not consider the power and function of apotheosis, a quality that we will explore later in this book. Her position as a deity is relatively new, but do not be fooled: whilst open to criticism from some Pagan sceptics and other misers, her position as goddess in the twenty-first century has much value and merit, and is profoundly indicative of a spirit that has long been prevalent in Wales and early Britain. Suffice to say that for this introduction to who Cerridwen was to my ancestors, we will put aside any exploration and relevance of her status as a goddess and focus our view on how those who perpetuated her mythos—the bards—perceived her. In order to achieve this, we must delve into the deep past.

Cerridwen cannot be separated from the systems that gave birth to her mythology, both within the oral and literal traditions of Wales. The familiar tale of Cerridwen and her cauldron, and the eventual transformation of the innocent Gwion Bach to the radiancy of Taliesin, is, as I have touched upon previously, a relative latecomer. The tale is not the point of origin when exploring the nature of Cerridwen, but rather it is a process of bardic and magical distillation that was centuries in the making. The processes that brought about this distillation are found in a system that is uniquely Welsh in expression: the Welsh bardic tradition. In order to understand the process that distilled the familiar tale, we must journey through time to the individuals and collective that served to perpetuate and preserve Cerridwen.

An individual born into Welsh culture is programmed on many levels to understand the power of the bard and the function of bardism as a vital aspect of Welsh cultural expression and identity. Within the Welsh educational system, the majority of Welsh-speaking children are exposed to bardism from infancy, but it is not necessarily an avenue of expression that all children will actively pursue. The bardic tradition has a vocational element that calls those who might go on to excel in the craft; those not drawn to it certainly take immense pleasure in listening to the bards and their battles, which is itself a vital component of the bardic tradition—more on this a little later.

It is easy to trivialise the term "tradition" as something that might refer to an act or practise that happens at Christmas or the office tradition of giving a birthday cake. It is a word that is easily flung about to refer to anything that might be perceived as having a pattern of repetition, but it is so much more than this. A tradition that has any value is something that is alive and living and expresses an inherent creativity that transcends the deeds of the individual. In the Welsh bardic tradition, the Awen-fuelled talent and genius of the individual bard works with their literal and oral inheritance, expanding upon it whilst nourishing the seeds of wisdom contained within the tradition for future generations. However, when the literal inheritance becomes of utmost importance and to the denigration of the oral component, this invariably leads to limitation and the subsequent oppression of the individual bard, forcing them into a logocentrism, where the tradition will stall, stagnate, and die. Any tradition that has merit must demonstrate elements of consistency, adaptability, and continuation, but it is a mistake to look at tradition as an unchanging thing.

In Wales, the collective term for the organisation of this tradition is the Bardic Order. Its current title is *Gorsedd Beirdd Ynys Prydein*, the Gorsedd of the Bards of the Island of Britain. However, regardless of the collective title, what is evident is that the Bardic Order of the Welsh bardic tradition has existed for centuries, and whilst its origins in the deep past cannot be ascertained by an actual date, the literal and historical evidence for such an order is compelling, as you will discover through the course of the next several chapters.

The bards were a continuation of a system that perpetuated and maintained a tradition that reached back into the Brythonic era of the deep Celtic past.[21] Not only did the Bardic Order enjoy autonomy and privilege, it demonstrated a remarkable resilience to the turbulence of time—that is, until it slowly diminished and changed its shape owing to powerful sociopolitical change. To a modern Pagan, the inclusion of what may well appear on the surface as an obscure history may well seem perplexing. I do, however,

---

21   Koch, *Celtic Culture*, 176.

maintain its necessity in demonstrating the complex systems that were in place to preserve Cerridwen and her retinue. It is the magic of this history that has kept her alive.

The Welsh bardic tradition contains three living and vital principles:

- learned
- oral/aural
- literary

The sequence that I present these principles to you is of utmost importance in gleaning an understanding of the function and importance of the Welsh bardic tradition.

The Learned Element

First and foremost, the tradition is one that is learned; it is not something that one can naturally or instinctively do. It was and continues to this day to be a strict process of learning the craft of the bard. Within established *Gorseddau*,[22] cultural or otherwise, the tradition continues to maintain an initiatory quality, implying that one has embarked upon a system of learning and achieved a certain status within the tradition that is recognised by a ceremony of initiation or membership. Within the current Welsh tradition, the bard undergoing initiation and admittance to the *Gorsedd* adopts a bardic name that is different to his or her given name, and this theme is recognisable in modern occult practises. But herein lies a quandary, for you will note that I casually used the term "craft" in relation to the bard, and I do so intentionally.

Not only is bardism considered to be an art and a craft, the term for craft in Welsh is written thus: celfyddyd. This contains different levels of meaning, as is often the case with the Welsh language, where words and terms frequently work on up to three or more distinct levels of meaning. The dictionary of the Welsh language defines the term "celfyddyd" as not only a

---

22 *Gorseddau* is the plural of *Gorsedd*, a term used to describe a tumulus or mound, the seat of a sovereign, or the organisation of bards.

process of vocational learning of a craft, in particular the craft of bardism, but also specifically the craft of magical incantations and spellworking.[23] It is a tradition that has at its core a learned foundation of metaphysics and a profound understanding of supernatural forces.[24] It is evident from the use of language throughout the different eras of the Welsh bardic tradition, that the function of bardism as an expression of magical or supernatural forces was understood, and whilst the relevance of this may have taken a back seat in modern bardism, it cannot wholly be separated from it.

Relevant to our exploration of Cerridwen, the literal works of Wales identify the bards who recorded the function of Cerridwen as practitioners of *celfyddyd barddoniaeth* (bardic craft), learned and proficient crafters. This quality is one that is later emulated in the tale of Cerridwen, who was said to be "learned in the three crafts of magic, witchcraft, and sorcery,"[25] and she took to the "crafts of the book of the Pheryllt to boil a cauldron of Awen."[26] If we can take any inspiration from the above quotes, it is that Cerridwen epitomised the power of effective learning and its dissemination. Her admiration for the virtues of learning is seen in the Book of Taliesin poem "The Chair of Cerridwen," where she sings the praises of Gwydion, the son of Dôn, whom she considered to have the best of learning.[27]

If Cerridwen and her adherents are attempting to tell us in the present anything at all, it is that the task of learning is not only an admirable and valuable trait, but also one that cannot be separated from magic; they run hand in hand. The extensive period of learning that the tradition serves to this day is intense, profound, and deeply transformative. Whilst elements of bardic education increase the mental skills of the bard, they simultaneously affect other aspects of the individual, notably the subtle skills. It is said that by the process of learning, the bards received and were in possession of supernatural keys that were awe-inspiring and dreadful all at once. The

---

23   Bevan, *Geiriadur Prifysgol Cymru*, 457.
24   Thomas, *Y Traddodiad Barddol*, 13.
25   Translated by the author from manuscript NLW 5276D, Ellis Gruffudd's *Chronicle*.
26   Translated by the author from Peniarth Manuscript 111, John Jones.
27   Haycock, *Legendary Poems from the Book of Taliesin*, 316.

power of the bard had the capacity to not only bring about transformation, healing, and inspiration, but could also bring about great illness and even death. Such was the power of the bard's song.[28]

The act of learning focuses the mind and brings discipline to mental practices and skills; learning simultaneously expands the mind. In a ready-made, let's-have-everything-prepared-on-a-plate-and-offered-to-us world, learning can sometimes feel jarring and an intrusion to one's sensibilities, and yet, paradoxically, learning contributes to one's sensibilities in a way that challenges and eventually transforms. Cerridwen herself was learned, a fact that is clearly stated in the legendary material. It is a quality that she expects in her children.

The Oral/Aural Element

The magical quality of bardism can be elaborated upon when we look at the second element of the Welsh bardic tradition: the oral/aural aspect. The umbrella term for this system is called *Cerdd Dafod*, which literally means the craft and music of the tongue. Within this complex system of bardism is a particular form of poetic structure called *cynghanedd*,[29] and it is a specific form of bardism that on one hand can be classified as a form of poetry whilst simultaneously containing an element that can be defined as music. Cynghanedd in a simplistic sense is the sound arrangement within a line of poetry that uses stress, alliteration, and rhyme. However, the Welsh language is fickle and magical all at the same time, and if we look for clarification of this magical craft in the dictionary of the Welsh language, we find an alluring and intriguing definition. On one hand, cynghanedd means music, harmony, symphony, chord, agreement, consistency, and concordance. Simultaneously it refers to a system of consonance or alliteration in a line of Welsh poetry presented in strict metre and internal rhyming[30]—all of that encapsulated in one single word! We are programmed to accept that poetry and music are

---

28   Thomas, *Y Traddodiad Barddol*, 14–15.
29   Cynghanedd is pronounced kyng-HAN-eth.
30   Bevan, *Geiriadur Prifysgol Cymru*, 737.

not necessarily one and the same thing; in Welsh culture they are not defined as being different; music, in particular song, has always run hand in hand with metred poetry and the crafting of magic.

The craft of cynghanedd is not something that comes instinctively; it must be learned and is classified as a form of science, which in Welsh is identified by the word gwyddoniaeth. This continues to be the modern word for "science," and yet the roots of the Welsh word gwyddoniaeth have within them the term for tree, magician, Druid, and magic. Science is literally the language of magic—or, in a modern sense, magic is the science that we have not quite figured out yet. The magic of cynghanedd permeates Welsh culture both orally and literally, and according to Chief Bard Mererid Hopwood, the origins of cynghanedd cannot be pinpointed to a certain time; it is not something that was suddenly invented out of thin air. It was centuries in the making, a process that she also describes as a distillation.[31] Its literal countenance developed between the sixth and ninth centuries after generations of refinement.

In its basic form, the term cynghanedd can be adequately translated to mean "harmony," and yet something is lost in translation—its essence or spirit perhaps. It would be erroneous of one to consider that cynghanedd is mere recitation, for it exists in a liminal state that is neither prose nor music, neither speech nor song. Instead it swims somewhere betwixt and between all of those four disciplines. Whilst on the surface it appears unnecessarily complex, its complexity is only exacerbated by the immense amount of time that it has existed. In her book *Singing in Chains*, Hopwood explores the tendency for non-Welsh-speaking critics to assume that the Welsh language lends itself wonderfully to the use of cynghanedd, and yet she claims that they actually miss the point. Cynghanedd and the Welsh language evolved together, and they cannot be separated.[32] Cynghanedd is the spirit of the language.

The power of cynghanedd is not to simply demonstrate the ability of the bard, but to also satisfy the ear of the listener. It is a truism that not all

---

31 Hopwood, *Singing in Chains*, 7.
32 Ibid., 4.

native Welsh speakers are fully versed in the complexities of cynghanedd, and many do not have a learned understanding of its technicalities, but the ear is trained from birth to appreciate and understand the beauty and magic of it. In my opinion, there is another subtle quality that stems from the ethereal edges of cultural consciousness: an inherent understanding. This is not something that can be quantified or examined in any objective manner, but it is a vitally important function of bardism in that it embodies an oral and aural quality, and one cannot exist without the other.

For bards to be effective in their abilities, there must be an audience who understands the magic they are expressing. This is exemplified every August during the modern annual National Eisteddfod, a week-long festival that celebrates Welsh language and culture. One of the main events for thousands of Welsh fans of the cynghanedd is the Battle of the Bards that takes place every day of the festival in the literature, knowledge, and lore pavilion. This battle is televised daily, satisfying the thirst for cynghanedd that the nation naturally has. This aural component is the reciprocated aspect of bardism that is not learned; this is the only element of bardism that is instinctive and embedded in the cultural consciousness of the Welsh. It is something that we do. The power of bardism and the bard is one of profound relationship between the bard (the combined learned and oral element) and the audience (the aural element) and the narrative spirit that breathes life into it.

The oral/aural aspect of bardism uses another form of magic: sound. Essentially the lines of cynghanedd and other forms of bardic crafts such as storytelling are spells of making. They bring something to life; they cause something to change within the listener. Within the modern Welsh bardic tradition some have claimed that the cynghanedd form of poetry is not something that is worked on in a way that one would work out the contents of a book. Neither are they constructed by a form of disciplined composition alone, but they are also channelled by unknown means. There is an implication here that at least some of the bard's skills are supernatural in origin.[33] By itself this channelling would be meaningless if not imbibed

---

33 Hopwood, *Singing in Chains*, 63.

with intent, but owing to the learned skill of the bard, the words that he or she pulls from the ether are structured and brought to life by the craft that they have studied and learned. As a result, they evoke and invoke emotional responses in the listener. The bard's task is to get the audience to remember whilst also telling story, satire, philosophy, and wisdoms, which are all transmitted through the power of structured sound.

This oral/aural component hearkens back to a time when the craft of writing was exclusively the domain of what Caesar noted were the Druids, the elite learned of society at the time. The power of the spoken word held its allure and magical connotations into the medieval period, a concept that was relevant to both Pagan and Christian traditions. Words were believed to have immense power and contain seeds of intention that could elevate by means of praise or destroy by means of satire and imprecation. The belief that the words of the bard's could profoundly affect those who would listen stems from the power bestowed on the craft of bardism, a power that causes the internal constitution of both bard and recipient to be influenced and transformed. And therein lies the profundity: the intrinsic constitution of both bard and listener are affected and transformed by the power of bardism; this is its magic. In Celtic society, past and present, the voice of the bard was and is held in great esteem, as are the words that they present or write. In preliterate centuries, when only the elite could read and write, those who yielded the power of spoken and written word were venerated, respected, and also feared.

One might easily fall into the trap that it is the literal element of any tradition that ensures its longevity or strives towards the longing for immortality. This would be a wholly incorrect assumption to make regarding the Welsh bardic tradition. Whilst for over one thousand five hundred years the oral/aural and literal elements have ran side by side through the tumults of time, it is the oral/aural component that perpetuated and maintained the survival of the tradition. One would be forgiven to place less emphasis on the oral aspect of a tradition when it has a literal counterpart, but this would be doing a disservice to the power of the bards.

The key to the immortal nature of the Welsh tradition is held within the collective memory of the bards themselves. Essentially the bards were the guardians of memory; they immortalised and caused the memorialisation of people, events, trials, tribulations, triumphs, satire, comedy, learning, and magic.[34] To achieve this consistency in practise, the components that made up the tradition were wholly memorable and designed in such a way that the symbiotic relationship between the discipline of cynghanedd and the language itself resulted in a tradition whose main skill was that of memorisation. The bards relied entirely on memory to perpetuate the poetry, songs, and stories, and they were able to do this because the structure of cynghanedd enabled them to memorise the material fairly easily.

The internal structure of each line caused the bard to direct the memory in a consistent fashion and transmit the poetry in a way that most listeners could remember.[35] The poems lived on, beyond the performance of the bard, and it was the magic of cynghanedd that enabled this. Whilst the study of cynghanedd is interesting and worthy of pursuit, this book does not advocate the necessity of learning the system to connect with the spirit of Cerridwen. However, what I am advocating is that cynghanedd and other bardic skills, as an occultist, seem to be something that Cerridwen enjoys, is familiar with, and recognises, so an appreciation of the system is, I believe, not only necessary, but it also honours the memory of those who preserved Cerridwen for the future.

Rhyming verse is pleasing to the ear and still requires an aptitude and a degree of skill to practise. Whilst the English verses throughout this book cannot be classified as cynghanedd in its pure sense, they are essentially *englynion* (singular *englyn*). An englyn is typically four verses in length; they may contain a structure of cynghanedd and consist of ten, eight, seven, or six syllables per line. The most pleasing and easiest to remember are four lines with a total of thirty syllables.[36] In my working as a Druid, I prefer to use the term englyn to describe the verses that I use for devotional and magical

34   Thomas, *Y Traddodiad Barddol*, 17.
35   Hopwood, *Singing in Chains*, 8–9.
36   Hopwood, *Singing in Chains*, 63–66.

practises as opposed to poem or verse.[37] I do not use this word to appear quirky or in some way arcane. What is essential for the reader to appreciate is that my first language is Welsh, so englyn is the most natural and obvious choice for me. For non-Welsh speakers, using the term englyn connects one to the stream of consciousness that preserved Cerridwen and her mysteries.

The Literal Element

The third element of the bardic tradition, the literal component, has documented and preserved the material that pertains to Cerridwen in a unique and magical manner. One of the primary reasons for its survival is that it is so culturally specific to Wales that until recent centuries nobody beyond our borders was able to make heads nor tails of it. It was irrelevant to the rest of the world—that is, until it fell under the gaze of the Romantic movement of the eighteenth century and the occultists of the early twentieth century. Suddenly, by means of the literal material, new avenues of exploration were open to a new age that craved them. Many modern occultists found inspiration in the Welsh material. Not only did the Welsh bardic tradition span new wings that would take its wisdoms beyond the borders of our nation, but the characters, archetypes, and spirits that swam within the old manuscripts became relevant to a new group of people. The fact that you are reading a book about Cerridwen is testament to the power of the seeds of bardism.

The literal element has been both a blessing and a curse, causing those within the tradition to become fixated on the written word to the extent that no development or evolution of the craft was possible for them. For those who are culturally removed from the Welsh bardic tradition, mistranslations and ulterior motives have served to muddy the waters and occlude the true magic of the tradition. It has been a blessing, for it has maintained the magic of this truly ancient system for the benefit of every generation to come. But this comes with responsibility and the ability to respond to the tradition in

---

37   Other examples of englynion exist, with some being more popular than others. Five examples of englyn structure exist in the Welsh bardic tradition, with the most popular being called the Englyn Unodl Union. See pages 63–70 of Hopwood's *Singing in Chains* for an in-depth account of the rules and structure of englynion.

a manner that perpetuates its wisdom whilst simultaneously honouring its ancestry. In a literal sense, it is the physical ink on parchment collection of poetry and myths that has served to preserve the Welsh bardic tradition in perpetuity. Whilst on paper I make the distinction between the three elements that compose the tradition, it is vital that you understand that the three work in unison.

It is evident from the scant material that predates the sixth century that little, if anything, was written prior to the first literal bards of the early medieval period, so the addition of the literal element is a relative newcomer, being only approximately 1,500 years old at the most. Its position as a vital element of the tradition is, however, here to stay. Today the rules of strict meter are written in textbooks and instructional booklets; it is a tradition that can be learned from books, but for it to be living, it must be spoken, it must be sung. One can learn the system of cynghanedd by studying the craft from the various books that are available on the market and by receiving tuition from an established and experienced bard.

The literal aspect of the tradition serves as a gift by which we can honour the bards who strived to guard, maintain, and germinate the seeds of magic and mystery. The seeds that gave rise to Cerridwen's position in the twenty-first century started with the ancient bards of Wales; each one planted a seedling that, in turn, grew into a sapling in the grove of the great world tree. It is now our responsibility to water, nourish, and care for these trees, to take their fruits as seeds of future wisdoms and plant them in honour of those who are yet to come.

Our literal knowledge of Cerridwen comes directly and exclusively from this system; it and she were found nowhere else on earth. It is the Welsh bardic tradition that preserved and germinated the seeds of Cerridwen and the power of Taliesin for each subsequent generation; with this in mind, the bard is essentially in service to the future. But who are the bards, and what was and is their function?

6

The Four Eras of the Welsh Bardic Tradition

As I examine the systems that preserved her wisdom for the future, it will be apparent that I do so from the literal element of the bardic tradition. From a historical and heritage point of view, this is the best platform to begin our journey; anything prior to this period existed only in the oral/aural sense, and its exploration would be purely conjecture on my part. Conjecture and vision are two very different things. I will cast my focus on the spiritual and visionary dimension in the next part of this book, for it too has merit. Suffice it to say that for this historical section, the most effective and honourable filter is the literal element of the tradition.

The Welsh bardic tradition has four significant eras of development and expression, and a basic understanding of them is vital to our exploration of the mechanism that caused Cerridwen to survive the ravishes of time, new ideas, and progressive bardic and religious thinking. Welsh bardism spans a dizzying amount of time, from the 500s to the present day. That is truly a shocking amount of time to even attempt to conceptualise, but it's also worthy of pause for its remarkable tenacity to survive such a span of time.

The approximate timeline of the four eras of the Welsh bardic tradition are as follows:

- the Hengerdd era (era of the old songs)—500s to the 1100s
- the Gogynfeirdd era (era of the not-so-early bards)—1100s to the 1300s
- the Beirdd yr Uchelwyr era (era of the bards of nobility)—1300s to the 1650s
- the Modern era[38]—1650s to the present time

Each era is marked by a point of crisis, either sociopolitically or socioreligiously, and whilst each school differed somewhat from the other, what they represent is the spirit of continuation. Let us look a little closer at these four eras.

The Hengerdd Era
500 CE–1100 CE

The oldest form of native Welsh literature belongs to this period and does not, as surprisingly as it may sound, come from the region that we now identify as Wales, for there was no such place in existence at that point in time. The land that is now identified as Wales consisted of a number of different kingdoms, some of which stretched beyond the current political delineation of Wales. The Hengerdd stem primarily from what is referred to as *Yr hen Ogledd*, or the Old North, the regions that we now delineate as Cumbria, the northwest of England and southern Scotland, but those borders were not in place during the Hengerdd era.

If we look a little closer at the word *hengerdd*, we will note that it consists of two words—*hen*, meaning old, and *gerdd* (a mutation of *cerdd*), meaning song. In combination they are translated as meaning "the old songs."

---

38 Times given are approximate generalisations and estimated time period given for each era of the bardic tradition. Movement from one era to another was subtle and in all likelihood took several decades.

The name given to the bards of this era was the *Cynfeirdd*, which can be translated as the "before bards," a title afforded them by the second era of bards. Modern scholars have claimed that the early bards had survived the Druids and were in all probability intimately connected to the Druids of the last Celtic golden age.[39] Hidden in plain sight, any vestiges of the ancient British Druids are likely recorded in the works of the Welsh bardic tradition. The function of the bards was recorded by early classical authors who consistently stipulated that the bards sang songs of praise and satire, and were often accompanied by musical instruments.[40] They are identified as a caste within the Druidic collective, with some authors claiming that the bards possessed many of the functions and abilities of the Druids, namely those of divination, and there is a plethora of bardic literal material to suggest that this was probable.[41] However, the primary function of the old bard is not to preserve philosophy or theology per se, but rather to sing in praise of those who were the philosophers, leaders, kings, and Druids. Any suggestion of philosophy or deep spiritual thoughts that do appear in the bardic works occurs inadvertently.

Whilst many members of modern occulture obsess about the significance and importance of "apostolic succession," this was never a function of the bardic tradition; in fact, it was quite the opposite. The tradition did not rely on the principle of personality. What is being preserved is practise, not apostolic succession. However, I do make the claim that if anything survives from the period of the Iron Age Druids, it does so in the narrative spirit of the bardic tradition. From this earliest bardic period until the present time, the bardic tradition seemingly and inadvertently preserved the wisdom of the past—or was it perhaps wholly intentional all along? Whilst we can never truly answer that question, what is significant is that it does indeed survive.

The bards were not the only people who had a voice. The most influential writers of the period were also stirring the cauldron. Gildas, writing in his sixth century *De Excidio et Conquestu Britanniae*, refers to the bards of this

---

39 Caerwyn Williams, "Gildas, Maelgwn, and the Bards," 23.
40 Koch, *The Celtic Heroic Age*, 12–16.
41 Aldhouse-Green, *Caesar's Druids*, 183–184.

time who were singing in praise of a North Wales chieftain called Maelgwn. Gildas had nothing good to say of the bards other than they were inheritors of a Brythonic and Celtic tradition that was, in his opinion, pre-Roman and pre-Christian. His agenda to champion the rise of the Christian tradition served to paint the bards as primitive and ungodly.[42] Whilst conjecture on my part, I wonder if Gildas's irrational loathing of the bards as vestiges of something pre-Christian rises directly from a knowledge at the time that the bards were a continuation of the Iron Age and Celto-Romano Druids?

Writing in the ninth century, Nennius in his *Historia Brittonum* identifies an elusive figure called Talhaearn Tad Awen (Iron or Strong Forehead, Father of Awen) as being renowned in poetry, together with Aneirin and Taliesin.[43] This is the first known written reference to Taliesin and, interestingly, to the Awen—a connection that would gain momentum and eventually lead to Taliesin's association with the source of the Awen, the cauldron of Cerridwen. This brief reference implies that a historical figure known as Taliesin worked as a bard at some point during the sixth century. The old poetry suggests that Taliesin and the other famed bard of the time, Aneirin, were contemporaries, and whilst we know little, if anything, about their actual lives, their poetry, in the style indicative of the time, has survived. Their work demonstrates aptitude of rhyme and alliteration that hint at the earliest stirrings of the cynghanedd tradition.[44]

It is not known what Nennius's sources were, although it is possible that he was recording these tales and sagas from an earlier chronicle or record from the Welsh monasteries of the time. If he was copying from earlier literal material, the material would have been written in Latin and would not have given him the epithets for Talheararn and the vast number of nicknames for various Anglian kings. It is probable that Nennius's sources were directly from the oral tradition of the existent bards, which Rachel Bromwich called the professional guardians of past history.[45]

---

42   Jarman, *The Cynfeirdd*, 4.
43   Caerwyn Williams, *The Poems of Taliesin*, x–xi.
44   Hopwood, *Singing in Chains*, 7
45   Bromwich, *The Beginnings of Welsh Poetry*, 44.

The period of the Cynfeirdd covers a vast chunk of time that is commonly referred to as the Dark Ages, from the sixth through the eleventh centuries until the arrival in Britain of the Normans. The material from this period, however, only survives in later medieval manuscripts. On the surface, this may seem a contradiction; however, the style of language and the evolution of written Welsh allowed later scholars to identify the idiosyncrasies and styles of poetry that belong to a significantly earlier period than they were scribed, notably to the period of early and Old Welsh. It must be appreciated that the common Brittonic language of Britain was evolving, and this took centuries to morph into what is identified as the "Old Welsh" language of pre-1100.

The distinctive thing about this period of early poetry is the nature of the poetry in question and the prose; there is a lot of mysticism here. Aneirin, Taliesin, the poet Llywarch Hen, the prophecies of Britain called Armes Prydein, and even the poetic material from the later Black Book of Carmarthen and the Red Book of Hergest belong to this period. With only five to six hundred years separating the Cynfeirdd from the time of the Iron Age Druids, it is possible that the mysticism of the past continued to influence the bardic tradition. Whilst it is possible that a historical figure that went by the name of Taliesin may have existed in the time that Nennius writes about, we have no evidence to pinpoint the individual to a specific location. The fourteenth-century Book of Taliesin contains at least twelve poems identified as belonging to the pre-ninth-century period, by means of the language used in their compilation.[46]

With the evolution of language and the first foundations of the literal bardic tradition, there is a vagueness to this era, one that inspired the next phase of the bardic tradition to have a somewhat Romantic opinion of the early bards. In all likelihood, the Hengerdd period inspired future bards to don the title/name of Taliesin for themselves, which would account for the dizzying amount of poetry attributed to Taliesin over an impossible span of several centuries. It cannot be known for certain if the name Cerridwen

---

46   Lewis and Williams, *The Book of Taliesin*, xv.

was significant in the minds and schooling of the early bards, but with later emphasis placed on the name and her function, it is likely that she was known to the earliest bards. Whilst the later material identified as belonging to this era certainly contains her name, we cannot with 100 percent certainty know if her name had been highly developed at this point in time.

The Gogynfeirdd Era
1100 CE–1300 CE

Gogynfeirdd—derived from "go" and "cynfardd," to mean "the not-so-early bards"—differed from their earlier counterparts in that they were professionals: they received training, they were paid a wage, they were members of an exclusive guild of bards, and their rights were protected by Welsh law.[47] The bards received formal training that spanned several years, and this system of bardic schooling persisted in Wales in various forms consistently until the seventeenth century, at which point it evolved into the current modern bardic system.[48]

It is evident that bardic schools of medieval Wales were singularly responsible for the guardianship and also the preservation of Wales's native traditions, a span of some 1,500 years in totality. The Black Book of Carmarthen is birthed from this era, 1225–50, and the themes within it belong to and are inspired by the period of the Hengerdd. This was also a period of identity crisis when Wales lost its independence in 1282 and was incorporated into the English political system by Edward the First. Perhaps the Romantic notions of the Hengerdd were particularly appealing during this volatile sociopolitical period. It is from this period in time that we learn remarkable things about Cerridwen—more on this in chapter 7.

---

47 Hopwood, *Singing in Chains*, 11–12.
48 Thomas, *Y Traddodiad Barddol*, 9–18.

· Yr Uchelwyr, the Bards of Nobility
1300 CE–1600 CE

From the period of 1300 onwards, we see a marked change in the bardic tradition as it became more formally structured and pervasive. Towards the middle part of the 1300s, with Christianity dominating the landscape, Cerridwen begins to lose her status and the admiration of the bards. By the late fourteenth century she has been pushed off her throne of honour and respect, and we start to witness the bards of the nobility denigrating her traditional attributes. She is subject to the worst and most horrific of fates: dismissal and disregard. What I need you to pause and note here is the amount of time that this denigration took: from approximately 1300 to the latter half of the 1600s—a staggering three centuries and a number of generations. This was not something that happened overnight; it was a gradual and slowly developed idea indicative of the vast changes to society and culture.

As far as the bards of the nobility were concerned, Awen was under jurisdiction of the Christian god and was not something indicative of the mystical qualities of Cerridwen's cauldron. By the end of the fourteenth century, the bards were reluctant to relate anything at all to Cerridwen, but they did, however, maintain their connection with their icon Taliesin. They placed great emphasis on the authenticity and wisdom of Taliesin's Awen, whereas in stark contrast Cerridwen is subjected to denigration, whilst paradoxically she cannot be wholly separated from the Taliesin figure. The dominant patriarchal society of the time preserved the identity of the assumed masculine figure of Taliesin.[49]

It would not have been beneficial for the bards to dismiss the Taliesin figure, for it gave them the authority to span time and to connect the archaic nature of their particular tradition. In this manner, the figure of Taliesin was purposefully developed and made appropriate for each generation of bards. It was essential that Taliesin moved on with the times and current thinking,

---

49 The title Taliesin is assumed to be male only by function of narrative. It simply means a radiant brow and has increasingly become a gender-neutral title.

adopting and expressing Christian thought rather than stagnating like a worn-out old Druid in an ancient Pagan past.[50]

Arguments as to the origins of the Awen prevailed, with perhaps the most famous being the battle of wits between two bards of the nobility, Llywelyn ap y Moel and Rhys Goch Eryri. Eryri asks Llywelyn, "If you are indeed a Chief Bard, say then what is the nature of Awen and where its beginnings can be found?"

To which Llywelyn answers, "From the Holy Ghost and pure battle, the light of song." Eryri accepts the answer and affirms that the Awen was first revealed to man from heaven on Whit Sunday.[51]

One of their contemporaries at the time, a bard by the name of Siôn Cent, blatantly attacked the bards themselves and what he perceived as the inappropriate use of the Awen. In his opinion, the Awen had two sources: the first and foremost being a gift directly to the bard from God and the Holy Spirit. The second source arose from the *ffwrn natur uffernawl*, meaning "the furnace of hellish nature."[52] Cent attacks the bardic schools, claiming that increasing numbers of bards were spouting lies by means of the infernal source of the Awen. This had an enormous impact on the psychology of the bards and was perhaps the turning tide of thought against the original source of the Awen: Cerridwen's cauldron. What we see during this time is in stark contrast to the pervious era of the bards and a turn against anything that may be perceived as anti-Christian or anything that contained thoughts contrary to Christian ideology.

The following example, from the hand of Iolo Goch in his *Marwnad i Hersdin Hogl* (Death Song of Hersdin Hogl), serves to demonstrate the often-strong feelings some of the bards had towards Cerridwen:

> She is a ridiculous, stupid stock character, demonic and devilish, or so it would appear. And the image of her pulls on every familiar anti-feminine, anti-womanly motif; she is a loathsome, odious mock of a woman with her ugly, diseased, infectious, devouring, and odious

---

50 Haycock, *Studia Celtica* XVIII/XIX, 58.
51 Ford, *Ystoria Taliesin*, 33–34.
52 Edwards, *Gwaith Siôn Cent*, 1914.

body and her hideous consuming nature. No wonder that she should be mated with one who emulates so perfectly her demonic countenance. But let us now bury her and her ugly clubfoot and her magical strikes, this pointy wide-nostriled hag, for we have lived long enough in the times of old Ceridfen.[53]

It must be noted that Goch, in the above statement, did not use a word associated at the time with a witch; the original word he used was *widdon*, a mutation of *gwiddon*, meaning giantess, female monster, and hag. It would be another century or so before the common early modern word *gwarch* was used to mean a witch; more on this a little later. Whilst his statement is derogatory and scathing of Cerridwen and those associated with her, it must also be seen in the wider context of enormous sociopolitical and religious change. Cerridwen slowly became a victim of the changing times and profound, long-lasting influences from the English-speaking world. Goch's statement is one of the first to denounce Cerridwen as anything that could be inspirational or sacred; it is the earliest example of her transformation to the stereotypical idea of a late medieval witch.

The bards of the nobility and their conservatism and sense of ownership of the material and its content caused a gradual stagnation of the tradition until it finally stalled after two hundred years of impending decline. The increasing anglicization of the Welsh gentry, and in turn the bards, saw a further distancing from a tradition that had maintained Welsh identity for centuries. The strict metred practise of bardism and its intractability failed to attract the new poets, who preferred to write in free verse. The rise in intellectualism steered the learned away from what was increasingly perceived as a stale and old-fashioned system. The bards gradually lost their privileged state and became no better than the poor minstrels who served to entertain in return for money.

The decline happened gradually over a period of one hundred years, from approximately 1530 to 1650. This entire span of time heralded great crisis in Wales, with the Acts of the Union profoundly affecting the countenance

---

53   Translated by the author from Johnston, *Gwaith Iolo Goch*.

of Welsh identity between 1536 and 1543.[54] English became the legal language of the Welsh court systems, and those found using the Welsh language were denied roles in public offices of the king. By this point in time, the Welsh gentry were already mostly fluent in English, with many denying their mother tongue for fear of losing status. The Welsh language slowly became the domain of the working and lower middle classes. Gradually, the works of the Union, gentrification, and an increase on the emphasis placed on intellectualism diminished the power of the Welsh language.

What followed was a barren period of degeneration within the bardic tradition, with few references recorded of the gatherings of bards through the latter half of the seventeenth century. By 1701 the bards were gathering once more, and in a timely fashion, for the rise in "Celtomania" was about to sweep the country, with the rise of the Romantics and those who would serve to revive the dying tradition.[55] There is magic to be gleaned from the silent decades of bardism. The social structure of the Bardic Order may well have lost its momentum, but something else was bubbling under the surface, just waiting to rise, waiting patiently for the right people to awaken to its power.

The Modern Era
CIRCA 1650–PRESENT

Following the lull and the decline of the organised bardic schools, the popularity of all things Celtic created an interest in Welsh culture and literature and traditions far beyond the confines of Wales. For the last 230 years, the tradition has been perpetuated by an organisation called Gorsedd Beirdd Ynys Prydein (Gorsedd of Bards of the Island of Britain). This was a concept dreamed into being by the infamous Edward Williams, who went by the bardic name Iolo Morganwg. He was determined to revision the role of the bard in Wales and bring about enormous change in Welsh culture, and he

---

54   Koch, *Celtic Culture*, 182.
55   Miles, *The Secret of the Bards of the Isle of Britain*, 34.

succeeded in doing so. His influences can be felt and seen not only in Welsh culture but throughout modern occulture.[56]

The role of the Gorsedd (which means a ceremonial throne and a mound of earth or a hillock) is to supervise the bardic rituals and competitions of the Welsh annual cultural extravaganza called the National Eisteddfod.[57] At this popular event every August, the Chief Bard of Wales is chosen, and prizes are awarded for the best demonstrations of bardism, resulting in the winning of a chair, a crown, or a medal in various competitions. The Gorsedd conducts examinations of bardic materials and individuals who wish to rise to the honour of being a member of the Gorsedd and are subsequently awarded by admission to the grades of blue (bard), green (ovate), or white (Druid) robe.

Those observing the National Eisteddfod ceremonies with no cultural understanding of the event will see, for all intents and purposes, what on the surface is a full-blown Pagan ritual, but this observation would be incorrect. Whilst appearing particularly Pagan in appearance, the Gorsedd of Bards and its Eisteddfod Druids are by definition cultural Druids. They do not express an animistic or a Pagan theology or philosophy. In fact, the National Eisteddfod doesn't express a Christian theology—the rituals are a tradition of cultural expression, but they do not contain a spiritual dimension to them. That is not to say that members of the Gorsedd are not spiritually or religiously inclined; some of them may well be. The function of the rituals is not to perpetuate a spiritual agenda, but rather to express a cultural identity and the promulgation and celebration of the Welsh language.

The mission of the Gorsedd is the excellence of the bardic tradition. The great achievers of bardism are honoured at the annual event with much pomp and ceremony, which is both entertaining and profoundly moving. But the key word in all this is "honour." The pinnacle of the event is to honour the efforts of the bards, and the highest honour of all goes to those who have excelled enough to win the chair and the crown. Bubbling under the surface

---

56   For further details about the life and influence of Iolo Morganwg, see *A Rattleskull Genius* by Geraint H. Jenkins.

57   *Eisteddfod* is translated to mean "the abode of the seat."

of the colourful ceremonies is a deep magic that may pass right over the heads of those observing, for at the moment the Archdruid of the Gorsedd invites the bard to sit on the great throne, they become in that moment the sum totality of all the bards that have gone before them. By ritual and proclamation, with the three gleaming rays that represent the Awen behind them, they are transformed forever—in effect destined to never be the same individual they were only moments before. The ceremony changes the internal psychic constitution of the bard, and at that still point in the centre of the Gorsedd, they fall into an ancient tradition of Chief Bards.

Whilst there is barely any mysticism intentionally transmitted, acknowledged, or expressed through the modern bardic schools, there is a deep appreciation of the tradition itself and its power to inspire. The modern bardic movement is strong, thriving, and a testament to the power of the bard and bardism and their ability to survive through the ages.

7

Songs of Praise: Cerridwen and the Gogynfeirdd

There are a number of references in the Gogynfeirdd material that are particularly interesting and worthy of elaboration. The nature of these differ greatly from the later bardic material, which moves from praise to derision. With only a handful of early references to what I refer to as "Cerridwen Adjacent Material," i.e., the Awen, the cauldron, and Taliesin in the Hengerdd poetry, there are significant examples available to explore in the Gogynfeirdd era. This is likely reflecting a maturation of tradition and the concreting of certain principles and ideas; of particular note to this book are several references to the origin of the Awen, the power of the bard and where that power comes from, and how the cauldron of Cerridwen herself is central to the bardic tradition. The bards have found their feet under the table, and in doing so, they have expanded on the idea that Cerridwen was a significant detail in their evolution, their development, and their expression. So, let us now turn our attention to some of the poems that record what might seem to be only minor details of Cerridwen, which, when examined closely, turn out to be quite revealing.

Please note that this current work will focus on only a small number of examples. I do this for several reasons. Upon reading and examining the poems, you will note that there is significantly more going on in these short verses than is immediately apparent. Many of the themes that I explore are repeated in other poems, and therefore I have omitted those poetic works that only serve to emulate and reflect the themes that are discussed here.

◆ ◆ ◆

The first example is brought to us from the manuscript of the Black Book of Carmarthen (Llyfr Du Caerfyrddin), dated 1225–1250 and preserved today at the National Library of Wales, in the form of a poem that has been offered the title "A Poem in Praise of Cuhelyn Fardd (Cuhelyn the Bard)." In the opening lines of the poem, we read:

> Devs ren, rymawy Awen, amen fiat.
> Fynedic waud, fruythlaun traethaud, trybesttaud heid.
> Hervit urten, autyl Kyrridven, ogyrven amhad.
> Amhad anav, areith awyrllav, y cav keineid.
>
> Lord God, grant me Awen, amen so may it be.
> A steadfast song of praise, fruitful utterance, in the tumult of the crowd.
> Because of the dignified song of Cerridwen, the ogyrfen of various seeds,
> Rich seeds, the generous song of the refined magician.[58]

The opening line's exaltation of the Christian god and beseeching of the gift of Awen is not unusual or unique. On one hand it is reflective of the changing times and the dominant Christianised culture of Wales, whilst also simultaneously and covertly hiding a bardic mystery. It has been noted by academics and visionaries alike that not all the poems of the bardic tradition begin in this manner—only a select few do. Why? Several scholars have claimed that the poems starting with a blatant exaltation of the Christian

---

58 Translated by the author from the text of Peniarth Manuscript 1, designated Llyfr Du Caerfyrddin (Black Book of Carmarthen), National Library of Wales.

god are those most replete with pre-Christian lore. This is a bold state-ment to make, but one which I believe has some merit, for it identifies the poetry that contains themes and subjects that belong to the old world long before the arrival of the Nazarene to these shores. The possible inclusion of the Christian deity in the opening line not only serves to identify those poems that are mystical in nature and allude to a pantheon of British gods and spirits, they also served to protect the material by using Latinised forms of words pertinent to the religious beliefs of the scribes who were actually doing the copying. Whilst there is seemingly some consistency of thought and planning that went into this mechanism of identification and survival, I believe that there is significantly more going on beneath the surface than is immediately apparent. I attribute this to the narrative spirit, which I will explore later in the visionary-applicable section of this book.

Our bard is beseeching the Christian god for the gift of Awen, which is identified as a steadfast song of praise, but one that is powerful enough to produce fertile gifts through its utterance alone—the implication here is that the Awen and its utterance have the power to produce something. Even when amongst a tumultuous crowd, all clambering for attention, the Awen will be heard.

The third line goes on to identify Cerridwen's song of Awen as being the highest ranking, most dignified, and splendid of all songs; this contra-dicts the function attributed to the Christian god in the opening line. On the surface of things, the bard is beseeching a deity for the gift of Awen whilst simultaneously attributing the power held within the Awen to the dignified and high-ranking song of Cerridwen herself.[59] This contradiction would have been lost on non-native speakers, and lost further through allit-eration and rhyme of metre, but to the trained ear, the power held within the expression of Awen originates with Cerridwen. The second half of the third verse demands significantly closer attention, owing to the inclusion of

---

59 *Urten*, written as *urdden* and *urddasol* in modern Welsh, has several meanings attrib-uted to it: dignified, honourable, noble, high-ranking, esteemed, revered; Bevan, *Geiriadur Prifysgol Cymru*.

the word *ogyrfen*. For an examination of the application of the suffixes *fen* and *wen*, see chapter 10.

The word *ogyrfen* appears in the bardic material with several spellings: *ogrfen, ogyrfen, ogyrwen*.[60] The prefix *ogr* is a soft mutation of *gogr*, which is translated as "sieve" or something that facilitates a sieving. Primarily in the Welsh language, a *gogr* is a wooden framed tool with a fine mesh base used for winnowing and the separation of seeds from the seed body, or from smaller particles that are not required or considered as waste. The suffix *fen* can be taken to mean woman or womanly, whereas the suffix *wen* implies holy and blessed. There is little consistency of form in the old manuscripts, and the name has taken the same fate that is strikingly similar to the name of Cerridwen herself. The suffix *fen* is no longer seen in modern renditions, where the name has stabilised into the forms *(g)ogyrwen*.[61] The translation of ogyrfen / ogyrwen throughout all bardic eras would appear thus:

A woman who sieves, or the blessed and holy sieve.

Just when you were expecting high profundity, I present to you a sieve! But if we scratch at the surface a little, what we found swimming beneath is, in fact, a profundity, but one hidden in plain sight. Cerridwen is not only a woman or blessed and holy personification that sieves, she is the person who sieves various seeds. You will find the word "seed" throughout this work, and for good reason, for the bardic tradition often refers to the Awen as being seeds, and not one alone but various and abundant. The Awen is not simply one thing: it is not just writing poetry or singing or playing an instrument, it is a myriad of qualities that invoke and evoke the creative powers of the Awen. Cerridwen acts as a sieve, sieving the seeds—truths from untruths, knowledge from ignorance, creation from destruction. She acts as the process of eliminating what does not inspire—the flimsy, the all too whimsical,

---

60 In this book, *ogrfen* will appear as *gogyrwen* when I refer to the use of the name in modern Pagan / polytheistic practise.

61 The G in brackets is only vocalised when the name is not subject to a soft mutation; this only occurs within the structure of a sentence. As a stand-alone name, the G would be pronounced.

the ethereal, procrastination, arrogance, ignorance, discouragement, hindrance, disempowerment.

When Cerridwen is approached and worked with by means of sacred relationship, the antithesis of Awen falls through the fine mesh, leaving behind the very things that bring to our lives the most inspiration—unadulterated Awen. It is a form of blessed or holy winnowing. This function of sieving or winnowing was known to the bards, and it is important that one understands that much of the bard's knowledge and wisdom is a *cyfrinach,* or secret that only they were privy to; words and their function conceal mystery. The peculiarity of the term *winnowing* is mentioned almost fleetingly yet tellingly by the late Hywel Teifi Edwards, an expert on the history of Wales's National Eisteddfod, who, when writing about the bard Dafydd Ap Edmwnt, said:

> Far more important than this winning the cywydd in praise of the Trinity was his revision and winnowing of the strict metres and the cynghaneddion.[62]

His casual reference to winnowing marries beautifully with this peculiar trait of the gogyrwen as the personification of Awen, and one that acts as a filter and director of the universe's inspirational life force. Land without the breath of spirit is simply matter; sea without the breath of spirit is only water; it is the holy and sacred breath that breathes life into these things: this is the song of Awen. The bards, those of the past and of the present, step into the currents of the Awen; they can do nothing other than sing within its flow, and in return they commence to shine, their brows radiant and splendid. They act as gogyrwen, as holy sievers of truth.

The Awen and the gogyrwen go hand in hand. If the bards speak of the gogyrwen, it is always in relation to the Awen or to Cerridwen and her bards. Examples of this can be seen in the Book of Taliesin, which tells us:

> *Seith ugein ogyrfen, yssyd yn yr Awen.*
>
> *There are seven-score ogyrfens in the Awen.*[63]

---

62   Edwards, *The Eisteddfod,* 7.
63   Translated by the author from the Book of Taliesin.

In essence, the Awen does not have a singular gogyrwen that serves it; it has a number of them. In my opinion, the term is indicative of a rank or a function of an individual who is intimately connected to the ways of the Awen. The function of gogyrwen in relation to Cerridwen is found in another poem in the Book of Taliesin:

> *Neut amuc yg kadeir, o peir Kerritwen;*
> *Handit ryd vyn tafawt, yn adawt gwawt ogyrwen.*
> *Gwawt ogyrwen, uferen rwy digones*
> *Arnun a llefrith a gwlith a mes.*

> *Defended is my song that rises from Cerridwen's cauldron;*
> *Free is my tongue, in the song of praise and exaltation of ogyrwen.*
> *My song in praise of the ogyrwen, who is satisfied,*
> *Together with milk, dew, and acorns.*[64]

The above verse, whilst elements are lost in translation, clearly identifies Cerridwen as a gogyrwen, which Marged Haycock in her commentary on the Book of Taliesin identifies as "inspiration, a component of the Awen." Yet again we see another example of the term song or to sing, continuously referred to when the bard speaks of the Awen.[65] Interestingly, the above verse also contains perhaps the only example in the Welsh bardic tradition of a suitable offering that satisfies Cerridwen in her role as a gogyrwen—the offerings of milk, dew, and acorns.

The other example from the same body of work, the Book of Taliesin, reiterates the previously stated function:

> *Ban pan doeth o peir,*
> *Ogyrwen Awen teir.*

> *Exalted wisdom from the cauldron,*
> *Ogyrwen of the three Awen.*[66]

---

64   Translated by the author from the Book of Taliesin.
65   Haycock, *Legendary Poems from the Book of Taliesin*, 280.
66   Translated by the author from *"Kadeir Teyrnon"* in the Book of Taliesin.

The most poignant term in the above verse is the use of the word *doeth*, meaning wise/wisdom, adding another quality to the myriad of meaning that we can attribute to the cauldron and the Awen. In the latter two examples we can ascertain that the Awen and its song is intimately connected to the cauldron, specifically to Cerridwen's, although there is often some ambiguity as to who owns the cauldron in the later poetic material, as Cerridwen's loses her station amidst the later medieval bardic tradition.

The Gogynfeirdd bards, and later manuscripts copied from earlier sources identify Cerridwen as a conduit and guardian of the Awen, and that the Awen arises from the depths of her cauldron, with the suggestion that it is somehow held or incubated by it. She has a role which is offered the title of *gogyrwen*, the blessed separator of seeds, a divine filter of sorts, and it is her song that causes this sieving to occur. We can see a function of separation emulated in the chase sequence of the later myth of the birth of Taliesin, culminating in Cerridwen as the black-crested hen, pecking at various seeds to find the one that would become the radiant brow. However, Cerridwen is not alone in being a *gogyrwen*, and in the next example of Gogynfeirdd poetry, you will note that the bards refer to themselves as being "the bards of Ogyrfen." This suggests to me that the bards themselves occupied a rank whereby they participated in an act of sieving, the filtration of inspiration, that their job and task is to find the right seeds, those that will grow into the future. One could also perceive the bards as being representatives of the primary gogyrwen, Cerridwen.

The role of the gogyrwen, the blessed and holy sieve, is to seed the future with Awen in the same manner that the function of the bard is to seed the next generation with wisdom.

The next poem from the Gogynfeirdd period that I shall focus on is one from the prolific medieval bard Cynddelw Brydydd Mawr. The poem in question is titled "Marwnad Rhiaid Flaidd ac Arthen (The Funeral Song of Rhiaid the Wolf and His Brother Arthen the Bear)." Of note here is the word *marwnad*, or funeral song, which inadvertently highlights the idiosyncrasies of the bardic tradition. The function of the funeral song was to honour an individual by immortalising them in poetry. It was the highest form of praise and accolade one could dream of having. Thousands of these funeral songs exist to this day, but they were written by bards for the bards, and therefore they contained themes specific to that school of thought and training. They offer us a glimpse into the mindset of the bards and of concepts and ideas that were important to them. Relevant to this work is their continuous references to Cerridwen, her cauldron, and the power inherent within the bardic tradition.

This is exemplified here from the mouth of Cynddelw Brydydd Mawr:

> *Mor wyf hyglau fardd o feirdd ogrfen,*
> *Mor wyf gŵyn gyfrwys, nid wyf gyfrwen,*
> *Mor wyf gyfrin a ffyrdd cyrdd Cyridfen;*
> *Mor eisiau eu dwyn yn eu dyrwen.*

> *As clear and resonant a bard I am, of the bards of ogrfen,*
> *As experienced as I am with grief, I am not merry,*
> *As privy to the secret and mystery I am in the ways of*
>   *the crafts of Cerridwen,*
> *The more I long to induce and bring about joyous sound.*[67]

What Brydydd Mawr is expressing in this verse, in line with the remaining element of the poem, is a sense of loss and grief for the subject of the funeral song—Rhiaid Flaidd and his brother Arthen, who were both killed in battle around the year 1160. Whilst simultaneously eulogising the subjects of the funeral song, he also cannot help but sing his own praises and the qualities that make him such an excellent bard. The words he chooses to epitomise this are carefully selected and offer us an insight into the magic of the bardic tradition.

First of all, he identifies himself as a clear and resonant bard, but on the next breath he claims he is a bard of ogyrwen. He directly connects his gift to the separator of seeds. To note, it is unclear in the original language if he is associating himself with another gogyrwen—in this case, that would be

---

67   Translated by the author from "Marwnad Rhiaid Flaidd," Hendregadredd Manuscript, NLW 6680B.

Cerridwen—or whether he is identifying himself as a *gogyrwen*. It is possible that both interpretations are valid.

The third line is particularly interesting, for it tells us something about the magic associated with Cerridwen and her crafts. The key word here is *gyfrin* (mutation of *cyfrin*), which means one who is privy to a secret or a mystery, a participant that is in the secret, mysterious, esoteric, mystical. Brydydd Mawr is telling his audience that he is privy to the secrets of the mystical crafts of Cerridwen, implying that he has been taught them. He is alluding to the fact that the bards are initiates of a school of practise that ordinary civilians were not privy to. The more he knows and the more he practises that craft, the more inclined he is to bring about a joyous sound. In the bardic tradition, the joyous sound is the Awen.

Brydydd Mawr remarks that Cerridwen possesses certain crafts, and he is aware and familiar with their nature. The bards of Wales have been continuously crafting one form of this magic—words—for a staggering amount of time.[68] They are privy to one of her crafts, and whilst emphasis on magic has waned within the tradition over the last four centuries, it is still there, swimming beneath the surface.

---

68   It is apparent that the bards have existed as a disciplined school in the literal sense
     for the last 1500 years and from accounts by the classical Roman authors, who were
     aware of the function of bardism. It is highly likely that the bards existed as an inte-
     gral aspect of Iron Age Celtic society, albeit no record in their own language sur-
     vives to substantiate this claim. Farley and Hunter, *Celts: Art and Identity*, 240–243.

8

The Book of Taliesin

Ironically, it is from the period of the bards of nobility that some of the most well-known resources arise. Regardless of their attempts to denigrate the material that records Cerridwen and her attributes, we must not lose heart. A significant amount of scribing and copying continued throughout this period. Distances and various disciplines served as a vacuum that allowed for swathes of manuscripts to be recorded that contradicted the attitudes of the bards of nobility. The palaeographer J. Gwenogvryn Evans attempted to date the collection now known as the Book of Taliesin to around the year 1275; this has been proven to be incorrect, with the accepted date being sometime in the early decades of the fourteenth century. The date is significant, for it posits the manuscripts at the earliest era of the bards of nobility; it would be over a century before Cerridwen's denigration by the bards was to take speed. The poetic content in the Book of Taliesin does not belong exclusively to the era of the bards of the nobility. Much in the pattern of language used denotes a style that is indicative of pre-twelfth-century bardism. Whilst many of the poems can be attributed to events of pre-tenth-century Britain, Celtic scholars are reluctant to date them as such, and there remains an ambiguity regarding the actual age of many of the poems. Whilst it is accepted that several of the poems may have roots in the Hengerdd era, modern scholars and myself would be remiss to make such sweeping claims without adequate evidence to support it.[69]

If I move towards conjecture and unverifiable personal gnosis, it is notable (even in the corridors of academia and occulture there is a speculative acceptance) that several of the oldest poems belong to the earliest era of the bards.

The Book of Taliesin is significant, for it records several instances of the name Cerridwen and also peculiarities of her function and purpose, and these are important for this current discourse. What follows is a brief summary of the history of the Book of Taliesin to demonstrate the complex history of the bardic material.

Peniarth Manuscript number 2, as designated by the National Library of Wales in Aberystwyth, formed part of the body of work called Archaeologica Britannica, compiled from the library of Hengwrt by the eminent scholar Edward Llwyd in 1707. The subsequently titled Llyvyr Taliesin (The Book of Taliesin) formed part of the inventory of manuscripts held at the library. However, it is notable that the designation Llyvyr Taliesin was not a medieval title for the manuscript but one placed upon it by Llwyd or his colleagues at the time. The manuscript now forms part of the national collection at the National Library of Wales in Aberystwyth.

The Book of Taliesin is a small and unassuming manuscript measuring only 7 by 5 inches, containing, in rather plain text, sixty-one poems attributed to the Taliesin figure. It is written by a single "excellent" hand, according to the Celtic scholar Marged Haycock, using a regular textura script, which the scholar Daniel Huws dates to the first half of the fourteenth century.[70]

The first translated printed text of the Book of Taliesin in the English language appeared in the form of a compilation known as *The Four Ancient Books of Wales* in 1868, translated and edited by W. F. Skene. This tome was to have significant influence on later exploration of the Celtic material and the history and culture of the old Britons. The majority of translations

---

69   Haycock, *Legendary Poems from the Book of Taliesin*, 36.
70   Ibid., 1.

available today are inspired by this authoritative work, and it continues to be the most popular quoted translation available. However, it is important to note that the collection, whilst being the first of its kind, is poorly translated, with much nuance lost in translation. In 1910 J. Gwenogvryn Evans, the palaeographer and adept of Celtic literature, provided an exceptional facsimile and typography, text, and translation of the Book of Taliesin, and although heavily criticised for his conclusions, his collection forms a formidable and impressive record of the British/Welsh body of Celtic literature.

The material of the Book of Taliesin has been the subject of much academic analysis, with several hundreds of papers written in an attempt to make sense of a body of work that Sharon Turner described as "elaborately incomprehensible."[71] Several writers attempted to utilise the material to serve their own ulterior motives and vision of history that were at times highly imaginative. Celtic scholar pitched against Celtic scholar, and by the turn of the twentieth century the battle had become an almost bloody and sadistic pastime, stripping the material to shreds with inconsequential arguments that served only to befuddle the layman further. By the early 1980s a new breed of academic arose that served the material from a neutral standpoint, with little ulterior motive other than the appreciation of the material as relics of culture and language. And this is when the tide began to turn.

The most obvious references within the Book of Taliesin to Cerridwen are those that directly name her. However, there are other instances of consistency found in the themes of the later tale of Cerridwen, Gwion Bach, and Taliesin that allude to her function. Perhaps the most striking fact of them all is not only the inclusion of the name "Cerridwen," but that it refers to a female. There is one reference to Aranrhod, two references to Dôn (albeit one of those refers to her only by proxy of her son Gwydion); Modron, the great mother, receives one mention, and there is a fleeting reference to the nine maidens that tend to a magical cauldron. Other than these, women are mostly absent from the text of the Book of Taliesin,[72] a

---

71   Turner, *History of the Anglo-Saxons*, 636.
72   Lewis and Williams, *The Book of Taliesin*, xv.

sign of medieval Welsh values no doubt. However, it must be significant that Cerridwen is mentioned several times, as are the themes and function of her later story and zoomorphic counterparts. The same applies to the text of the Black Book of Carmarthen. She was evidently so integral to the mindset of the bards that they could not help but attribute a crucial role to her in their work. This point alone is a startling revelation to Cerridwen's momentous importance.

Our first example comes from the poem "Prif Gyuarch Geluyd (Chief Greeting of the Skilful One)," where Taliesin claims:

> Neu bum gan wyr keluydon,
> Gan Uath Hen, gan Gouannon,
> Gan iewyd, gan elestron,
> Ry ganhymdeith achwysson.
> Blwydyn yg Kaer Ofanhon,
> Wyf hen, wyf newyd, wyf Gwion;
> Wyf llwyr, wyf synhwyr keinon.

> I was with the craft/skilled/magic men,
> With ancient Math and Gofannon,
> I was with liverwort and iris,
> I was in company of powers,
> I was a year in the fort of Govannon,
> I am old, I am new, I am Gwion;
> I am complete, I am the conscious wisdom of the first drink.[73]

Taliesin tends to be associated with the divine family of Dôn from the fourth branch of the Mabinogi, a pattern that will be explored more comprehensively a little later in this discourse. Earlier in this poem, the characters of Gwydion and Lleu from the fourth branch are also mentioned. But here it is Math and Govannon that are called by name. Math is the great Druid magician king of the Kingdom of Gwynedd in modern-day North Wales.

---

73 Translated by the author from the *Facsimile and Text of the Book of Taliesin* by J. Gwnogvryn Evans.

He is the brother of the divine mother goddess Dôn, whilst Govannon, the divine smith, is Dôn's son. The company also consists of herbs and flowers, namely liverwort (iewyd) and iris (elestron), and whilst Celtic scholars have argued over whether or not the actual plants are being alluded to or if they are indeed the personal names of characters who are lost to us, I believe that the plants in themselves are worthy of exploration.

In the fourth branch of the Mabinogi, Math and Gwydion take to the flowers and plants of the earth to create a woman of flowers, Blodeuedd, to circumnavigate a fate that the goddess Aranrhod had placed on her son Lleu. It was the powers of the flowers that caused the magic to be effective, and I believe that the powerful company that Taliesin refers to is that of the magicians and the flowers combined. Taliesin then goes on to state that he was a year in the fort of Govannon, the divine smith. It is tempting here to associate Govannon and his fort with fire, and one might be sensible to do so, especially in line with a verse from the Book of Carmarthen where Taliesin claims:

> *It was with seven faculties that I was blessed,*
> *and with seven created beings that I was placed for purification;*
> *I was gleaming fire when I was caused to exist.*[74]

Taliesin then continues by stating, "I am old, I am new, I am Gwion," the protagonist in the much later tale of Cerridwen and Taliesin. It appears that whilst Taliesin holds the title of having a radiant brow, he maintains his identity as Gwion, or at least as having been Gwion in some other earlier guise. In his Taliesin form he claims to be complete and that he embodies the conscious wisdom of the first drink. I claim that the reference to the first drink is directly linked and subsequently inspired the story of the drops of liquid leaping from the cauldron to land on Gwion's thumb, thus imbuing him with all the wisdom and knowledge of all the worlds and their sciences. Whilst Cerridwen is not mentioned by name, the themes that surround her

---

74 Translated by the author from the Black Book of Carmarthen, Peniarth Manuscript 1, National Library of Wales.

in the later tale and the bardic material can be seen quite clearly in the above account.

Further potential references to these events are told in the poem "Angar Kyfundawt (The Hostile Confederacy)," which also contains references to Gwydion from the fourth branch of the Mabinogi.

Bum gronyn erkennis,
Ef tyfwys ymryn,
A'm mettawr, a'm dottawr,
Yn sawell y'm gyrrawr,
Y'm ry giawr o law,
Wrth vyg godeidaw,
A'm haruolles yar,
Grafrud, grib escar;
Gorffowysseis naw nos,
Yn y chroth yn was.

I was a perceptible grain,
I grew on the hill,
I am reaped and I am planted,
I am sent to the kiln,
I am freed from the hand,
And then I am roasted,
A hen got hold of me,
A ruddy, blood-stained one, a crested foe,
I rested nine nights,
In repose in her womb.[75]

We can clearly see references to the late themes of grain and the pecking of said grain by a crested hen, albeit the later tale identifies her as a black crested hen. However, in the Book of Taliesin the hen is described as being *grafrud*, meaning red-clawed. Consequently, Taliesin rests for nine nights in

---

75   Translated by the author from *The Facsimile and Text of the Book of Taliesin* by J. Gwenogvryn Evans.

the womb of the hen. Nine nights may well have been a euphemism for the common duration of pregnancy. Marged Haycock is of the opinion that it is a reference for the kilning time a grain is required to produce malt.[76] Once again, we can deduce a consistency of themes that course through the bardic material and eventually distill into the popular tale.

In the poem "Mabgyfreu Taliesin (The Youthful Adventures of Taliesin)," we see the first instance of Cerridwen being mentioned by name:

> *Kyfarachaf y'm ren,*
> *Y ystyryaw Awen,*
> *Py dyduc aghen,*
> *Kyn no Cherituen,*
> *Kyssefin ym byt,*
> *A uu eissywyt.*
>
> *I entreat the great parent,*
> *To consider the Awen,*
> *What brought its necessity,*
> *Before Cerridwen,*
> *In the primitive world,*
> *Which had its need.*[77]

In this verse we can see a reference to the Awen as a gift that Cerridwen was responsible for directing into our world. The bard is asking the audience to consider what ensured Awen was in the world before Cerridwen, when the world was in desperate need of its power. There is an implication here that little existed to direct Awen into the world until the concept of Cerridwen as its director came into being, suggesting that prior to this occurrence only chaos existed.

---

76 Haycock, *Legendary Poems from the Book of Taliesin*, 164–165.
77 Translated by the author from *The Facsimile and Text of the Book of Taliesin* by J. Gwenogvryn Evans.

9

The Chair of Cerridwen

I now turn my focus to the most significant poem of the Book of Taliesin in relation to Cerridwen, aptly titled "Kadeir Kerrituen (The Chair of Cerridwen)." I include the poem in full here; albeit elements of it seem to take us off-track, there is a beauty of interconnection that would no doubt be lost if I were to take verses out of context of the poem in its entirety. I offer the original Welsh with my translation:

Kadeir Kerrituen (The Chair of Cerridwen)
  Ren rymawr titheu.
  Kerreifant o'm karedeu.
  Yn deweint ym pylgeineu.
  Llewychawt vy lleufreu.
  Mynawc hoedyl minawc ap lleu.
  A weleis i yma gynheu.
  Diwed yn llechued lleu.
  Bu gwrd y hwrd ygkadeu.
  Auacdu vy mab inheu.
  Detwyd douyd rwy goreu.
  Yg kyfamrysson kerdeu.

Oed gwell y synhwyr nor veu.

Keluydaf gwr agigleu.

Gwydyon ap don dygynuertheu.

A hudwys gwreic ovlodeu.

A dyduc moch o deheu.

Kan bu idaw disgoreu.

Drut ymyt agwryt pletheu.

Arithwys gorwydawt

Yar plagawt lys.

Ac enwerys kyfrwyeu.

Pan varnher y kadeireu.

Arbenhic vdun y veu.

Vygkadeir am peir am deduon,

Am areith tryadyl gadeir gysson.

Rym gelwir kyfrwys yn llys don.

Mi ac euronwy ac euron.

Gweleis ymlad taer yn nant ffrangcon.

Duw sul pryt pylgeint.

Rwg wytheint a gwydyon.

Dyf ieu yn geugant yd aethant von.

Y geissaw yscut ahudolyon.

Aranrot drem clot tra gwawr hinon.

Mwyhaf gwarth y marth o parth brython.

Dybrys am ylys efuys afon.

Afon ae hechrys gwrys gwrth terra.

Gwenwyn y chybyt kylchbyt eda.

Nyt wy dyweit geu llyfreu beda.

Kadeir getwided yssyd yma.

A hyt vrawt parawt yn europa.

An rothwy y trindawt.

Trugared dydbrawt

Kein gardawt gan wyrda.

Great parent, I entreat you,
Forgive me of my sins,
In the dead of night and at morning prayer,
My radiance shines brightly,
Piercing was the life of Minawc the son of Lleu,
Who I saw in the past,
His end was in the stone grave of Lleu,
He was forced fiercely into battle,
Avagddu, my own son,
It was the gracious tamer who made him,
In contentious song,
But his senses were superior to mine.
The most skilled man I know,
Was Gwydion the son of Dôn who made splendid things,
And by magic made a woman of flowers,
He who stole pigs from the south,
For he had the best of learning,
Who was bold in battle, with the interlace of chain, *
And formed the shape of horses,
In order to appease objection, *
As well as wondrous saddles. *
When the chairs come to be judged,
Mine will be the best of them,
This is my chair, my cauldron, and these are my rules,
My perfect language is a consistent chair,
In the court of Dôn, I am the knowledgeable one,
I and Euronwy and Euron.
I saw violent fighting in Nant Ffrancon,
Early on Sunday,
Between birds of prey and Gwydion,
But on Thursday, certainly, they went to Anglesey,
To look for the skilled ones and the enchanters.
Aranrhod, her beauty exceeds the radiance of the dawn,

Her shame was the greatest shame for the Britons,
A raging river rushes about her court,
A savage river beats against the earth,
Poisonous its snare around the world,
The books of Bede do not tell lies,
My chair is kept, it is here,
And it will be maintained in Europe,
May the trinity grant,
Forgiveness on the day of judgement,
And the true kindness of noblemen.[78]

I fear that a comprehensive exploration of this poem would be well beyond the scope of this book. One could easily compose a dissertation of 30,000 words on this poem and still only scrape the surface. However, it is imperative that I offer you some insights to the details of the poem. What is not clear in the poem is whether the words are from Cerridwen herself or if Taliesin is acting as mouthpiece for her. This has invoked a quandary in academia that has raged for countless decades; no agreed consensus has been offered as to who, in fact, is speaking.

With Taliesin spanning an impossible stretch of time, it may suggest that various bards throughout time identified with the persona of Taliesin as their utmost ideal. At times the tone of the poem seems to suggest a third person is speaking, and at other times it speaks in the first person and is evidently the voice of Cerridwen. We could beat about the proverbial bush on this subject for a further handful of decades. So, for clarity and direction within this discourse, I offer you the following brief explanation, which will be explored fully in a later chapter. The voice that is speaking is the narrative spirit: it is the element of the bard that swims within the currents of Awen. In its written form, the poem loses the magic of relationship between bard and Awen; it becomes monodimensional. In performance the bard shifts by

---

78 Translated by the author from *The Facsimile and Text of the Book of Taliesin* by J. Gwenogvryn Evans, except for lines noted as * translated by Marged Haycock in *Legendary Poems from the Book of Taliesin*. Note that the title of this poem appears in Middle Welsh as Kadeir Kerrituen; in modern Welsh it is spelled Cadair Cerridwen.

power of Awen from speaking in the first person as him- or herself to also speaking in the first person as someone else entirely—a form of channelling, if you will. In this poem there are two voices, that of the bard and Cerridwen, who is speaking directly through the bard. It is not just the bard that possesses a radiant brow; it would be logical that Cerridwen herself, as the prototypic bard, is also gifted with the radiant brow. This peculiarity of bardism is lost not only in translation but in its literation.

In the first stanza are the words "In the dead of night and at morning prayer, my radiance shines brightly." If we consider that almost all references to Cerridwen are in relation to the Awen and the birthing of the radiant brow, this is important. The maintenance of one's own light and ability to shine. This is difficult. There are times in our lives when we do not feel like shining or when our light has dimmed by situations or problems. Often, those around us are affronted by one's light and strive to dim it. Bright lights will always cast the darkest shadows, and not necessarily in oneself but in others. Those who call for you to dim their light down to the level of theirs long to shine as brightly but are unable to do so. Cerridwen asks that you do not dim your light, that you keep your brow radiant—even when your heart is breaking and your spirit broken by the tribulations of life, maintain your light. In another poem from the Book of Taliesin, we are asked to ponder the nature of the body and spirit and the mysteries of sleep, where Taliesin asks us to consider the power of our inner radiance, our hidden radiance.[79] It is emulated here in the "Cadair Cerridwen."

It is apparent on first glance that another group of deities and archetypes are mentioned in this poem, as they were in the other poems that referenced Cerridwen, Gwion Bach, or her cauldron, that of the family of Dôn, matron goddess of the fourth branch of the Mabinogi.[80] The presence of Taliesin within the four branches of the Mabinogi is made clear as he is one of the seven survivors who return from the battle in Eire. His poetry continuously

---

79 *Mabgyfreu Taliesin*, lines 30–35, *The Facsimile and Text of the Book of Taliesin* by J. Gwenogvryn Evans.

80 Bromwich, *Trioedd Ynys Prydein*, 330, and Davies, *The Mabinogion*, 240.

alludes to witnessing the branches. Taliesin, or rather the radiant brow, is an ever-present radiance within the pages of the Mabinogi.

The poem appears to place Cerridwen in direct association with the family of Dôn, and indeed within the same poem she claims admiration for Gwydion, the son of Dôn, and speaks of the nature of Aranrhod, daughter of Dôn. With all these references to the fourth branch, one is inclined to wonder if she is present within that narrative of the Mabinogi at all, and whilst on face value she appears to be absent by name, I do believe that there is enough evidence to suggest that she exists in another form. I shall explore this function a little later.

Turning back to the poem at hand, the entire sequence of events that occur within the Mabinogi concerning the family of Dôn are, on the surface of things, very earthy—they concern themselves with magic, flowers, and the power inherent within the earth, and when language is combined with these elements, magic happens. When we look at Cerridwen's association with the family of Dôn, all examples of her name in the Book of Taliesin are in relation to this magical family. What can this be trying to tell us?

As we have previously seen, the bardic tradition, so intimately connected to Cerridwen, are by their very definition and practise magical. But these are limited to the crafting of magic by the power of words and sound and song. The family of Dôn possesses an additional form of magical skill, that of crafting magic, not only by the use of words and sound, but also by materials of the earth. Gwydion summons an army of trees in the epic poem "The Battle of the Trees." He and his uncle Math create a woman of flowers and steal pigs from the south, for they "had the best of learning." There is an implication here that natural materials contain within them a potential that can be utilised for the implementation of magic—that by some mysterious methodology, the innate power within the plants can somehow be released and harnessed.

Bardic magic changes the internal constitution of bard and listener. The magic of the family of Dôn combines this quality with a magic that causes change within the physical world. They cast spells, they change the shape and form of things, they perform a glamour that directly affects the internal and external constitution of things simultaneously.

Cerridwen takes to foraging the plants and herbs of the earth in the later tale to create the brew of Awen. There appears to be a symbiotic relationship and an understanding that voice and materials can be used for the crafting of magic. Not only is this stated as perhaps an example of effective magical crafting, but it is something that Cerridwen herself greatly admires. It is a magician that she admires above all else, and yet a quick glance at the shenanigans of Gwydion in the fourth branch clearly demonstrates a flawed magician, not an exemplary one, but still she admires him, and she does so because of his learning. This tells us something important, not only about the nature of Cerridwen, but of the expectations that she has of her bards and her children.

There is a humility and apologetic acceptance of her failings within the poem, and perhaps it is this which she sees emulated in the trials of Gwydion. Her son Afagddu is mentioned by name ("Auacdu" is Middle Welsh; "Affagddu" is modern Welsh), and that it was the divine tamer that created him, and whilst elements of the song of his creation were contentious, she admits that his sense was superior to her own. I find this quality interesting, especially the almost apologetic tone that it sets, albeit that tone is lost to some extent in translation. From the later tale we are informed that Afagddu, whose name means "utter darkness," is essentially the catalyst for the brewing of the magical Awen potion on account of his ugliness. However, other references to Afagddu in the Welsh bardic tradition exalt him as a peaceful individual, and whilst his countenance was terrifying, his internal constitution was quite the opposite, and he too was renowned for his bardic skills.[81] Cerridwen sought the potion to moderate his ugliness and make him acceptable amongst people and thus not offend their sensibilities. Yet at no point did she seek to ask her son's consent. His opinions, desires, or wishes were not consulted, and in the Chair of Cerridwen she humbly declares that his senses were superior to her own. Perhaps it is this quality of

---

81   Haycock, *Legendary Poems from the Book of Taliesin*, 321–322.

taking responsibility for one's actions and attempting to moderate them or correct them that she admired in Gwydion. His actions were neither good nor acceptable, and yet he took to his punishment and shaming and sought to correct his mistakes. He held his hands up and admitted he was wrong—a trait that takes courage and wisdom.

There is a lesson here in not taking things at face value, for what we may see on the surface may not be reflective of what is happening beneath the surface. Afagddu, whilst ugly, beheld an inner radiance and beauty not emulated by his looks. So often we can be quick to act when something appears contrary to our sensibilities or desires, and yet any attempt to transform those to our liking may cause untold collateral damage. Collateral damage is a theme that runs through the fourth branch in particular, and within the transformative tale of Cerridwen and Taliesin and the breaking of the cauldron, whose contents run as poison. Cerridwen and Gwydion may on the surface of things appear to be worlds apart, but there is much that they have in common.

When the chairs come to be judged, Cerridwen's chair will be the best of them. The judging of a chair—rendered in Welsh as *cadair*, meaning a song, a strict metre, and a physical chair—is a practise that continues to this day. During the primary bardic competition of the National Eisteddfod, it is the chair that is the most sought-after prize and yet, paradoxically, the 200 lines or more of bardic excellence that may win the chair is also considered a cadair. The chair is judged, and the prize is a chair. In the poem at hand, Cerridwen claims that when the chairs are judged, hers and hers alone will be the best of them, and with good reason: she is, in essence, the prototypic bard, the bard by which all other bards seek to emulate and mimic. Her song of Awen is the best of all the songs; it is the original song. She claims that her chair/song, her cauldron, and her rules bring about a perfection of language worthy of a prize. Consequently, even amongst the powerful magicians of the court or House of Dôn, she and she alone is the most knowledgeable one. The relationship between Cerridwen and the House of Dôn implies a reciprocity indicative of admiration and emulation. There is much that these deities have in common and much that we can learn from a closer inspection of those relationships.

One must learn in order to excel. She does not just wish this for her children, she demands it. She demands that we be the best that we can be, and as a stern mother, she is not afraid to punish or chastise us for sloppiness and for shoddy practise. She is the best at what she does and what she represents, and she wants for her children to be the best at their own skill sets. We see this emulated in her tale where it claims that she is learned in the arts of magic, the crafting of magic, and divination. This quality is evident within the Welsh bardic tradition, where bards are steeped in learning, the education is tough, the work is competitive, and the rewards are deeply fulfilling. Modern occulture also strives to learn from this quality, with many covens, orders, and groups striving to offer quality education and learned skills to their students, and long may it continue, for this is certainly a trait that Cerridwen wishes for her children: the betterment of the mind, the fine-tuning of mental aptitude, the integration of intent.

The learned arts work on three distinct levels: they affect the physical world, they transform the internal constitution, and they promulgate and encourage the ethereal, subtle, and magical attributes of the craft itself. Cerridwen is deeply and intimately tied not only to the bardic craft but to the entire spectrum of magical practise that circumnavigates the bardic tradition. It is the bringing of things into being by the power of words, it is the crafting of magic from elements and materials of the earth to bring about change, it is being skilled in prognostication and divination. In the twenty-first century, we must honour this; it is imperative that we do lest the spirit that is Cerridwen pass us by or we fall into patterns of self-indulgent, power-hungry stroking of one's ego for the sole benefit of the self.

The danger in all this is complacency and distorted vision. Magic lies at the heart of the modus operandi of Cerridwen's children, and when this quality is diminished, such as it has within the present Welsh bardic tradition, we no longer fulfil Cerridwen's rules. Learning and knowledge must be moderated by the visionary and subtle arts. Remember the bards were and should presently be magicians, learned, educated, and yet profoundly aware of the power of what is hidden from plain sight. The danger in modern occultism is that in an attempt to strive only for scholarship, we lose sight of the occult principles and inadvertently breed new occultists that lack any form of occult abilities. This is counter to Cerridwen's rules. We must moderate the intellect, the spirit, and the body.

Cerridwen is the divine personification of the virtues and quality of Awen. Her continuous evolution, development, and ability to change to the needs of her adherents is a function of her natural progression through time, but through all this, the fundamental properties of her virtues remain the same.

Her admiration for the skills of Gwydion are moderated by her references to Aranrhod, Gwydion's sister. Both were powerful magicians, but interestingly, Aranrhod's position as a powerful, independent woman emulates the qualities that we see in Cerridwen. There is much worth in exploring the interconnection between these two women in relation to the mysteries of womanhood, though it's a subject that, as a person who does not fully identify as female, I feel I would dishonour by attempting to discuss.

If we break down the poem, we can see that it comprises five distinct parts:

1. The radiance of one's own inner light.

2. The acceptance of one's own faults.

3. The admiration of the family of Dôn (magic).

4. The power of knowledge and learning.

5. The qualities of Aranrhod and womanhood.

We could take each of these sequences and apply them to a metaphysical analysis of our own living, and doing so consciously and in relationship with Cerridwen would serve to deepen our connection with her.

10

Cerridwen:
What's in a Name?

Throughout the previous chapters, it may now become apparent to you that an obvious element of Cerridwen has not been addressed—that of her name. Cerridwen's name can be spelt in a number of ways, and I must make it clear that none have precedence over another. Throughout this book and all my other written works on Cerridwen, you will note that I spell her name with a capital C and a double R. And there is reason for this, but it may not be one that will wholly satisfy your desire for literal and historical accuracy, for there is such diversity to the literal spelling of her name that whichever version one decides to use can neither be accurate nor inaccurate. With that being said, it is important that a reason for deciding to use a particular spelling comes from an informed platform, particularly if one might be questioned or challenged as to its usage. What is important to consider with the name of Cerridwen, as with any other personal names in the body of Welsh mythology, is that none of them were ever designed to be written down. They are essentially sounds.

In written form there is rarely any consistency of its spelling, but we are able to glean some information from the various ways her name is spelt. I will provide some examples here, but be aware that these are only a selection of examples in which her name appears in the literal tradition; it is not meant to be a comprehensive list, but it does represent the majority of instances where she is included in the bardic material.

- In the Black Book of Carmarthen (circa 1225), she appears as Kyrridven.
- In Peniarth Manuscript number 3 (circa 1250), she appears as Kyrrytuen.
- In the Hendregadredd Manuscript (circa 1300), she appears as Kyrriduen.
- In the Book of Taliesin (circa 1300–1350), she appears in three different forms: Cerituen, Kerrituen, and Kerritwen.
- The Red Book of Hergest (circa 1400) records her in two forms, Kerituen and Kyrrituen.
- In the Peniarth Manuscript 47 (circa mid 1300–mid 1400), she appears as Keritwen in its Triads.
- In Ystoria Taliesin, NLW 5276D (circa 1552), she appears as Keridwen.
- In Hanes Taliesin, Peniarth Manuscript 111 (circa 1607), she appears as Karidwen.[82]

To list these in alphabetical order, her name would appear in these variants:

- Cerituen
- Karidwen
- Keridwen
- Kerituen

---

82 Listing adapted and expanded by the author from "Cadair Ceridwen" in *Cyfoeth y Testun*, Haycock, 149–151.

- Keritwen
- Kerrituen
- Kerritwen
- Kyrriduen
- Kyrridven
- Kyrrituen
- Kyrrytuen

The various spellings of her name has led to the discombobulation of many modern writers, in particular those of the New Age spectrum, and rightly so. It is incredibly difficult to pick at the names in the attempt to understand what is going on unless one knows the key that is essential to deciphering this conundrum. That key is found in the magic and quality of sound.

First let's look at the structure of the word and the placement of some of the letters. It is important to understand that the name in all instances is composed of three syllables, although there is some uncertainty as to the placement of the sound of the penultimate syllable. In the Welsh language the stress is almost always on the penultimate syllable. Variations of the syllabic structure are commonplace and in all likelihood due to the constant sound changes that occurred in the oration of her name and in combination with regional dialects and accents. However, when combined they can sound something like *keh-rid-ven*.

Almost every written example of her name is spelled with the letter K. Anyone who has any awareness of the current Welsh alphabet will know that the letter K does not presently exist in it. However, it is the sound that is actually being conveyed here. In Middle Welsh, all initial C sounds were scribed with the letter K, perhaps to emphasise the hard C sound—being the C sound in *cat* and not in *cedar*.

You will note that in six instances the letter U proceeds the middle letter T and/or D. The differences in these individual sounds have served only to confuse, but this usually occurs because an English-programmed brain is looking at letters that are not in the English language. In Middle and Old

83

Welsh, the letter T immediately after a vowel is always pronounced as a soft D sound. Also of significance is that, as opposed to the five vowels one finds in English, the Welsh language has seven vowels: a, e, i, o, u, w, y.

To add to this quandary, whenever one observes the letter U that immediately follows a D sound, the U is vocalised as a soft V sound. In modern Welsh this would be written *fen*. Essentially, whilst there is seemingly a plethora of the letter U in the above examples of her name, they all carry the V sound, meaning that with the exception of those that carry the suffix *wen*, every example ends with the suffix *fen* (pronounced in English as *ven*). Except for the example of the suffix *wen* in the Book of Taliesin and the significantly later versions from the common tale of Cerridwen and her cauldron and the birth of Taliesin, most medieval examples demonstrate that the final syllable sound of her name was *fen* (*ven*).

Her name is more frequently spelled with a double R throughout the numerous renditions. The most realistic explanation for this is that the scribes were not hearing a soft R sound but rather a pronounced rolling R, which continues to be heard in modern Welsh. The double R is telling us that there was great emphasis on that sound in the internal structure of the name. Today, in the English tongue, when her name is spoken, the R is often so soft that it is barely audible, similar to the R sound in the word "there." But listen to a native Welsh person and the R sound is quite prominent; whilst incomparable in the English language, the closest one might get to the sound is in the word "mural." The vowel sounds that bookend the rolling double R are, by contrast, significantly softer. The sound of the letter R within the structure of the name has a certain ringing sound to it and gives the name a musicality. This rolling, ringing R sound is often difficult for a non-Welsh palate to easily pronounce and requires a little practise. The sound slams the airways shut during the vocalisation of the soft vowel sounds that bookend it, making it even more tricky for the English palate to attempt.

Pause for a few moments here and re-read the previous paragraphs, and then go back to the list of different spellings, but do so in the knowledge that what you are seeing in written form poorly represents the vocalisations of a phonetic language. With that in mind, and with only a mere hint of slightly different vowel sounds, every example is more or less vocalised to the same sound (with the exception of *wen*, which I will explore later): *Ker-ID-ven*.

Bear in mind that we are not as yet exploring any meaning attributed to the name, but only the sound that constructs its composition and how that sound may have been audibly perceived in the past. The manuscripts in which her name appears were all copied from earlier and earlier versions. If we had a time-travelling device, the further back that we would travel, the closer we would get to the point where they were being written for the very first time. Imagine the scene—a bard is reciting a poem that is over 100 lines in length, yet the bard is able to recite it all from memory. With his eyes straining in the candlelight, a scribe is attempting to write down what he is hearing. Now factor in regional dialects, accents, presentation style, and the significant possibility that the scribe is not fully versed in the language itself, and very quickly one can see how and why various words appear with a myriad of spellings, but when scratched at, the sounds are more or less the same.

Finding Meaning

Ask a room full of a dozen Cerridwen devotees for the meaning of her name and you will no doubt get a dozen answers. Ask a dozen Celtic academics for clarity, but don't make a mess on the walls when your head explodes. What can be certain is uncertainty. Many a scholar have offered suggestions, with R. Geraint Gruffydd abandoning any thought of meaning and naming her as the wondrous "Mam yr Awen Gymraeg (Mother of the Welsh Awen)"[83]— whilst not a translation of the name itself, it is a beautiful and appropriate designation for such an enigmatic figure. What we can be assured of is that whilst meaning may be difficult to ascribe to the name, her function in relation to the Awen is consistent. But does her name imply a connection to the Awen itself or does it mean something else entirely?

Cerridwen was subject to the ravages of time in a unique and perplexing manner; bias towards her can still be seen in the academic evisceration of

---

83   Gwaith Llywarch ap Llewelyn—Prydydd y Moch, Gruffydd.

her in the twentieth century. Perhaps one of the most vocal and literal influences on the myth of Cerridwen and indeed even her name was the now legendary Welsh scholar Ifor Williams.[84] His work on the Taliesin material so influenced Celtic academia that one can see strong elements of his various hypotheses continuously perpetuated by present scholars. His most influential work in regards to Cerridwen and Taliesin was his 1955 O'Donnell lecture entitled "Chwedl Taliesin"[85] presented at the University of Wales and later printed by the University of Wales Press. In his opening remarks, he explained the name Cerridwen:

> Ceridwen was not the real name of this witch; it is too pretty and loving a name to be put on someone like her. In the old manuscripts, for example the Black Book of Carmarthen, she is called Cyrridfen. There is no difficulty understanding the suffix *fen*, a mutation of *ben*, meaning wife/woman. The *cyrrid*, I suspect comes from *cwrr*, but two Rs are necessary nonetheless, and I suggest that *cwrr* means something akin to crooked or hooked. Similar to *corran* in Irish, meaning hook, sickle. Do you know what kind of nose a witch has, in illustrations at least? Well, I suspect that Cyrridfen was herself with a crooked body and a hooked nose, her clawed hands, and her evil iniquitous craft. It was a dreadful error, nonetheless, to turn her name to Ceridwen.[86]

Whilst the above explanation gives some examples of the potential meaning hid in the name, it also does not hold back in openly comparing Cerridwen to a stereotypical witch. I have enormous admiration and respect for Ifor Williams—without him the corridors of Celtic academia would be a poorer place—but sadly he was also a product of his time. He arrived in the halls of the University of Wales with a Presbyterian filter that was commonplace and normal.

Sadly, this filter affected the abilities of so many twentieth and twenty-first century scholars to appreciate that a female character within our native

---

84 Sir Ifor Williams (1881–1965): Celtic scholar at Bangor University and editor of the *Bulletin of the Board of Celtic Studies* from 1937–1948.

85 Williams, *Chwedl Taliesin (The Taliesin Story)*, University of Wales Press.

86 Translated by the author from the original Welsh *Chwedl Taliesin*, Williams, 3–4.

myths could have a status that was profoundly inspirational and deific. It is an opinion that within modern occulture is baffling and obviously biased. Modern Pagan practitioners see a graceful, powerful, and knowledgeable woman gathering the tools of her craft and foraging for the correct plants. She takes to boiling her brew with dedication and commitment. But, on the other side of the fence, she is seen as devilish, practising an evil craft, her body twisted and deformed, none of which is suggested in the tale itself. Ifor Williams's opinions rippled through academia, influencing future scholarly works. Her associations as a witch is unquestionably presented even by modern scholars and bards of the Welsh tradition, with even one of our Chief Bards casually associating her as "Ceridwen the witch."[87]

Williams's proposition that the common suffix *fen* (pronounced *ven*), is a soft mutation of *ben*, which itself is derived from *benyw*, meaning woman and womanly, has been openly criticised. Marged Haycock claims that the evidence for the suffix *fen* to mean womanly is rather thin, but she does not offer a counter explanation.[88] Consequently, and to this day, it is taken as fact that *fen* does indeed imply "woman" or "womanly."

In the Triads of the Island of Britain, scholar Rachel Bromwich suggests that her name means fair and loved, but she does not offer a reason or hypothesis for this, she simply remarks on it as fact. However, she goes on to point out the explanation provided by Williams, which contradicts her own suggestion, and concludes that the meaning of the name is consistent with the traditional concept of a witch.[89] Her exploration of Ceridwen's name is neither conclusive nor conducive to clarity but is indicative of simply towing the accepted academic line. Haycock, on the other hand, whilst fleetingly disparaging of the name containing a reference to someone who is either a woman or womanly, does go on to offer five different suggestions for the meaning of the name but does not commit to one or another. Her suggestions are as follows:

---

87 Hopwood, *Singing in Chains*, 11.
88 Haycock, "Cadair Ceridwen," in Daniel, *Cyfoeth y Testun*, 152.
89 Bromwich, *Trioedd Ynys Prydein*, 312–313.

1. Cwrr-rhid-ben = an angular or crooked woman who copulates with female animals

2. Cryd-fen = a woman who brings terror and disease

3. Creid-fen = a violent, wrathful, or angry woman

4. Cer-ŷd-fen = a crooked woman of corn or grain

5. Credid-fen = a woman that one has a belief or faith in[90]

Whilst generally inconclusive, Haycock does propose that the name itself has been subject to metathesis and the transposition of sounds and/or letters in any given word—a quality that I have exemplified in the earlier discourse of this section about the various literal spellings and the transposition of sound into literal form. It is no great surprise that clarity cannot be gleaned, and there continues to be uncertainty regarding its meaning. There are examples of some academics offering absolutely no explanation at all, one being perhaps the most seminal work on the legend of Taliesin in the twentieth century by American Celtic scholar Patrick K. Ford titled *Ystoria Taliesin*.[91] In this valuable work, there is an obvious elephant in the room in the guise of Cerridwen, in which he offers no hypothesis, translation, or opinion as to the meaning of her name. Subjected either to blatantly being ignored or denigrated, the academic trend from the last two centuries demonstrates that the most learned of individuals cannot, by means of their culturally programmed filters, separate the figure of Cerridwen from the stereotypical image of the witch, or a stock character that does not warrant, deserve, or require an explanation. Haycock is among the rare modern scholars who states that there is no direct suggestion in the poetic material that

---

90   Haycock, *Cadair Ceridwen*, 152–153.
91   Ford's *Ystoria Taliesin* was published by the University of Wales Press in 1992 and is currently no longer in print or circulation. This is perhaps the most extensive exploration of the popular tale of Cerridwen and Taliesin and the magical cauldron of Awen. Ford's examination of the tale is second to none, and yet no explantion is offered or suggested for the name Cerridwen.

Cerridwen was perceived or identified as a witch, and that her debasing and denigration is a product of the later bardic schools, including the present.[92]

So where does this leave us? If we can be assured of anything, it is that the various renditions are most likely indicative of regional dialects and accents, which in itself implies that her name was known widely. Nobody can definitively say with 100 percent surety that they know the meaning of the name; the sounds are contradictory, and even the number of syllables change depending on who might be vocalising them or which scholar is eviscerating it. But this is the perfect ground for ploughing and planting new ideas from existent seeds that are only starting to germinate.

The ground in which modern occultism has planted the idea and divinity of Cerridwen is fertile and growing, and it does so by the power of apotheosis and polytheistic practises of the modern era. Essentially her definition is up to us. The spirit of Cerridwen is a constant, flowing energy that has for centuries moved through time to settle in the hearts of people who are touched by her. In so doing, the spirit that is Cerridwen morphs itself to the needs of that community; she is adaptable and applicable, essential qualities for the narrative and prophetic spirit to be imbibed in each generation.

I have been devoted to the spirit that I identify as Cerridwen for nearly three decades of my life. I have studied and learnt as much as I possibly can to arrive at an informed opinion. The literal form of her name in the twenty-first century is usually as follows, with the first example being the version that I consistently use:

Cerridwen

or

Ceridwen

Only the addition of an extra R demonstrates a slight difference in the spelling—as I suggested earlier, I believe that the double R places emphasis on the rolling R sound, which is as applicable today as it was in the past. I include both spellings to exemplify the difference between the Welsh tongue

---

92 Haycock, *Legendary Poems from the Book of Taliesin*, 314.

and the non-Welsh-speaking tongue but hasten to add that neither is more correct than the other. What you will note that has been transformed is the suffix *fen* to the current *wen*. The settlement of the suffix *wen* is magically appropriate to twenty-first-century polytheism, for it suggests that the subject of the name is pure, fair, blessed, and holy. When we consider that it is the process of apotheosis that has elevated Cerridwen to her station as a goddess, the suffix *wen* is wonderfully relevant. But we do not use it without foundation owing to the handful of instances where the *wen* suffix is utilised in bardic literature. Whilst it is clear that no indisputable translation can be offered from the various hypothesis available, it does afford modern-day Paganism and Polytheism the luxury of defining the name in a manner conducive to effective orthopraxy. This must, however, arise from an informed and calculated opinion that respects and honours the past, and takes the seeds of scholars and practitioners and plants a new and valid concept in modern occulture.

So, what about a cohesive meaning—are we afforded one or do we have to look to the visionary? I believe that we can glean meaning if we consider the discerning powers of both scholarship and vision. Having pondered the literal evidence of her name over the last several years, I have concluded that Ifor Williams and his successors are correct in their hypothesis of the first sound of her name being derived from an old Welsh word to mean angular or bending. However, I would add that the "bending, angular" element can be perceived as the ability to see what is currently out of sight or just around the corner. In addition, Haycock suggests the possibility that the second syllable contains within it the soft sound for the word "hud" to mean magic, and whilst there is not one example in the literature that contains a literal H, it is equally plausible that following the rolling R, the H would be rendered so soft as to be almost imperceptible to the human ear.[93] Sounds, particularly in the colloquial, are often muted. An example would be the present word for "thank you" in Welsh, which is diolch. Its vocalisation in North Wales renders the L sound practically inaudible, and yet it is undeniably there. It

---

93   Haycock, "Cadair Ceridwen in Cyfoeth," in Daniel, *Cyfoeth y Testun*, 152–153.

is possible that the original form of Cerridwen's name may well have contained the sound for the word "magic." Whilst there is no literal evidence to support this particular hypothesis, I do believe that owing to the consistency of Cerridwen's association with the Awen and, by proxy, magic, I consider it to have merit and value in twenty-first-century Pagan practise.

By taking all of this to heart, I offer a version and translation of her name that is appropriate and applicable to current Pagan and polytheistic expression, based on an examination of the literal and oral/aural traditions and in conjunction with the visionary:

Cerridwen/Ceridwen

Syllabic and phonetic: cerr-ID-wen[94]

Meaning: A blessed holy woman of angular, bending magic

Whilst I offer this as an informed opinion, I also present it as a valid twenty-first-century designation for Cerridwen in her role as a goddess. The manner by which we connect to Cerridwen today is different to that of the medieval bards, and rightly so; as I have previously explored, there is nothing to suggest that the bards identified or connected to her in her guise as a goddess. She is not exclusively a product of the past—the past cannot claim ownership of her—but rather, she acts as a concept, an archetype, and now as a deity that is valid for the present time and culture, and one that will continue to be relevant for future generations of polytheists. Cultures do not retain aspects of lore if they become irrelevant to said cultures.[95] However, this will only succeed if we make her relevant. Without relevance she will sink into obscurity and forgetfulness. The responsibility for seeding Cerridwen into the next generation is ours and ours alone, this being inclusive of developing a deeper understanding of the mechanism that breathed life and continuity into her.

---

94   Note the emphasis is always on the penultimate syllable. Emphasis on syllabic sound is also altered slightly by means of this definition, with the rolling R sound moving to the first syllable as opposed to the penultimate.

95   Ford, *Ystoria Taliesin*, 38, footnote 83.

More Than Just a Name

There is magic here, for the last 1,500 years of Cerridwen's literal legacy, there has been a shift of focus. Cerridwen is no longer limited to definition and exploration by the Welsh alone; instead, the fragrant steam that arose from her cauldron has taken her and her mythology to the farthest flung corners of the world. This is a quality that surprisingly emulates the past, albeit in ways that our ancestors could barely imagine. The concept of the archetypal bard Taliesin and the mechanism and faculties that brought about his transformation was known throughout the majority of Celtic Britain, even as far as the lower Scottish territories. We have long been led to believe that the Iron Age and Celto-Romano peoples of Britain were tribal and warring, with little if any consistency of common heritage. This is not true.

It is apparent from the works of the Gogynfeirdd, who themselves seemingly hearkened back to a romantic period of yesteryear, the whimsical longing for times gone by, to the idealism of the ancient bards, the Cynfeirdd. This is not new; this is equally present in human mentality today, where we long for the good old days when, in fact, there are no good old days. What the Gogynfeirdd bards offer is a snapshot of time that not only records the name of Cerridwen, but demonstrates that she was known amongst the many bardic schools and respected for generations. Their works express a consistency in her role and function. Even during her denigration by the bards of the nobility, hints at her function can still be seen persistently swimming beneath the surface of bias. Her name, inseparable from the Taliesin persona, was known north and south, perpetuated by the bards, who themselves were intimately connected to her, and this affords us a glimpse through the mists of time.

There was undeniably considerable locality-specific diversity among the British Celts until the early middle ages, especially concerning their common cultural heritage. To have such diversity is not inconsistent with the expression of traditions that demonstrate a uniformity and contain themes that were important to the people over numerous generations. So, when we cast our gaze at the bardic tradition—as we have done thus far, and in particular to the bard Taliesin and, by proxy, Cerridwen. What we see is something that transcends local diversity and survived throughout the various regions for well over a thousand years, until it was eventually and vividly recorded in writing in a number of manuscripts during the 1500s.[96] These did not arise in a vacuum; the numerous manuscripts that record, either whole or in part, come from a number of regions where variants of the tale were perpetuated. Each version contains elements found in the earlier bardic poetry. What the tale and poetry demonstrate is the importance of the narrative spirit and the archetypal bard within the Celtic cultural continuum and the origin of its power in the cauldron of Cerridwen.

Cerridwen now finds herself in a new age, where it is not the power of cynghanedd and the bardic tradition alone that is responsible for her continuation. She has found a new mechanism in modern polytheism and Pagan practise. She has transcended local diversity to bring a uniformity of inspiration to a new generation of people who are only just starting to get to know her. Potentially you, the reader, are one of those bards.

With that being said, it is vitally important that we honour the bardic tradition that seeded her in the present whilst simultaneously taking to heart Cerridwen's message to be learned, to be committed, to have the best of knowledge—to be magical practitioners that are worthy of her admiration.

I ask that you cast your mind back to the earlier pages of this book where I describe a process of bubbling distillation, where each bubble carries a consistent theme through the depths and passage of time to reach the surface, each one imbibed with the narrative spirit. All of those little bubbles, each one carrying a memory, a thought, rise to the surface of your experience—they rise within you.

---

96   Ford, *Ystoria Taliesin*, 38.

11

Cerridwen and the Cauldron

The bards considered that Cerridwen held an item in her possession, one intimately connected with the source of Awen: the cauldron. Arguably, at the centre of Pagan symbology and iconography stands the cauldron, a symbol and tool that has continuously influenced and inspired the current Pagan traditions. Its history is as colourful and varied as the traditions to which it can most commonly be found, and its continuous presence is testament to its sacred nature. But where does it come from and why do we utilise it as a symbol of the divine feminine? In this section it is pertinent that we take a wider look at the cauldron and its position in Celtic myth before considering the nature of Cerridwen's cauldron and the necessity for its presence in the myths and bardic traditions.

On a purely physical level, the cauldron symbolises the nourishing qualities of the hearth and the centre of the home. It epitomises food, sustenance, status, hospitality, and power. During the Bronze and Iron Ages, chieftains would impress their guests and demonstrate their wealth and efforts by providing gargantuan feasts, and at the centre of this display of power hung the cauldron. The hearth, with all its accoutrements and firedogs, became the focus for the amount of power the chieftain possessed and his ability to reward those loyal to him.[97] In typical domestic situations, the cauldron beheld similar properties, albeit on a humbler level; it expressed the attributions of home, warmth, comfort, safety, and nourishment. It is only a small leap from those functions to adopting the allegorical and symbolic qualities of the cauldron as a representation of the divine feminine.

The functionality of the Celtic cauldron as a purely practical vessel is evident by the staggering quantity that have been discovered within domestic and ritualistic archaeological sites. However, the eventual focus of this discourse is the sublime qualities of the vessel as a symbol that captures not only a physical attribute, but also as a symbol of mystery and secret. The latter quality can be seen reflected in the myriad of cauldrons found at sites that were clearly sacred to the Celts; these vessels were rarely previously used, and generally new and intentionally damaged before being offered to the gods or spirits of a place. One could argue that the presence of cauldrons found in bogs and lakes might not necessarily be present for their assumed supernatural qualities; they may have been offered in order to feed the objects or subjects of the people's attention. Either way, cauldrons were offered to unseen worlds and unseen forces, to spirits or gods whose names are lost to us.

It seems evident that the cauldron, by association of its physical and nourishing qualities, evolved naturally to represent spiritual sustenance and fulfilment in the mind of the Celtic people and onwards into modern Pagan practise. The Gundestrup Cauldron is perhaps the most ornate and visually impressive vessel to have survived the centuries, and it presents a snapshot of the cauldron as a spiritual symbol. One of its panels depicts the immersion of an individual into a cauldron, a motif that appears throughout Celtic mythology and mimics the properties of the cauldron of rebirth found in the second branch of the Mabinogi, where the dead soldiers of Ireland are cast into a giant cauldron and the next day they arise, animated yet unable to speak. Archetypes, giants, and mythical creatures appear on its other panels, offering tantalising windows onto the past. One can only imagine the

---

97   Lynch, *Prehistoric Anglesey*, 270–271.

power, wealth, and status of the person who commissioned it purely as a ritual offering to the spirits or deity of a bog in Jutland. Archaeologists have concluded that the cauldron's iconography is of pre-Roman origin, and the images portray deities and archetypes pertinent to the Celts of that region.[98]

Cerridwen's cauldron is not unique; it is one of a number of cauldrons present in the Celtic mythological and archaeological record. If we look to the chronicles of the British and Irish Celts, we can surmise that the cauldron as a symbol of the spiritual had three defined functions:

- a vessel of inspiration
- a transformative device
- a vessel of testing

All of the above attributes are contextually expressed within the Celtic material almost exclusively in relation to the divine feminine. Akin to the body of the mother whose womb sustains us before our birthing, she becomes the physical and spiritual representation of the cauldron. In the Welsh language the word *crochen,* meaning cauldron, shares the same prefix, *cro,* as the word *croth,* meaning womb. References to the cauldron within the British and Irish Celtic sagas perpetuate the position of the cauldron as a vessel of divine, feminine qualities. The importance, relevance, and magical significance of the cauldron are continuously reinforced throughout our native mythology, where it is perceived as a vessel of profound spiritual function.

The Cauldron of Inspiration

"I received my Awen from the cauldron of Cerridwen," said Taliesin in reference to the prophetic, narrative, and enchanted spirit of inspiration that is imbued within him. He claims that his Awen was received from the cauldron of a witch in whose womb he resided for nine nights of the moon, before his placement into another womb-like structure, the coracle. All three aspects can be perceived as symbolic of the cauldron. Initially we have the actual physical representation in the form of an iron vessel, which epitomises the

---

98   Farley and Hunter, *Celts,* 262–270.

primary tool of Cerridwen, wherein the brew of Awen is boiled. Secondly, we have the cauldron properties of Cerridwen's womb, in which the initiate undergoes assimilation of the mysteries; and thirdly, the nurturing qualities of the coracle on water. The coracle or *Bol Croen*, meaning skin belly, further reinforces the quality of the womb as a cauldron-like structure, within which we have access to sustenance and also mystery. Ultimately the initiate is birthed almost by means of caesarean section at a salmon weir.

The primary cauldron of the tale of Taliesin is the cauldron of inspiration; it initiates the querent into the mysteries and causes him or her to poetically express that connection. This connection by means of the Awen disseminates the wisdom and magic of the mysteries and inspires others to seek out the qualities of the cauldron.

It can be deduced that poetry, inspiration, and the narrative, enchanted, and prophetic spirits are expressions of the cauldron. One can find references to the vessel as being synonymous with inspiration continuously reiterated by Taliesin.

There is no doubt that it was a common motif amongst the Celts that the cauldron was and continues to be a symbol of inspiration, forever connected to the womb of the divine feminine. The three cauldrons of the Irish tradition can be conceived as the three drops of Awen that rise from Cerridwen's cauldron to land upon the initiate's thumb. It is reasonable to suggest that each drop contains the requisite components of poetic knowledge.

The Cauldron as Transformative Device

It could reasonably be argued that the womb of Cerridwen and the coracle in which Taliesin is placed for his final voyage to the salmon weir are, in fact, transformative vessels, albeit linked to the primary cauldron of inspiration. The purpose and intent of these cauldrons are varied, but overall they exemplify a transformative process whereby the initiate undergoes isolation and separation tantamount to death. Within these cauldrons there is a period of reflection and assimilation wherein the mysteries are incorporated into the spirit and body in a cohesive manner. The mysteries have been transmitted, but the mind, body, and spirit are yet to coalesce it into meaning, thus enabling the initiate to articulate them fully. The magical implications of the cauldron as transformative device suggest that in order for the initiate to be fully immersed in the mysteries, he or she must undergo a secondary period of gestational isolation in a womb-like vessel. Upon completion of this period of sustained assimilation and nourishment, the initiate appears different; he or she is changed by the experience and steps forth as an adept of the mysteries.

There are examples of vessels within the Celtic material that demonstrate the quality and necessity of transformation within the Celtic spiritual continuum. I am limited in their exploration in this short book, so I offer the following two examples from a list of many. In the second branch of the Mabinogi, we encounter a vessel described as this:

> For I will give you a cauldron, and the property of the cauldron is that if you throw into it one of your men who is killed today, then by tomorrow he will be as good as ever, except that he will not be able to speak.[99]

This cauldron is generally referred to as "the cauldron of rebirth," where the dead undergo some form of mysterious transformation within its depths, the mystery of which we are not privy to. This is further emphasised by the inability of the warriors to speak, perhaps a function which purposefully disables their ability to articulate their experience within the cauldron. Whatever we experience within these vessels is deeply pertinent and indicative of individual connection; to attempt to ride in the slipstream of another's initiatory experience could potentially cause irreparable collateral damage.

My next example does not share the physical attributes of a cauldron, yet its nature is identical. In the fourth branch of the Mabinogi, the figure of Aranrhod steps over the magic wand of the god/king Math in order to prove her virginity. Alas, she gives birth to a fully formed large boy and a "small thing." The latter is placed into a *cist*, which can be translated as a "chest" or "coffin"—these may appear contrary to the form of a cauldron,

---

99   Davies, *The Mabinogion*, 25.

yet the Mabinogi informs us that the "small thing" Aranrhod birthed is transformed within it into a fully fledged boy. It acts as a secondary gestational vessel that prepares the initiate—in this case, the yet un-named Lleu Llaw Gyffes—for immersion into the mysteries. It is his uncle Gwydion, who Cerridwen admires above all magicians, the primary enchanter of the Britons, who instigates this transformation process by adopting the child as his own and instructing him in the arts of magic. This vessel is similar in nature to the coracle in the tale of the birth of Taliesin that facilitates a secondary gestation.

The cauldrons of transformation are imperative for assimilation without which the initiate is in danger of attaining only a cerebral or armchair philosophical understanding of the mysteries. The mind absorbs the teachings, the spirit sings in harmony with it, but only after a period of gestation can this be put into effective practise. This is the purpose of the cauldron of transformation.

The Cauldron of Testing

This peculiar vessel is abundant in Celtic mythology, and its primary purpose is to test the integrity, courage, and stamina of the querent. Scattered throughout the pages of Welsh mythology is the elusive and often dangerous search for a cauldron that is itself evasive. The search for the cauldron that is never found is significant, for it connects threads of mythology one to the other. In the epic poem "Preiddeu Annwfn (The Spoils of Annwfn)" in the Book of Taliesin, Arthur leads a small army in search of a cauldron that does not boil the food of a coward, a cauldron that is warmed by the breath of nine maidens, and it is never found. The journey into Annwfn is so perilous that none but seven return to the apparent world, and the cauldron does not accompany them. The cauldrons of Celtic mythology are predominantly elusive; at times they are dangerous, and more often than not, they either vanish from sight or are destroyed.

The journey is never easy and implies that for one to approach the mysteries, one must do so fully prepared and willing to have one's intent challenged and questioned. This allegorical cauldron that hides in the depths of the indigenous underworld is indicative of a deeply personal journey that explores the nature of self. We are informed by Taliesin:

> My first utterance was spoken concerning the cauldron kindled by the breath of nine maidens. The cauldron of the Head of Annwn, what is its disposition [with its] dark trim and pearls? It does not boil a coward's food, it has not been destined to do so.[100]

This and further lines in "The Spoils of Annwfn" poem reiterate the difficult nature of the journey in search of the cauldron, and that cowardice is a fault that it will not tolerate. This can be seen emulated in one of the thirteen treasures of the Island of Britain:

> The Cauldron of Dyrnwch the Giant, which is said that if the meat for a coward were put into it to boil, it would never boil; but if meat for a brave man were put into it, it would boil with haste and thus the brave could be distinguished from the cowardly.[101]

By informing us of integral qualities essential for the journey, the cauldrons of testing inform us of what the transmitters of mystery expect of the querent and would-be initiate. In primary position is the quality of bravery, implying that immersion in the mysteries is certainly not for the faint hearted—its ability to transform may overwhelm and damage the weak or cowardly. Testing talismans were essential to ensuring the quality and integrity of those admitted into the mystery schools. These concepts may be seen as antiquated remnants of a distant past, curiosities of history and tradition, irrelevant to modern practise. But I argue that what is of no relevance falls out of practise, and this material continues to survive and perpetuate its wisdom.

Qualities of the cauldron can be seen emulated in current Pagan practise, particularly in the initiatory traditions that are based on systems of teaching and reflection. The cauldron continues to this day to be perceived and utilised as a vessel of inspiration, transformation, and testing, and it is

---

100   Haycock, *Legendary Poems from the Book of Taliesin*, 435.
101   Bromwich, *Trioedd Ynys Prydein*, 259–260.

synonymous with the divine feminine. The symbol of the cauldron is, in essence, a goddess motif symbolic of the nurturing and sexual qualities of the feminine. They serve to nourish, assimilate, gestate, sustain, and even sometimes scorn, but above all they continue to inspire our modern practises as tendrils of inspiration and transformation reach out from the mists of the distant Celtic past to tantalise the present. They are not useless relics of a bygone age. The teachings of the cauldron act as templates that bring an authentic applicability to our modern traditions.

The cauldron as a source of inspiration is a common theme in both Irish and Welsh Celtic tradition. In both traditions it is claimed that the power of the bard originates deep within a cauldron and is contained by it until its imbibing within the bard.[102] In the later tale of his birth, Taliesin reiterates and affirms the origin of his Awen as being the cauldron and womb of Cerridwen, but so do the Gogynfeirdd bards, hundreds of years before the tale was written in its current form.

The famed bard Llywarch ap Llewelyn, who went by the bardic name Prydydd y Moch, in his "Mawl Llywelyn ap Iorwerth o Wynedd (In Praise of Llywelyn, Son of Iorwerth of Gwynedd)," said:

> *Gair fy ngair o'r pair yn perthyn.*
>
> *The word of my word is the cauldron's kindred.*[103]

In the above verse, the bard is claiming that his own words have within them hidden words that belong to and are kindred to the cauldron. It is the cauldron of Cerridwen that he references here. The word has always been a concept laden with mystery and power in a number of traditions, and here the bard claiming that words are hidden within words, and each arise and belong, like family to the cauldron itself. They reflect the mysteries contained within the cauldron.

In his "Mawl Gruffydd ap Cynon o Wynedd (In Praise of Gruffydd, Son of Cynon of Gwynedd)," he offers an origin for the Awen:

---

102 Ford, *Ystoria Taliesin*, 27–28.
103 Translated by the author from NLW MS 6680B.

Duw dofyt, dy-m-ryt, reitun Awen—ber,
Fel o bair Kyrridfen.

God the tamer, who gave so I can give Awen—of pure sound,
As from the cauldron of Cerridwen.[104]

This is perhaps one of the finest examples of the Gogynfeirdd era of a bard laying claim to the origin of his Awen in the form of a pure sound, and one that originates from the cauldron of Cerridwen. According to Celtic scholar Marged Haycock, the material from Prydydd y Moch is in all likelihood the earliest datable mention of the cauldron of Cerridwen.[105] The exaltation to what on the surface appears to be in praise to the Christian god is not so clear when we look closer at the word he chose—duw dofyt (spelled *dofydd* in modern Welsh)—the word *dofydd* means "tamer" or "subduer" and implies a role or function of a deity. The Welsh bardic tradition, particularly in the later Romantic era, claims that the divine has seven divisions to it. It is unclear if each division is indicative of a separate divine spirit or if they are faces of the one entity.[106] This exaltation to a god is, however, not uncommon in the bardic tradition, but we see a marked difference in style between the Gogynfeirdd era and the next, which initiated the denigration of Cerridwen. The Gogynfeirdd bards were remarkably enamoured and perhaps even indebted to the spirit of Cerridwen, in whatever guise they may have personified her.

Later in the poem "Canu Bychan (The Small Song)," Llywarch says:

Cyfarchaf i'm rhen, cyfarchfawr Awen,
Cyfrau Cyridfen, rwyf barddoni,
Yn null Taliesin, yn nillwng Elffin,
Yn dyllest barddrin beirdd fanieri.

---

104   Translated by the author from NLW MS 6680B.
105   Haycock, *Legendary Poems from the Book of Taliesin*, 313.
106   Much of the information that exists that refers to the divisions of the divine comes from the pen of Iolo Morganwg in the late 1700s and early 1800s, and whilst marred for his elaborate poetic forgeries, there is still much wisdom and inspiration to be gleaned from his work. See bibliographical entry for ab Ithel's *Barddas*.

> *I greet the great ruler, great summoner of Awen,*
> *Which is the song of Cerridwen, the paddle/steerer of bardism,*
> *In the manner of Taliesin, the liberator of Elffin,*[107]
> *In the shape of the muse of the bannered bards.*[108]

The bard greets the mighty ruler, the great summoner of Awen, but who exactly is being summoned? Whilst the majority of modern scholars have translated the *cyfarchaf i'm rhen* element of the poem as a reference to the Christian god, I do believe that elements of this comes from a natural bias that those eviscerating the poems beheld. The Welsh word *rhen* is derived from the same etymological root as *rhiaint*, meaning parent, a role that was often offered, and continues to be, to Cerridwen as the parent/mother of Awen. I would argue that the first line is not as straightforward as a verse in praise of the Christian god being the great summoner of the Awen, but instead that it is indeed referring to a function of Cerridwen as the parent spirit and guardian of the Awen. Note that I referred to the summoner as a function of Cerridwen, and I did so wholly intentionally, for it is not Cerridwen herself that pulls the Awen from the depths of her cauldron; it is her song that fulfils this role. In so doing, she serves as an example to her bards, to steer and paddle their journey through the bardic crafts, acting in a manner that is akin to a bardic/magical ally. This is also one of the earliest examples we have of a poem directly referring to several elements from the significantly younger Tale of Taliesin. In this one verse, we see references to the Awen, Cerridwen, Taliesin, Elffin, and bardism.

In the poem "Marwnad Madog Fychan o Dir Iarll (Funeral Song of Madog the Small from Earl's Land)," he elaborates:

> *Am Fadog ddeifniog, ddofn Awen,*
> *Am nur pur fel pair Ceridfen.*
>
> *Madog of the falling drops, of deep Awen,*
> *Like the pure essence from the cauldron of Cerridwen.*[109]

---

107 Elffin being the figure who discovers and names the baby Taliesin at the salmon weir.

108 Translated by the author from NLW MS 6680B.

109 Translated by the author from NLW MS 6680B.

In this verse, Llywarch reiterates even more familiar attributes from the later tale. In two fairly short but beautifully constructed lines we see references to the falling drops, the Awen, and the cauldron of Cerridwen. Whilst we cannot be entirely certain if the bard is referring to the three drops that arise from the cauldron to descend onto the thumb of Gwion Bach, the similarities are striking enough to make a decent assumption that this may well be the case—that the concept of the Awen being brewed down to its purest essence will rise to fall like drops.

What all of this tells us is that whilst the later tale of Taliesin was not necessarily fully structured in its literal form as a mythology in the early bardic eras, the themes, iconography, and essential elements of the tale were certainly known to the early bardic schools of Wales. It is important to stress that the tradition was not limited to one location or time; these concepts were known over vast distances and across centuries of time. The function of Cerridwen may have been understood by the bards, who not only frequently reference Cerridwen's function as a separator of seeds, but also emulate that function themselves.

As the bardic attributes of Cerridwen distilled into the later tale, we can see the qualities of the three cauldrons emulated within it: inspiration, transformation, and testing. At times the cauldrons are not clearly defined, yet they are present nonetheless. The perpetual search for the cauldron in mythology can often lead one to assume that the cauldron is a physical prize, but that is not what is happening here. The cauldron is a holding metaphor for the creative and inspirational powers of the universe. Cerridwen's cauldron exists within you as potential, and whilst its attainment is challenging and often testing, its transformative qualities are profoundly cathartic.

12

Witch?

Prior to the middle of the sixteenth century, there was no evidence to associate Cerridwen with what we would currently and culturally associate with the practise of witchcraft. She is not once referred to as a witch, and there is good reason for this: witchcraft did not exist in Wales. Or, to clarify, what the English-speaking world perceived as witchcraft had no relevance in the Welsh cultural consciousness. They had no point of reference for the evil, demonic, and devilish portrayal of a witch popularised during the decades of witch hunts in Britain and Europe.

The subject of witchcraft, particularly in Wales, has been extensively researched by the historian Richard Suggett in his books *A History of Magic and Witchcraft in Wales* and *Welsh Witches*. He suggests that the comparatively low cases of witchcraft persecutions in Wales, particularly when compared to areas such as Essex in the southeast of England, were incredibly rare. For example, during the period from 1568 to 1698, there were 42 cases in relation to witchcraft in Wales. Most of these never led to a prosecution, with the majority being thrown out by the judges even before they came to trial. Only eight guilty verdicts were recorded, with five leading to execution.[110]

---

110   Suggett, *Welsh Witches*, 14–15.

It is important to note the enormous amount of time these cases spanned: 130 years! Those brought to trial were border cases, where the influence of England and its new fear of witchcraft was at its greatest.

The Western coastlands of Wales and the heartlands did not suffer from Witchcraft persecutions. The greatest influencing factor in all of this was the use of language, for the majority of ordinary Welsh natives during the so-called Burning Times could not speak English. They could barely understand any of it, and they certainly could not read English; this skill was one afforded only to the elite of Welsh society. The Welsh, particularly those further away from the border lands, had no direct knowledge and little interest in English society. Those who did practise what was known in Wales as swyngyfaredd, or enchantment/sorcery/magic, were essential components of society—who else would you turn to for help when sick? There weren't many doctors around in those times in rural Wales. The closest approximate word to describe what the twenty-first century would equate as a witch would be swyn.[111] This term also describes a charm or spell but contains none of the negative connotations of late medieval witchcraft. A swynwr would be the masculine designation for a practitioner of swyn, with swynwraig being the feminine.

The idea of witchcraft and the words associated with it were essentially borrowed into Celtic language cultures, a fact not unique to Wales but also found in Scots and Irish Gaelic.[112] With little to no concept of what a witch was, loan words were incorporated into the Welsh language, but these were new words for an alien concept.[113] In the witchcraft trials of Wales, we see the use of the word *wits* to describe the culturally specific witch of the English-speaking world. This is not a genuine Welsh word but rather an English word with essentially a Welsh accent. The early modern Welsh term for someone who practised what was becoming understood as witchcraft was

---

111   Pronounced with two syllables as "Zoo-inn," with an exaggerated "oo" sound in the zoo component.
112   Suggett, *Welsh Witches*, 17.
113   Suggett, *Welsh Witches*, 16–17.

gwrach, although its original usage was in reference to an old woman, a hag, or anything otherwise that was ugly, loathsome, or repugnant.

The term gwrach was never used in witchcraft trials; it seems the word was gradually associated with witches by influence of the English language to anything that was repulsive. It is during this time, approximately the middle of the 1500s, that we start to see the word gwrach being attributed to Cerridwen, a natural progression of identifying a character that for decades had been vilified as repugnant and hideous by the bards of the nobility. In his 1552 version of the Tale of Taliesin, Elis Gruffudd identifies Cerridwen as being versed in "witshkrafft,"[114] a loan word to describe a function of magic that was unacceptable to the cultural mentality of the time. If one looks at that word closely, it can easily be identified as comprising of two words— witsh and krafft, essentially witch and craft but with a Welsh accent. These words do not exist in the Welsh language. At the time no single word existed in the English popular and academic imagination to adequately describe the gifts and the crafts of Cerridwen as anything other than the medieval English concept of witchcraft.

Later in the same tale, Taliesin says:

> A myui a uum naw mis haiach,
> Ynghroth Keridwen y wrach.
> Myui a vum gyntt Wion Bach;
> Neithyr Taliesin wyf I bellach.

> And I was nine months long,
> In the womb of Cerridwen the "witch,"
> I was once Gwion Bach,
> But I am now Taliesin.[115]

The above poem is strictly metred, with the word wrach (mutation of gwrach) rhyming with the terminus of each line. This is obviously not something Gruffudd appropriated or changed; he was merely copying what he

---

114 Gruffudd, NLW 5276D.
115 Gruffudd, NLW 5276D. Translated by the author.

was hearing or reading. However, the term "witshkrafft" is contained in prose, not verse, and what is unknown to us is precisely what word Gruffudd was substituting. It is likely that he approximated a word that captured the essence of what he would have understood as a form of witchcraft. Gruffudd was also influenced by earlier examples of the tale in written form, some more complete than others, and it is likely that they, too, were influenced to denounce the magic expressed in the tale as anything other than negative and verging on evil. Whilst Gruffudd plainly states that the tale is against faith and reason, the implication is a deep influence from the Christian mindset at the time. Whilst we cannot be entirely sure of what word or term he was replacing, it is highly likely that his "witshkrafft" replaced "swyn" in one form or another. In a similar spirit, the renowned bard Lewis Môn maintains the continuity of her cauldron's power in stark contrast to the predominant bards at the time. Môn said:

> *Awen Rhys yn yr oesoedd,*
> *O bair y wrach berwi'r oedd.*
>
> *Rhys's Awen through the ages,*
> *Boiled in the cauldron of the witch.*[116]

Cerridwen is branded as a gwrach, and whilst Môn's description of her is not wholly derogatory, we can clearly see the influence of the changing times in the words that he chooses to describe her. It is unheard of for a modern Welsh-language magical practitioner with an etymological understanding of the words associated with magic to refer to themselves as gwarch.

Other words for magical practitioners can be found in the Celtic language of Wales, including *Gwyddon/Gwiddon/Widdon*, meaning a practitioner of magic associated directly with the root words for tree and a female monster or hag. *Hudolwyr* is a title attributed to the magicians of the myths of the Mabinogi. The magic that the *swyngyfarwyddon* (charm/sorcery/magic users) practised bore a striking semblance to the qualities that the classical writers attributed to the Druids. However, if the bards were essentially a

---

116 Translated by the author from Môn, *Gwaith Lewis Môn*.

caste of the Druids, then their words were the conduit for the making of magic. Elements of this can be found in the precisely recorded court documents of the Welsh witchcraft trials, which contain examples of the complex bardic verses that the practitioners utilised to activate and direct their magic.

Perhaps one of the finest examples of the power of spoken word in relation to what was increasingly understood as witchcraft comes from the trial of Gwen Ferch Ellis (Gwen the daughter of Ellis) in 1594, the first individual accused of what was increasingly being understood as witchcraft in Wales. Her use of various charms was impeccably recorded during her trial. It is evident that a physical charm alone was not sufficient for the magic to be effective; a sequence of spoken verses was required. From the trial documents, it was evident that Gwen was indeed a swyn-wraig who had inherited the skills of swyn from her eldest sister,[117] implying a continuation of magical folk practises that utilised skills of verse and memory akin to those of the bardic schools.

The sixteenth- and seventeenth-century occupants of England regarded Wales as a stronghold of magic, to the extent that some English practitioners would claim Welsh influence or lineage to boost the kudos of their own practise. And as Richard Suggett explores, it is likely that the attitude towards witchcraft in Wales was influenced by the predominance of the Celts and their ancient priests, the Druids, to be practitioners of magic.[118] This is commonplace today, where modern occult practitioners often will align themselves to what are imagined as Welsh/Celtic lineages to give an illusion of authenticity and authority.

A peculiarity was to arise in modern occulture related to the above discourse: the claim that one is in apostolic succession to a secret and organised system of Welsh witchcraft. Our history clearly demonstrates that this is factually incorrect and in essence does more harm than good. It serves only to dishonour the magic of the Welsh bardic tradition by overlaying it with a fantasy that has no basis in truth. This results in the futile searching

---

117 Suggett, *Welsh Witches*, 31.
118 Suggett, *A History of Magic and Witchcraft in Wales*, 8–13.

of genuine seekers to find authenticity from a past that never existed, and in turn they miss out on the wealth of magic and wisdom that arises from the bardic tradition.

The culture of the ancient Celts was one where magic was commonplace and where they simply did not have the word "witch," at least not with its current anglicised meaning. The common people, the bards, and the Druids expressed certain elements of magical thinking that we would align today with modern witchcraft practises, this being the practical aspect of natural manipulation and transformation by supernatural means.

When we look at the wider cultural context of magic and witchcraft and its impact on Welsh society, it becomes evident how the learned bards of the nobility took new ideas and thoughts and incorporated them into their practise. Add religiosity to this and opinions and attitudes towards themes and icons from the deep past begin to transform. What the material of the bards of the nobility demonstrate is the shifting patterns of beliefs and superstition. Slowly, with the influence of England and its witch trials, the religiosity of the bards, and their desire to associate bardic skills as a divine gift from the Christian god, the concept of witches and witchcraft became a reality in Wales. By the end of the sixteenth century, the fear that had been imbibed into the English world was affecting the Welsh. Cerridwen was to fall victim to this change.

Cerridwen & Modern Witchcraft

A contradictory factor that must have perplexed many of the bards of the nobility was the preservation of ancient bardic materials. Huge numbers of the old bardic material were preserved in manuscripts dating from this era. Their saving grace was the fact that the common people were not privy to the material being copied in Welsh scriptoria, and the bards were too fixated on creating new material to worry too much about what the old books may or may not contain. And with this, they largely flew under the radar and were fated to that most peculiar of paradoxes, insignificance. These copies found their way into the palaces and manors of the Welsh gentry, who in all probability could not understand the archaic language within them. Whilst indicative of the bardic tradition, they were, ironically, not in the possession of the bards. Their intense schooling no doubt preserved some of the songs from the old manuscripts, but the books themselves became commodities for the wealthy, and eventually for Neopaganism, modern Druidry, and witchcraft.

Whilst Cerridwen was denigrated as wits and gwrach in the later medieval period, something remarkable happened as a result. As the centuries passed, a new phenomenon was to occur in the mid decades of the twentieth century: the revival and development of witchcraft as a valid and authentic practise. Cerridwen's guise as ridiculed gwrach was transforming into the general idea of what a witch might be. Consequently, twentieth-century depictions portray her as the stereotypical and often Disneyfied version of a witch, replete with pointed hat, warts, and riding a broomstick. This ridiculous characterisation was to have an unforeseen consequence: a ridiculous individual does not pose a threat to the status quo. Times had changed; the bardic tradition had evolved into the current form of the Gorsedd of bards, with less emphasis on the magical arts. The distance between the bards and their muse Cerridwen stretched into a wide canyon.

The birth of a new witchcraft sparked an interest in ancient mythology and legends, and suddenly Cerridwen swung into focus once more. After centuries of ridicule, she found allies in the unlikeliest of places and beyond the cultural limitations of the Welsh language and the bardic tradition. In Cerridwen the new witches saw an ally, for here was a powerful woman who was in charge of her own magical abilities. Centre stage was her cauldron and the brewing of potions and spells; the symbols could not have been more perfect. The literal stage had also been set, with early and mid-twentieth-century metaphysical writers influencing the countenance of Cerridwen, making her even more appealing to the New Age world.

British libraries were replete with nineteenth-century works heavily influenced by the Celtic Romanticists and revivalists of the previous two centuries. Hidden among them were books that claimed Cerridwen's status as mysterious and goddess-like, and most importantly to note, many of these books were written in English and not Welsh. In 1889 Morien O. Morgan in his work *The Mabin of the Mabinogion* claims that Cerridwen is the great mother spirit and a great mother goddess.[119] In 1911 J. A. MacCulloch was one of the first modern twentieth-century writers to assume her role as a fertility goddess:

> ...the cauldron was first of all associated with a fertility cult, and Cerridwen must therefore once have been a goddess of fertility. She may also have been a corn goddess, since she is called a goddess of grain, and tradition associates the pig with her.[120]

MacCulloch's works and influences directly impacted on Robert Graves and his influential book *The White Goddess*. Cerridwen features heavily in this work and is unquestionably identified as a goddess. Graves also claims that the devouring of the grain and consuming of the initiate marks Cerridwen as a death goddess,[121] a role that continues to be held by some modern adherents of Cerridwen. *The White Goddess* and its conclusions were to have enormous impact on later occult and Pagan writers, who, with limited resources, took Graves at his word. The mother of modern witchcraft, Doreen Valiente, writing in 1973, said:

> [The grail chalice] has a good deal in common with the Sacred Cauldron of Cerridwen, the goddess of Nature, of the moon, and of poetry, who was invoked by the Druids. The cauldron so frequently associated with witches as one of their ritual objects, is really another version of the miraculous Cauldron of Cerridwen.[122]

Valiente's influence on modern witchcraft is profound, and whilst authors such as Spence and Graves made sweeping assumptions and reached inaccurate conclusions, modern witchcraft writers were inspired by these correspondences that were perceived as sympathetic to the evolution of a new tradition of magical practise. By the 1980s Cerridwen's attributions had found their feet under the table of modern witchcraft.

---

119   Morgan, *The Mabin of the Mabinogion*, 13, 25
120   MacCulloch, *The Religion of the Ancient Celts*, 117.
121   Graves, *The White Goddess*, 400.
122   Valiente, *An ABC of Witchcraft*, 30.

Janet and Stewart Farrar in their 1987 book *The Witches' Goddess* wrote:

> Cerridwen: Welsh mother, moon and grain goddess...owner of an inexhaustible cauldron called Amen (sic), in which she made a magic draught called "greal" (grain?) from six plants which gave inspiration and knowledge. One of her symbols was a sow. Most of her legends emphasise the terrifying aspect of the Dark Mother; yet her cauldron is the source of wisdom and inspiration.[123]

What is evident in these influential works is the assumption that previous conclusions regarding Cerridwen were correct, when in fact they were not. Nineteenth-century writers were attempting to create a past and a philosophical school of thought that was counter-culture in nature. They mostly failed. Early to mid-twentieth century writers, the likes of Frazer, Spence, and Graves, were not practitioners or adherents of Paganism, and yet their greatest influence was to be seen in the new Pagan traditions. With few resources available to them, late twentieth-century writers of witchcraft, Druidry, and Paganism, without the filter of academia, were wholly reliant on the flawed research that they could find. They did not act or write from ignorance; they expressed the only ideas available to them at the time.

By the late 1990s and the early decades of the twenty-first century, Cerridwen had been taken under the wings of the Pagan traditions and assimilated into their worldview, philosophies, and teachings. Essentially, Cerridwen had become synonymous with the new witches, and she fit their world perfectly. She flew beyond the confines of the bardic tradition that had preserved her, and in the new witches she found fresh voices to carry her message of inspiration and transformation. Once scorned as a medieval witch, her guise as twentieth- and twenty-first-century witch goddess would have the bards of the nobility spinning indignantly in their graves. Ironically, her denigration would eventually lead to her rebirth as not just a muse, but a powerful and modern goddess with an army of witches and Druids claiming to be devoted to her.

---

123   Farrar and Farrar, *The Witches' Goddess*, 209.

Modern witchcraft traditions continue to be lacklustre and weak in modern-day Wales, as if something in our cultural consciousness and linguistics continues to misunderstand it. Yet it undeniably exists in the modern sense. As a Welsh person, the term *witch*, especially in translation, is jarring; there is no fault or blame here but simply the fickleness of language. *Swyn* is the most appropriate term in my native tongue to describe what is now identified in the English-speaking world as witchcraft. It is also a useful term in the Welsh language that I use to describe a spell or charm. Cerridwen is now a goddess of more than one tongue. She exists to inspire peoples beyond her native Wales. She is goddess and mother of Awen to modern Druids, but she is also a powerful witch goddess.

As a Druid I practise the bardic magic of song-spells, utilising the power of words to bring about internal and external change. I practise spell casting and conjuration; I use incantations, tools, and amulets to express the connection I have to the natural world, the spiritual dimension, and the subtle senses utilised in acts of magic. However, it is the term *swyn* that I employ as a modern Welsh Druid to these skills. This is not to denounce the now-accepted term "witch" and "witchcraft" and the traditions of witchcraft that have emerged in the twentieth century, but rather to honour the complex evolution and development of magical practise within Wales, the bardic tradition, and the Welsh language. The practice of swyn embraces the Welsh bardic tradition, modern Druidry, and Witchcraft simultaneously.

Today, the two great expressions of modern Western Paganism, witchcraft and Druidry, grew together, often hand in hand. There are witches who are Druids and Druids who are witches. And yet we are more than the sum of our parts; we are siblings travelling along a new road of expression, and uniting us is Cerridwen, Mam yr Awen, great witch goddess. She has found in us the fertile ground in which to plant new seeds of Awen.

13

Cerridwen and the Mabinogi

At this point I must digress somewhat and delve into the corpus of Welsh mythology commonly referred to as the Mabinogi, for like the intricate weaving of Celtic knotwork, there is much we can glean about the function of Cerridwen by looking at the greater mythological landscape of Wales. This seemingly complex system of interlacing mythologies is made simple when we move into relationship with them, and in order to achieve this we must first secure our understanding of them, where they came from, what they do, and why they have survived for over 1,500 years in various written forms.

Wales is the land of legend; it is a landscape that has long since breathed life and vitality into story and myth. They sing from the fertile plains of the Isle of Anglesey in the extreme north, they whisper from the summit of the tallest mountains of Snowdonia, they are written in the deep valleys of the south. The entire landscape gave birth, nurtured, and developed a body of myth and legends that are world renowned. These myths do not pertain to history as we would currently understand that concept, but instead they sing of a history of the heart, the history of a people and their relationship with the land.

Our ancestors took their stories from the undulating patterns of the landscape, from the way in which weather played its role on the stage of life. A hillock renowned for witnessing a miracle became famed as a place between the worlds; a lake deep, dark, and mysteries and the pattern of the wind upon its surface spoke of the mysteries of the otherworld. Over time, and by the tongues of countless generations, these stories that exemplified a locality-specific nature took to their feet and by the power of the bards and minstrels embarked on a journey throughout the land. By doing so, they captured the imagination of the people and developed consistency of plot and character. Just like a tree, they took root, their trunks growing wider and stronger, their branches dancing to the cycle of the seasons.

Without a doubt, the most famed of these tales lie in the body of work known as Y Mabinogi, a corpus of myth containing eleven tales that in compilation are given the umbrella title of the Mabinogi, which you may be familiar with as the Mabiniogion. The erroneous term Mabinogion has become commonplace and arose from a scribal error in which a scribe, perhaps candle-light weary, rhymed the term Mabinogi with a word in a previous sentence: "dyledogyon," a place name.[124] This error was perpetuated by the most famed translator of the work—Lady Charlotte Guest, who between 1838 and 1849 brought the myths into the English language. She believed that the erroneous "Mabinogion" was the plural for Mabinogi and did not consider that it was, in fact, a scribal error; however, it offered her the perfect title for her collection, and the term stuck.[125]

Mysteries of the Mabinogi

Of the eleven individual tales that are collated as the Mabinogi, the most renowned are the four branches, but there is a peculiarity and a magic to be found here. The term "four branches" arises from a terminus that is utilised

---

124 The term Mabynogyon does not appear in any other text, save for one erroenous example in the White Book of Rhydderch; consistently they are referred to as Mabinogi, notably at the end of each branch.

125 Davies, *The Mabinogion*, ix–x.

at the conclusion of each branch. In Welsh the term is *cainc* and mutated as *geinc* within the structure of a sentence. The examples are as such:

The First Branch—*"Ac yuelly y teruyna y geinc hon yma or mabynogyon."*
(And so ends this branch of the Mabinogi.)[126]
Second Branch—*"A llyna ual y teruyna y geinc honn o'r Mabinyogi."*
(And here ends this branch of the Mabinogi.)
Third Branch—*"Ac yuelly y teruyna y geinc honn o'r Mabinogy."* (And so ends this branch of the Mabinogi.)
Fourth Branch—*"Ac yuelly y teruyna y geinc honn o'r Mabinogi."* (And so ends this branch of the Mabinogi.)[127]

What is presented here are not four individual myths, but rather one body of mythology expressed on four branches. The branches grow upon a single tree, and herein lies the mystery. The Mabinogi are perceived and have been perpetuated as the song of a tree. I like to coin the term world tree when describing the mythological being upon whose body grow the branches of the Welsh bardic and storytelling traditions. The tree holds the power of myth, but it is the nature of a tree to not do so statically, or in stasis; it is in a continuous state of flux.

The tree gives forth great branches that in themselves split into numerous twigs, each with a bud or a number of buds, and with every passing season the branch is never the same, and yet it is connected to the tree, to the source, until its ultimate demise. With this in mind, the branches of the Mabinogi are not separate, they share the same parent: the world tree. Each retelling, each rendition is a new bud on the terminus of the branch, the leaves of which stretch towards the sun and in turn take in vital energy to feed the parent tree.

These branches contain another form of magic, the magic of words. In Welsh, the word for branch is cainc; however, as is often the case in Welsh, the word has a multitude of meanings depending on the context in which one is

---

126 Scribal error from the White Book of Rhydderch, designated as Peniarth Manuscript 4.
127 Examples taken and translated by the author from Llyfr Gwyn Rhydderch, National Library of Wales, Peniarth Manuscript 4.

using it. Other than meaning "branch," cainc also refers to a strand or yarn of a rope. This is not unlike the previous analogy that I offered of the myths being similar to the intricate interlacing of Celtic knotwork. A single strand of yarn in and of itself is not strong nor stable, but when interwoven with others into a rope, the result is something that is both steadfast and powerful. Cainc has another meaning in which it refers to a song and a tune, and this is by no means accidental, for there is much to suggest that the power of song, of music, is tantamount to the expression of the mysteries that are held in the myths and poems of Wales.[128] It is indicative of the Awen itself, a force or power that is immanent in all things, including myth and story.

On a magical level, each telling, each new expression of the branches nourishes the world tree and keeps it strong, vital, and living. Each rendition adds lyrics to the song of the world tree, and whilst the words may always be different, the music remains the same. The inspiration that is gleaned from storytelling nourishes the tree—whenever storytellers or bards open their mouth to sing the old songs, they are engaged in a sacred dance of preservation and perpetuation. To consider their expression to be merely storytelling in its simplistic sense of offering entertainment is to miss the point entirely. The myths and poems are symbiotic; one cannot survive or thrive without the other.

From their first literation in the later medieval period from undoubtedly earlier sources, they have continued to be relevant and current. Many of the characters from the Mabinogi appear in the much earlier work known as Trioedd Ynys Prydein (The Triads of the Islands of Britain), and it is generally accepted within academia that the entire collection refers to a much older body of work that existed in the vernacular and has been lost to the mists of time. The last time that the Mabinogi were scribed occurred in two specific and important manuscripts, the Llyfr Gwyn Rhydderch (The White Book of Rhydderch), circa 1300–1325, and the Llyfr Coch Hergest (The Red Book of Hergest), circa 1375–1425. Note that I used the phrase "the last time" to describe the penning of these manuscripts, for there are fragments pertain-

---

128   Bevan and Donovan, *Geiriadur Prifysgol Cymru*, 390.

ing to the myths in other manuscripts of the same and slightly earlier period. Neither of the manuscripts mentioned contain the original text of the four branches and other tales; they are only later copies of them. There is some speculation as to the exact origin of the myths in written form. The consensus is that their earliest literal form does not precede the year 1100.[129]

Lady Charlotte Guest played an important role in popularising the Mabinogi and bringing them to the eye of the non-Welsh-speaking world. Her collection presents in English the eleven tales that in chronological order appear thus:

- Culhwch ac Olwen
- The Four Branches
- Lludd and Llefelys
- The Three Romances—The Lady of the Fountain, Peredur, and Geraint
- The Dream of Macsen Wledig
- The Dream of Rhonabwy

In a continuous logocentric world, we are wont to give credence to that which is written over and above that which is spoken. And as is oft the case, one can easily be led to the belief that bodies of mythologies only sprang into existence once they were written. This is incorrect, and there is evidence to suggest (ironically from the written word) that the Mabinogi in particular, at least in part had existed in the oral tradition of Britain long before they came to the scribing desks of the medieval period. The myths are highly developed, suggesting that they were perhaps centuries in the making. This development and evolution have caused even our academics to make increasingly bold statements about the nature and function of the Mabinogi.

Rachel Bromwich, the editor of the *Triads of the Islands of Britain,* said:

> The four branches are to be distinguished from the other chwedlau (tales) as much by an essential difference in their basic subject matter, as by the developed artistry of their narration. They are

---

129   Charles-Edwards in Sullivan, C. W. III, ed., *The Mabinogi: A Book of Essays,* 44.

fundamentally the stories of the old Brittonic gods from whom the leading Welsh dynasties claimed descent.[130]

This is quite the statement to make, in which Bromwich claims that the characters or archetypes of the Mabinogi are reflections of earlier deities. She is not alone in this hypothesis.

In his introduction to Dafydd and Rhiannon Ifans' translation of the Mabinogi, Brynley F. Roberts went even further by saying:

> These are not tales solely for the purpose of entertainment, and nei-
> ther to explain the wonders of a region or the lineage of a nation,
> but they do clearly contain elements of folk-lore. They are the rem-
> nants of the mythology of the Britons, and their belief about the
> Other World—Annwfn, and about the dealings of Gods and men,
> the heroes of the four branches are characters from the Pantheaon
> of Celtic religions in Britain.[131]

In the above quote, Roberts makes use of the word "pantheon" when referring to the characters of the Mabinogi, and he is perhaps the first aca-demic to do so in modern times. To this day, counter arguments persist over the nature of the divine in the Mabinogi, in particular the often-strong response that is invoked by the identification of Mabinogi characters as dei-ties in twenty-first-century Pagan practise. There is enough evidence to sug-gest that the names recorded in the myths demonstrate linguistic develop-ment of earlier nouns that did indeed refer to deities. In his gigantic tome *The Four Branches of the Mabinogi*, scholar Will Parker claims:

> The hero of the fourth branch is the one character in the Mabinogi
> for whom we have definitive evidence of a pre-Christian cult. Lleu is
> literally a druidic god in medieval clothing.[132]

He goes on to elaborate:

---

130 Bromwich, *Trioedd Ynys Prydein*, lxxii.
131 Translated from Welsh by the author from the inroductory material of "Y Mabino-gion," Ifans and Ifans, by Brynley F. Roberts, xiii.
132 Parker, *The Four Branches of the Mabinogi*, 447.

It is a truism that more or less everything about the Mabinogi is rooted in the pre-Christian past. The name of the tradition itself, as we have seen, appears to derive from the name for the seasonal celebrations of the Romano-British boy-god, Apollo Maponus.[133]

None of the above statements claim that the material, as it is preserved, perfectly records the liturgical component of ancient Celtic religion, none of which was transcribed into writing. But what it does claim is that there is significantly more hiding beneath the syncretic medieval layer, and that by lifting the skirts of the Middle Ages, one can catch a tantalising glimpse of an older time. Claims that the Mabinogi are in some way a Christian text can be dismissed by the lack of Christian doctrine and teachings that appear therein. The elements of language and courtly practise certainly reflect a culture that has at its core a Christian expression, but that is the extent of it. Essentially there is more concerning folkloric practise and belief than there is of Christian religious doctrine.

However, there is a subtle trap in this exploration in search of the old and antiquated: one can be led down a path of seeking authenticity and validation only by emulating the past. The mythologies themselves tell another story, not only of continuous development but also of the deep change that occurs to all peoples throughout all times. The pantheon that Brynley F. Roberts is referring to may be lost to us, and we may know little of the dynamics of ancient practise and expression, but what we can be assured of is that the elements and characters did survive, and they are here today as the modern pantheon of Welsh deities. Rhiannon is no longer Rigatona in her ancient guise; she has evolved with the needs of the people, and it is the reason she survives today. There is deep magic in the power of relevance and consistent practise. I will explore the nature of this and the process of apotheosis a little later in this book.

Myths have always served to further the ideas, philosophes, and ideologies of people, be they religious or otherwise. Dr. Gwilym Morus-Baird sums this quality up nicely when describing the tenacity for the Taliesin figure to

---

133 Parker, *The Four Branches of the Mabinogi*, 653.

survive the thrashes of time, as well as the manner by which various schools of thought and individuals have connected to and made use of myth:

> Different tellers of myth, be they renowned bards, literate monks, advertising agencies, modern druids or academics, will use popular figures such as Taliesin to further their own particular ideology. Myths are made almost always for this one reason, to promote the myth-makers' own values.[134]

Academic criticism of modern polytheistic practices often misses the point and power hid within myth. The function of Celtic academia is to preserve, collate, and study the linguistic structure of language, trends, and to an extent explore a cultural archaeological expression. Their function is not to examine existential issues or to delve into spiritual and religious significance of mythology, a mechanism that underlies every world religion and spiritual tradition. The often-blatant criticism from Celtic academia towards those who perceive an element of the spiritual in mythology is unfounded.

Cultures and peoples have since time immemorial found meaning in patterns, and myths and poems offer one such pattern of significance and ultimately transcendence. The values of modern Celtic polytheistic Pagan practise and its worldview are inspired by the past but not defined by it. It takes old concepts and breathes new life into them, but this is not a unique feature. My examination of the bardic tradition itself and its four distinguishable eras exemplifies the frequency by which myth and poetry is taken, adapted, and altered to fit the needs and values of the people. This is not a new quality, but one that is continuously renewing itself in response to the people. It demonstrates the vitality of myth, story, legend, and song, and its ability to impact and transform the human heart and expression. It will, however, always have its critics, but the criticism arises from a camp that will never understand the existential and spiritual thirst of those who utilise these principles to better their own lives, glean a sense of place and being, and imbibe their traditions with elements that bring value and worth to that community or individual.

---

134 Morus-Baird, *Understanding Welsh Myths*, 26.

Myths do not belong to one period of time, and they are not possessions; academia may have preserved the material for the present generation to enjoy, but it does not own the material. The material belongs to the spirit of the people. The Welsh are guardians of the material; we served to perpetuate and protect them. The Mabinogi and myths like them reflect the continuous human search for meaning, significance, and transcendence. Myths express organised and developed images that recall the experiences of the people and their relationships with the world around them; stories develop organically from the ground up and record actions, worldviews, cultural expression, and the idiosyncrasies of the human spirit.

They are truly a history of the human heart.

Cerridwen in the Mabinogi

One could easily assume that Cerridwen is entirely absent from the four branches of the Mabinogi. However, if we take Ifor Williams at his word—that the tale of the birth of Taliesin combined with the poetry of Taliesin is key to the mysteries—we will discover that she is, indeed, quite present.

Modern academia agrees that the indigenous Celtic material was fragmented, and whilst the actual motive for this intentional fragmentation cannot be fully proven, many have speculated. I cover elements of this in my book *From the Cauldron Born*, but suffice it to say here that many agree, and others like Will Parker have gone all out and referred to the mechanics behind this fragmentation as the School of Taliesin.[135] Therefore, if we entertain this idea and explore it, our understanding of Cerridwen and our relationship with her will be transformed.

I do believe that Cerridwen is present in the fourth branch and can be found in the form of the hwch (sow) that leads Gwydion on his search for Lleu to the base of the world tree. This is not without controversy, as Ronald Hutton in his *Stations of the Sun* states that any notion of Cerridwen as a divine sow is one popularised by the mid-twentieth-century writer Robert Graves in his seminal work *The White Goddess*, where he identifies Cerridwen

---

135   Parker, *The Four Branches of the Mabinogi*, 91–93.

as the sow goddess. Hutton goes on to claim that this supposition is entirely without supporting evidence.[136] However, what is not explored in both *The White Goddess* and Hutton's *Stations of the Sun* is the magic hidden in words and the power of language to occlude one's vision of what is happening beneath the surface. The following chapters will explore the hidden relationship of Cerridwen in her animal countence and their connection to the magic of the Mabinogi and other native tales and traditions.

---

136   Hutton, *Stations of the Sun*, 368.

14

The Zoomorphic Faces of Cerridwen

Things are rarely what one assumes them to be, a fact that holds a truism in twenty-first-century life but that was certainly significant in Celtic culture as well. Within the Welsh myths, there are several examples of characters/ archetypes that appear as integral aspects of the narrative and yet are not afforded a name. The wife of the King of Annwfn in the first branch, followed by the wife of Lord Teyrnon, are not afforded a name; only their attire is described—the same attire worn by Rhiannon. These themes and the identities of such characters would have been understood by the audience. Several important characters of the myths display shapeshifting abilities, Cerridwen, Gwion Bach, and Taliesin included. Shape and form are evidently temporary states in the Celtic imagination and something that can be changed and influenced by the power of magic.

In the poem "Kat Godeu (The Battle of the Trees)," Taliesin states that he had assumed a multitude of forms, only one of which was anthropomorphic:

Bum yn lliaws rith,
Kyn bum disgyfrith,
Bum cledyf culurith,
Or ardaf pan writh,
Bum diegyr yn awyr,
Bum serawl syr.
Bum geir yn llythyr,
Bum llyfyr ym prifder.
Bum llugyrn lleufer,
Blwydyn a hanher.

I have been in many forms,
Until I was set free and wild.
I was a narrow sword,
Made by hand,
I was a droplet in the air,
I was the radiance of stars.
I was a word in a writing,
I was a book in my prime.
I was the light in a lantern,
For a year and a half.[137]

Simply because an individual or character is not named within the written accounts does not immediately suggest that they are not present. Within the living structure of the narrative as bardic performance, this would have been understood and utilised for tension and suspense whilst simultaneously transferring the latest elements of learning and technique to the bards in the audience.

With this in mind, we would be foolhardy to assume that Cerridwen exists wholly as an anthropomorphic entity—in fact, there is further magic to be gleaned when we examine what happens to Cerridwen when she interacts with the apparent world in a non-humanoid form. My previous explora-

---

137   Translated by the author from *The Facsimile and Text of the Book of Taliesin* by J. Gwneogvryn Evans, 23–24.

tion of the nature of the lake as both setting for the tale and also allegory for liminality comes to the fore here, for in my musings I claim that Cerridwen's form as anthropomorphic is only present in the otherworld, beyond the very fabric of the lake itself. When she steps from the edge of the cauldron and interacts with the apparent world, it seems that she is unable to sustain her anthropomorphic form and assumes a complex sequence of zoomorphic countenance. Her guise in the shape and form of otter, salmon, hawk, and hen are obvious and belong to the sequence of the chase itself; I explored this fully in my book *From the Cauldron Born*. However, it is to her zoomorphic aspect as a hwch that the following pages will explore.

Let us examine the sequence of events to further explore this function. As the cauldron nears its boiling, Cerridwen takes to her rest. All the components and ingredients necessary for the Awen have been assimilated into the cauldron, and they are ripe for expression. As Cerridwen sleeps, the cauldron gives up its three drops onto the thumb of Gwion Bach, and then it gives out a loud cry and shatters, its contents now rendered poison. All at once the edges of the cauldron—that place between the manifest and unmanifest world—is shattered, and from this point onwards the sequence of events no longer takes place in liminality but spill out into the apparent world. Rivers run toxic and horses perish whilst drinking. The nature of the mysteries verge on the edge of poison. With the cauldron shattered, the force that holds and gives form to the unadulterated power of the universe is released, but it is unstable, undirected power. Without stability and form, its power is too great, and it morphs into toxicity.

Cerridwen responds by beating the primary symbol of liminality in the tale, the character of the blind man Morda, and takes to the chase; in so doing she loses her anthropomorphic form and assumes that of creatures of land and sea and sky. By the beating of Morda, the threshold between the worlds is made tangible, the veil shreds, and the worlds collide. In one particular manuscript that recounts the birth tale of Taliesin, Morda is given the name Dallmor Dallme, which can be taken to mean "blind sea" or "blind stone," further reiterating the power of liminality.

It is only upon her return to the realms between the worlds, as she gestates the future radiant brow, that she resumes her humanoid form. But pause here for a second and consider the nature of Cerridwen's pregnancy; could the state of being with child be considered liminal? In this position, she is neither one individual nor yet two; she must wait nine moons for the gestation of the child, a child that she intends on killing, and yet she chooses to wait. With her knowledge of herbs and plant wisdom, one would imagine her ability to abort the pregnancy would have been more than possible, and yet she chooses not to.

The initiate of the mysteries, Gwion Bach, returns to a proxy cauldron between the worlds in the guise of Cerridwen's womb in order to assimilate and digest the mysteries, to experience something tantamount to death, and yet essentially what he experiences is a state of profound liminality. It is the seed that holds the potential for growth and expressive inspiration; this is an important point to consider. It is false to assume that every acorn contains an oak tree; in truth, the acorn contains the *potential* of an oak tree. As I explored previously, Cerridwen herself in the Black Book of Caermarthen is referred to as "ogyrven amhad"—the gogyrwen of various seeds. She embodies the potential within the seed, the benign forces of growth and fertility, and the promise of inspiration.

I claim that only the sequence of the chase takes place in the apparent world, followed by the discovery of Taliesin at the salmon weir; the remainder occurs between the worlds, interwoven into the mists that weave a tapestry between realities.

One may argue that Cerridwen is apparently human during her sojourns into the Welsh landscape to gather her herbs; however, these sequences of events are not described at all—only the magical potential within the ingredients are alluded to. The remainder takes place in the otherworld or at a place deemed betwixt and between, at the edge of the cauldron, where its unmanifest potential is streamed into coherence and given shape and form, not just by the function of Cerridwen alone, but by a collaboration between Cerridwen and her consort Tegid Foel. Without the holding properties of Tegid, the Awen would be too expansive with nothing to hold its form long enough for the universe to perceive it. Cerridwen, Tegid, and the ingredients of the cauldron form the material that permits us, as initiates of the mystery, to not only perceive them clearly, but to also swim within them as those with radiant brows.

Cerridwen's zoomorphic aspects within the chase are indicative of the three apparent realms of land, sea, and sky. For now, we shall focus instead on the initiatory qualities of the chase and its connection to the Mabinogi, in particular the family of Dôn.

Most academic, visionary, and occult platforms accept that the sequence of events within the chase are initiatory in nature; that the innocent— Gwion—is pushed further and further through the experience and mysteries of the apparent world before assimilation in the cauldron that is now in the guise of Cerridwen's womb. The entire function of the initiation sequence is to imbibe within the initiate the power of Awen. Its rebirth is an indication of the successfulness of that assimilation; however, a ritual of integration, where the mysteries gleaned by the process of initiation are incorporated into experience, is yet to occur.

If we now cast our musings to the fourth branch of the Mabinogi, we will note that it too has a sequence of events that leads to initiation. The potential initiate of the Mabinogi, in the guise of Rhiannon and Pwyll's son Pryderi, has experienced the world, grown, loved, lived, and died. He is then reborn as Lleu, who in turn is gestated twice, once in the womb of Aranrhod and secondly in the stone cist at the foot of Gwydion's bed before ultimately being transformed at the top of the world tree and by the powers of magic. Look at the narrative closer and you will note a similar sequence of events as that contained within the tale of Cerridwen and Taliesin: the profane is devoured by an entity that represents the transformative powers of Annwfn, the hwch.[138]

---

138 Commonly meaning "sow" in modern Welsh.

15

A Pig by Any Other Name

Whilst the pig is absent from the sequence of events held within the chase, it is important at this juncture to pause and look at the mystery and magic held in words that may well be alien to you—words that allude to the magic of pigs. It is apparent that pigs were of great importance to the Celts, and in Welsh mythology they were perceived as gifts from the otherworld. However, there is a subtle distinction made that is invariably lost in translation. The Mabinogi collection contains a complex, dynamic, and magical tale called Culhwch ac Olwen, where the protagonist Culhwch must undergo near-impossible tasks to win the hand of Olwen in marriage. Throughout the tale a distinction is made between two Welsh words that, on the surface, appear to be describing the same thing.

The common plural word in Welsh for pig is *moch*, its singular counterpart being *mochyn*, which according to the *Dictionary of the Welsh Language* translates as "a quadruped mammal of the suidae family, notable for their bristles and long snouts; pigs, swine, hogs."[139] However, another word is often used to refer to another form of pig, namely the *hwch*; in translation this is usually taken to mean a sow or nursing pig, but on closer examination

---

139   Bevan, *Geiriadur Prifysgol Cymru*, 2468.

of its contextual usage, something else comes to light. In all appearances, the male character Culhwch contains the suffix *hwch* with the prefix *cul*, which is often taken to mean "long" or "narrow,"[140] although Eric Hamp associated *cul* with the Indo-European word *keul*, variants of which can be found in Celtic, Germanic, Baltic, and Slavic languages, which means "pig."[141] So why would this character be called a "pig pig"? Why use two words for the same thing? There must be something else going on here—and indeed, if we scratch at the surface, something remarkable swims into vision.

Within the tale of Culhwch ac Olwen the term hwch is used three times. The first instance is in attempting to explain the etymology of the name Culhwch, the protagonist. The remaining references all relate to another supernatural creature called the Twrch Trwyth. In a brief nutshell, the Twrch Trwyth is a hwch that has significant magical properties, often lost in translation as a magical boar. This boar became a subject of a sacred hunt undertaken by Arthur and his retinue to secure various and obscure items hid in the boar's coarse hair. The term *boar* is, however, loaded with gender misconception, for in the popular imagination (and according to its dictionary definition) a boar is defined as not only a wild pig that has tusks, but also as an uncastrated male pig. This presents a unique problem when attempting to not only translate a body of work from Welsh into English, but also maintain a storytelling narrative—we may miss out on the magic hid within the term hwch and its erroneous exclusive association with the female gender.

The Welsh word hwch fuses gender concepts and is identified by the *Dictionary of the Welsh Language* as a term that uniquely combines male and female properties into one word.[142] Interestingly, in modern Welsh, the word hwch is also taken to mean something that is dirty or unclean, and it is often used as a derogatory designation for an unwholesome individual or one who is dirty of body or mind. Is it a coincidence that what was once a sacred word has been demoted to meaning something unclean? It is likely that collective

---

140 Bromwich, *Culhwch ac Olwen*, 47.
141 Hamp, "Celtic Banuo," 214.
142 Bevan, *Geiriadur Prifysgol Cymru*, 1928.

forces within the later bardic traditions purposefully denigrated words that once held a sacred component.

To return briefly to the tale of Culhwch ac Olwen, the Twrch Trwyth was, in fact, a king upon whom a curse had been placed, and consequently he had been transformed into a magical porcine with remarkable qualities, but what is important for this discourse is that the term hwch is used to differentiate the Twrch Trwyth from an ordinary porcine. It is something other, a porcine of supernatural erudition. If we backtrack to the name Culhwch and assume that Hamp is correct in his analysis, then the name does not translate as "pig pig," but rather implies that the character is both pig in the ordinary sense of the term whilst simultaneously evoking the supernatural quality of the hwch. The protagonist's quarry, Olwen, meaning "white track" or "white pathway," also alludes to the possibility of something that is porcine in nature. The tale recounts that as Olwen walks, she leaves four clovers in her track. What is not clear is whether or not a cluster of four clovers appears in each footprint or if a single clover appears in each footprint, which happens to the pattern a pig's footprint makes. If we take the possibility of the latter, a clover in each footprint, it suggests that Olwen herself is nonhuman and is potentially a porcine.[143]

With this in mind, it is possible that the entire tale of Culhwch ac Olwen is reflective of a body of mythology recording the significance of pig deities of the ancient Celtic cultural continuum.[144] If this analysis is correct, it suggests that Culhwch represents a pig deity that expresses both aspects of the porcine, the secular and the sublime. Whilst pigs were afforded extraordinary importance to the Celts, it is clear that through the magic of language the audience would have known if the storyteller or bard was referring to an ordinary porcine or something significantly more mystical—a peculiarity lost in the modern world when a word is translated by reliance on a dictionary alone. Add in the complexity of gender principles that differ greatly between Welsh and English, and one can easily be scuppered.

---

143   Ford in Matonis and Melia, *Celtic Language, Celtic Culture*, 293.
144   Ford, *The Mabinogi*, 15.

There are another two examples of the term hwch occuring in Welsh mythology and lore that are worthy of mention, for in both instances there is an initiatory component that emulates the function of Cerridwen. The first comes to us from the Trioedd Ynys Prydein (Triads of the Island of Britain) and triad number 26 from the White Book of Rhydderch and the Red Book of Hergest, and concerns a hwch that went by the name Henwen, the blessed or holy ancient one. The triad concerns itself with the three powerful swineherds of the island of Britain, the third of which was Coll, son of Collfrewy,[145] who guarded the swine of Dallwyr Dallben in Cornwall. A hwch within that herd was pregnant, and it was prophesied that her womb burden would be the worse for the Island of Britain. Arthur set about an army to capture and destroy Henwen. In the north of Cornwall, the hwch took to the sea and emerged on the coast of South Wales.

In the wheat fields of Gwent, she birthed a grain of wheat and a bee, and consequently Gwent has the best wheat and honey. In Pembrokeshire she birthed a grain of barley and a bee, resulting in that county having the best barley and honey. At the barking hill in Snowdonia, she gave birth to a wolf cub and an eagle. And at Llanfair on the border of Môn, on the Black Rock, she gave birth to a kitten. The powerful swineherd threw the kitten into the Menai Straits for drowning, but the sons of Palug fostered it, which was to their own harm, for that was Palug's cat and it was foretold to be one of the three great oppressions of the island of Môn.

An interesting note within the triad of Henwen is the name of the owner of the swineherd, Dallwyr Dallben, whose name can be translated to mean blind man, blind head. This bears a striking similarity to the full name given to Morda, the blind man in the version of the tale of Taliesin in the hand of Llywellyn Sion, who names him as Dallmor Dallme—blind sea, blind

---

145   *Coll* translates as hazel; however, the surname, whilst containing the term coll, is unclear as to the meaning of the suffix *frewy*. Sugestions have been offered that the name may refer to the magician of hazel, whilst Rachel Bromwich has explored the possibility of the name being that of a woman and that Coll is referred to as the son of Collfrewy (his mother), an unusual titling in medieval Wales. Bromwich, *Trioedd Ynys Prydein*, 315.

stone.[146] There is a theme of blindness that runs through the material and may be suggestive of a requirement to perceive the subtle realms by means of another form of sight.

Triad 26 records a chase sequence where an animal is pursued. And yet, it feels in reverse order to the common tale, whereby in this instance it is the hwch, the symbol of initiation, that is being pursued. The pastoral and agricultural elements of her birthing are fortuitous and cause the southern counties of Gwent and Pembroke to prosper; however, the two birthings in the north bring about ill fortune, with Palug's cat bringing the worse for Môn, modern-day Anglesey. No explanation is offered to explain why certain animals brought misfortune. This island was attacked by the Roman army in 62 C.E. to destroy the Druid threat to the Roman Empire. There is a sense here of a profound journey being made and a symbiotic relationship between the human world, the animal world, and the plant world. The triad does not conclude as such, and we are not afforded a result, and neither are we told if Arthur and his army were successful in the destruction of Henwen.

If we cast our focus away from the literal tradition and to the pastoral, particularly community-centred folk practises and customs, we can glean a little more inspiration and perhaps therein find traces of an initiatrix that is temptingly similar in nature to Cerridwen. Whilst it is tempting to only seek wisdom substantiated by the written word, it is important that we consider elements existing in the human world that transcend or underlie the logocentric structures we place such enormous credence upon.

In the traditional Calan Gaeaf (Samhain) customs of Wales, another hwch is prevalent: the Hwch Ddu Gwta (tailless black hwch). Calan Gaeaf, translated as the Calends of Winter, is ancestor day, with the previous evening being Nos Galan Gaeaf, which equates to All Hallow's Eve, a liminal time where the dead are believed to wander the earthly realms. It is a divine fusion of Pagan, Celtic, and Christian traditions and customs, and one that holds a record of another hwch that functions as a devourer of the profane.

---

146   Bromwich, *Trioedd Ynys Prydein*, 328.

Local historians throughout Wales record the various customs of Nos Galan Gaeaf with various rites where children would sing for spiced cakes, called Solod, and food would be prepared for the dead, a custom known as *hel bwyd cennad y meirw* (collecting food for the messenger of the assembly of the dead). At some point in the proceedings and later taken to encourage young children to return home, from the shadows the Hwch Ddu Gwta would appear and songs would be sung, perhaps in an attempt to slow her progression or bewilder her. The overall threat was that the slowest in the chase would be caught and devoured by the hwch. A beautiful example of this can be seen in the works of T. Gwynn Jones and his reporting of a Caernarvonshire witness, who said:

> I saw the acting of the story of the Hwch Ddu Gwta in 1818, it was a dark, cold night and I was seven years old, having gone to see the bonfire on a neighbouring hill. Before the fire had burnt out some black object appeared, grunting and moving along. There was a shout that the sow had come, and we ran home in fear.[147]

Welsh customs record the bardic verses that were utilised for these events. The first example was particularly popular in the northeastern county of Clwyd:

> *Adre! Adre, am y cynta'!*
> *Hwch Ddu Gwta a gipio'r ola'!*
>
> *Home! Home, be the first,*
> *For the tailless black sow will take the hindmost!*[148]

Popular on the island of Anglesey as late as the nineteenth century was this song:

> *Hwch Ddu Gwta*
> *A Ladi Wen*
> *Heb ddim pen.*
> *Hwch Ddu Gwta*

---

147 Jones, *Welsh Folklore and Folk-Custom*, 149.
148 Jones, *Llên Gwerin Sir Gaernarfon*, 262–263.

A gipio'r ola.
Hwch Ddu Gwta
Nos G'lan Gaea,
Lladron yn dwad
Tan weu sana.

The tailless black sow
And the white lady
Without a head.
The tailless black sow
Will take the hindmost.
Tailless black sow
On the night of the calends of winter,
Thieves are coming
Whilst we knit our socks.[149]

Both recount a chase sequence initiated by the arrival of a hwch and a sinister companion, the ambiguous and headless apparition of the white lady. In the county of Arfon in northwest Wales, children would sing:

Nos Glangaua,
Ar ben pob camfa,
Hwch Ddu Gwta,
Gipio'r ola!

On All Hallows Eve,
On top of every stile,
Is the tailless black sow,
And she will take the hindmost![150]

In this example we see reference to a stile, a traditional symbol of liminality and a place betwixt and between the worlds. Whilst Cerridwen is evidently missing by name, literal and folkloric customs all record a consistent theme that emulates the function of Cerridwen as initiatrix. Whilst we

---

149   Jones, *Welsh Folklore and Folk-Custom,* 148–149.
150   Ibid.

cannot be entirely sure of their origins, it is tempting to see parallels and similarity of themes. When one considers that even the secular and often frivolous nature of the Calan Gaeaf verses were created by the bards at some unknown point in the past, I do believe that there is a commonality that links such practises to the old myths and the bardic tradition. Calan Gaeaf customs in Wales all demonstrate a belief that the point of separation between the apparent world and the unseen world is somehow tenuous or fragile; it belies a liminal quality so apparent and essential to the function of Cerridwen and bardic magic.

Hwch or Sow?

Which word should therefore be used to adequately express the qualities of hwch in the English language? I would suggest none and that, in fact, the term hwch be used, which in itself carries the profound meaning of a porcine of supernatural erudition. Take, for example, the word karma, which is Sanskrit in origin. The meaning of the word is understood in the English language and therefore it does not require a translated term to adequately describe it. It is often tempting to try appropriating a word into another language, but as is often the case with the Celtic languages, our attempts may be futile and serve only to muddy the waters. With that in mind, and the explanation given above, I would suggest that the term hwch is used contextually in English when expressing the function of magical porcine.

What does this have to do with Cerridwen?

I shall backtrack a little here to explore once again the mysteries of the Mabinogi. In the fourth branch, Gwydion follows a sow to locate his adopted son, but he does not follow a porcine to the base of the world tree that holds within its branches the potential initiate; he follows a hwch.[151] A differentiation is made in the tale between the hwch and the pigs to which she comes home to; seemingly she shares the same pigsty as the worldly, ordinary pigs, but she is also quite different in nature from the other swine. As soon as the pen is opened each morning, she takes her leave; however, she is not

---

151   Williams, *Pedeir Keinc y Mabinogi*, 88–89.

observed and nobody is aware of where she goes. Gwydion, being a power-ful magician, knows this to be indicative of magic and follows the hwch. The hwch does not take an ordinary path towards her destination. Instead, she enters a river and travels upstream and against the flow. The river in focus is the Afon Llyfni, or the sleek or smooth river in what is today the county of Arfon. A sequence of fields within the area of Pontllyfni records the name Llain yr Hwch, the piece of land of the hwch. Could this be the point at which the hwch entered the river and subsequently leads Gwydion towards the world tree?

The fact that the hwch enters running water and travels upstream is in itself interesting as an option that an ordinary pig would certainly not take voluntarily, and yet the symbolic significance of this parallels the sequence of events in the tale of Cerridwen and Taliesin. It is a river that flows from one degree of reality to another that is essential for the ultimate transforma-tion of the initiate into the radiant brow. Henwen also enters water to cross from one reality to another. Water holds and transmits a profound mystery that is utilised within the bardic material, implying that the audience under-stood this on some level.

Within the fourth branch of the Mabinogi, the initiate is found at the top of a tree in the valley of Nantlleu (the valley of Lleu), which is also its present designation. However, to reach the valley, the hwch would have travelled up the River Llyfni, through the Nantlleu Lake, and continued up the river called Afon Drws y Coed, the river of the door in the trees. There are few trees in this enormous glacial valley, and yet it is the location of the seemingly invisible world tree. It is my opinion that the hwch is indicative of Cerridwen and her function as devourer of the profane and facilitator of the rise of the sublime self, as seen in the saga of Lleu, meaning light or bright, which in itself implies a radiance akin to Taliesin.

In order for the initiate to be transformed, a sequence of magical bardic incantations is spoken by Gwydion, who by the power of language and his magic wand facilitates the transformation of the light one that is initiated by the devouring nature of the hwch. Cerridwen claims a deep admiration for Gwydion, who made a woman of flowers and stole pigs from the south, but there is more going on here than first meets the eye. We are consistently told that Gwydion excels at the crafting of magic, and he is evidently a word-smith. He is able to construct powerful englynion song-spells that call to the initiate to descend through levels or degrees of initiation. In the epic poem "Kat Godeu (The Battle of the Trees," we are informed that

Kenynt gerdoryon,
Kryssant katuaon,
Datwyrein y vrythron,
A oreu Gwytyon...
Trwy ieith ac eluyd,
Rithwch riedawc wyd.

Poets were singing,
Soldiers were battling,
Resurging from the wand,
The best of Gwydion...
By language and earth,
He formed the majesty of trees.[152]

It is evident from the above few lines that Gwydion possesses immense magical skills. Of interest is the suggestion that Gwydion fashioned the forms of battling trees by the use of language and materials of the earth. If it sounds like a spell, smells like a spell, and acts like a spell, it is in all probability a spell. However, what Gwydion is demonstrating in the Book of Taliesin poetry and in the fourth branch of the Mabinogi is a particular form of magic—bardic magic. His ability to create a song-spell, one of the few surviving examples of metred rhyme in the Mabinogi, is testament to the fact that in all probability Gwydion was also a bard. It is too easy in the modern world to perceive Gwydion as just a magician in its common meaning; he is significantly more than that. If we look at the *englyn* that Gwydion sang in the presence of the hwch, we can learn a little more about the function of bardic magic as an element of Gwydion's skill set:

---

152 Translated by the author from "Kat Godeu" in *The Facsimile and Text of the Book of Taliesin* by J. Gwenogvryn Evans.

Dar a dyf y rwng deu lenn,
Gorduwrych awyr a glenn.
Ony dywedaf I eu,
O ulodeu LLeu ban yw hynn.

Dar a dyf y nard uaes,
Nis gwlych glaw, nis mwy tawd,
Naw ugein angerd a borthes,
Yn y blaen, Lleu Llaw Gyffes.

Dar a dyf dan anwaeret,
Mirein modur yn nywet,
Ony dywedaf I eu,
Ef dydau Lleu y'm afret.

To maintain the metre and the spirit of the rhyme held within an englyn, which itself is a form of cynghanedd, the following translation is adapted to rhyme but still contains an approximate translation:

Oak that grows between two lakes,
Shadows cast on sky it makes,
Unless a lie I do tell,
It is the flowers of Lleu I smell.

Oak that grows in upland soil,
Rain nor heat can never spoil,
Ninescore gifts its branches hold,
And Lleu the skilful one so bold.

Oak that grows beneath the slope,
Grove to shelter fair prince in hope,
Unless a lie is spoke of me,
Lleu will come unto my knee.[153]

---

153 Translation by Barrie Jenks and Kristoffer Hughes, liturgy of the Anglesey Druid Order, Alban Arthan ritual.

It is unclear how Gwydion comes to the place where the hwch resides, albeit he travels extensively through the counties of Gwynedd and Powys beforehand. Owing to his status as a magician, one might assume he utilises powers of divination and/or prophesy to reach that place. The ultimate transformation of the initiate from eagle to human occurs by the striking of Gwydion's wand, but central to the process of transformation is the singing of the englyn above. Of further note is the object or personality that is initially petitioned; the great oak that stands between various elements and landscapes plays a significant part in the process of initiation. It is the sequence of words that are impeccably recorded, demonstrating the importance of the power of words and bardic magic.

Cerridwen's affiliation to the family of Dôn within the poems of Taliesin give further credence to her presence in the fourth branch of the Mabinogi as initiatrix and conduit of transformation. Evidently, there is no mention of Cerridwen by name, but the associations between the fourth branch and Gwydion in particular are such that I suggest her initiatory persona is present, and it serves to transform a profane and damaged creature into a being of light and radiancy. Another element of interest within the complex relationship between Cerridwen and the House of Dôn is her deep admiration for Gwydion.

He has become a somewhat contentious figure, judged by his actions in the fourth branch of the Mabinogi. When looked at through the lens of modernity, his behaviour is problematic. His actions can be seen as misogynistic. A conspirer, he facilitated the raping of Math's foot maiden, Goewin, and created a woman of flowers, Blodeuedd, who was subsequently punished for not playing the game according to his rules. There is a lot that one can find issues with in the twenty-first century, especially when we take these elements at face value and place upon them the values of modernity. Yet, with that being said, Cerridwen claims a deep admiration for Gwydion, which begs the question why. Is she condoning his actions? How can a female archetype admire someone whose deeds were seemingly atrocious? Much nuance and detail—and consequently so much magic—are lost in the translation of this material.

That the characters of the myths are apparently human in nature serves only to make the myths relevant to its human audience, ensuring that when presented by an achieved bard or storyteller, they will appeal and work on several levels. Every generation will see the details within the myths through the magnifying glass of their specific time, with various filters in place: social, cultural, political, religious, etc. The written form that we find them in today is superimposed with a medieval glaze, and that filter can be particularly problematic in the present. Perceiving the myths as anything other than the manner by which one group of human individuals treat another is difficult, and yet that is precisely what one needs to do in order to see the magic underneath.

We are wont to connect to Math, Aranrhod, Blodeuwedd, and the foot maiden Goewin as actual human personas that occupied a very human world, and yet they do not, and this is essential to understanding the meaning hid within their names. Their apparent names are not personal nouns. They all, without exception, describe a state of being, an aspect of the human condition, or a magical function. For example, *Blodeuedd* means "of flowers." In her owl guise her name changes to Blodeuwedd, meaning "flower face." Aranrhod means a large turning mound or wheel; Gwydion, the summoner or supernatural quality of trees. Goewin is the expression of sovereignty within the land; that is, what is being attacked and defiled. Whilst it is tremendously difficult to remove oneself from the apparent human beings that occupy the myths, it is vitally important that one understands these are mythological archetypes occupying a mythological landscape. To see them only as human beings to whom some injustice has been served is to miss the point and function of mythology. To not be able to move beyond the apparent injustices is to be caught in the trap of a bad story in which bad things happened. Instead, one can question the admiration Cerridwen has for an apparently flawed magician and seek to understand the magic that bubbles beneath it. To be caught up in mythological injustices is to miss out on the power of mythology to initiate deep transformation.

16

Initiatory Transformation

It is important at this juncture to consider the nature of that which is being transformed. Nobody is dying here—there is no death, at least not in the manner in which we currently understand death. There is, however, separation, a theme common to most initiatory rites of passage, where the initiate is separated from a familiar state and left in a transitory liminal place where assimilation takes place.[154] Gwion experiences this within the second cauldron of the tale, which is the womb of Cerridwen. In the fourth branch, Lleu experiences it upon the branches of the world tree. In his *Ystoria Taliesin*, Ford explores the necessity of initiation, separation, and isolation, that whilst on the surface may appear tantamount to the process of death, there are marked differences.[155]

To assume that the initiate is somehow experiencing a form of death negates the power of magical initiatory integration. Whilst death may be seen as an initiatory process, I would argue that passing into death causes the initiate to be released from the responsibilities and experience of being alive. In contrast, the process of initiation into the expression of Awen is

---

154   Sheldrake, *Science and Spiritual Practises*, 115.
155   Ford, *Ystoria Taliesin*, 33.

the opposite of death; it is the very act of expressing life in all its technicolour grandeur. It is the act of assimilating qualities that the bard, imbibed by the narrative, enchanted, and prophetic spirit, requires for the expression of Awen. Whilst one can argue that funereal rites are initiatory for the deceased in transferring them from a state of living to the status of being dead, and of assuming the role of ancestor, initiatory rituals within the course of living are quite different.

The later tale of Cerridwen and Taliesin has distilled within it an initiatory allegory within which we are introduced to an archetypal bard in possession of supernatural and magical abilities. The initiate undergoes a sequence of transformations through the guise of animals of land and sea and sky before becoming a seed that is swallowed into the belly of a black crested hen, after which he is subjected to a gestational period before being reborn and placed into yet another gestation vessel and put to water. Details within the manuscripts then vary: at times the initiate floats for forty years, at times for eighty. Eventually, on the eve of Calan Gaeaf/Hallowe'en or May's Eve, depending on the text being consulted, the coracle, or "skin belly," is caught in the salmon weir of Elffin, where the initiate undergoes another rebirth. What is not entirely clear is whether or not Gwion has physically died or is undergoing a tremendous transformative process tantamount to death, except that he is able to return to this world. Taliesin claims to have been Gwion once but has since become the radiant brow. What elements or aspects of Gwion Bach remain is not highlighted or made clear, and yet at times, the Taliesin persona makes claims to suggest that the Gwion Bach aspect continues to exist within him:

Wyf hen, wyf newyd, wyf Gwion.

I am old, I am new, I am Gwion.[156]

A ritual of integration occurs at the salmon weir when Elffin births the child from the skin belly/coracle by what appears to be a pseudo caesarean section. The description is vivid and visceral as he takes a knife and slits open

---

156   Haycock, *Legendary Poems from the Book of Taliesin*, 58.

the skin belly. Astounded by the glowing brow of the child, he proclaims its name as "y tal iesin," the radiant brow, at which point the child expresses the sagacity and wonder that it has beheld on its journey to the weir. This is in stark contrast to the Irish sagas whereby wisdom is contained within a hazel nut and consumed by a salmon, who in turn is consumed by the initiate, thus he is transformed. Within the Welsh tales what is caught in the weir is wisdom personified as opposed to wisdom by numerous processes of ingestion.

A similar sequence of events occurs within the fourth branch of the Mabinogi, albeit in this case it is the magician Gwydion who initiates the ritual of integration by singing a sequence of song-spells that have the power to summon the initiate down the tree until the initiate is transformed back into the guise of a human, yet one who is forever changed by the initiatory process.

I reiterate: no death occurs. There is no process of separation that results in bereavement or anxiety, only profound and radiant transformation. In modern Pagan traditions, it has been tempting to identify the function of Cerridwen as a dark, death, or psychopompic archetype, and yet there exists nothing in the bardic material to suggest this. One could argue that the cauldron itself is a treasure of darkness, and metaphorically this is a powerful concept. The cauldron's belly as a symbol of the potential within the universe is a vessel of no-thing, and within that no-thingness is the possibility for anything to come into being, pulled from the swirling, ethereal creative forces of the universe. It is the form of Cerridwen that brings the Awen into existence in our world, it is she that draws its potential shape and form from the no-thing and goes on to birth it in light and magic.

The historical discourse of this book alone has highlighted attributes that are light-filled, brilliant, radiant, pure, creative, illuminated, and enlightened. However, we do so long for things to fit a new way of thinking, and in that guise Cerridwen has often come to be associated with the popular Pagan deific assigned role of the crone. But look closely at her virtues and what one sees is a mother in the prime of her creative powers. She is both loving and vengeful, flawed and powerful.

The Awen is a creative force that brings things into being. As a representative and the director of the universal power of Awen, Cerridwen goes on to create over and over and birth numerous—nay, countless—individuals of radiancy who possess the Taliesin, the radiant brow. One may assume that Cerridwen ceases to birth new beings after the calamity of swallowing Gwion Bach, only to find herself with child. But, one must remember that this is also your tale, and the tale of all those who seek to glean and learn from Cerridwen. In that guise, she continues to be the Mam yr Awen, the Mother of Awen, the great parent of the Plant Cerridwen.[157] She has not evolved into a cronehood or into a state of being where she can no longer produce offspring, for I would argue that those whose brows radiate with the magic of Awen are her offspring. Had she ceased to produce children, the Awen would have stalled.

The reason the Awen is alive and well, and continues to be relevant today as it was centuries past, is because of its ability to be passed on, to be birthed and given countenance and expression in the Plant Cerridwen. To insist that Cerridwen has somehow grown beyond her own fertility is to the miss the point of Mam yr Awen; she will always be the mother, her seeds are numerous and varied, and they continue to grow, nurtured and encouraged by her.

What is evident here is the sense of a profound process of initiation, and that this initiation, as Ifor Williams claimed, is the key to understanding the mysteries that lie within the bardic tradition. And that without a beginning point, a point of initiation, the mysteries will continue to be elusive. Something of the initiate needs to change and be transformed within the quester for him or her to fully assimilate and understand the mysteries. There is initiation here on two very distinct levels. On one hand it is indicative of a true beginning, a journey that initiates one's exploration of the mysteries, whereas on the other hand it is initiation into a mystery tradition, a concept not alien to anyone who is well read in modern Pagan practise. Witchcraft, Wiccan, and Druid traditions are often initiatory in nature, where elements of the mysteries are kept secret within those traditions to heighten the integ-

---

157 *Plant* is the Welsh word for "children."

rity and occult significance of those traditions. The latter perfectly captures the nature of the Welsh bardic tradition, which was initiatory and continues to be so. In the twenty-first century, those honoured into the Gorsedd of Bards of the Island of Britain are given a bardic name, their heads covered and admitted into the Gorsedd with much pomp and ceremony.

Whilst we cannot be entirely certain of how the bards of old would have presented such rituals, we can deduce that the structure of their system in all probability had a way of marking one's progression and development within that institution as an expression of a mystery school.

With this in mind, and in a modern occult sense, I perceive Cerridwen as an initiator, as the guardian deity of the experience. Whether one embarks on the journey into initiation alone or as part of a mystery school, I believe that it is Cerridwen who activates the initiate's journey and pursues them through the subtle inner realms to a deep transformation.

In our ready-made society, where everything is available on a plate or at a price, the fact that we must sometimes take time to absorb anything is almost insulting to our sensibilities. But the mysteries take time. As Taliesin says:

Myfi a gefais Awen,
O Bair Cerridwen...
Ac ni wyddais beth yw fy ngahwd,
Ai chig neu pysgawd,
A myfi a fum naw mis haiach,
Ynghroth Cerridwen y wrach,
Myfi a fum gynt Wion Bach,
Neithyr Taliesin wyf I bellach.

I received the Awen
From the cauldron of Cerridwen...
And it is not known what is my flesh,
Whether it is meat or fish,
I was nine months gestating,
In the womb of Cerridwen the witch,

I was Gwion Bach once,
But now I am Taliesin.[158]

Our relationship with the mysteries of Cerridwen serves a vital and often overlooked function: to bring about the birth of the radiant brow—to initiate one into becoming a Taliesin, imbibed with the narrative, enchanted, and prophetic spirit and glowing with Awen. Immersion into the mysteries of Cerridwen brings about a wisdom gleaned from her cauldron, and in that state it is not known if one's flesh is meat or fish. Initiate undergo a transformation where they can sense and know the experiences and existences of all things. This state of being in profound relationship with all things must bring about a compassion and empathy that one gleans from having been in a myriad of shapes before attaining the consistency of the enchanted bard. The end goal of this initiatory function is to become Taliesin in the literal sense as a radiant brow.

---

158   Translated by the author from NLW 5276D.

17

The Children of Cerridwen

An effective way of making sense of the exploration of the bardic tradition is to use occult tools to absorb and assimilate the information into experience. The chase sequence in the tale of the birth of Taliesin can be used as a mechanism for exploring the development of the self and of the mechanisms that contribute to the promulgation of Awen. Let's look at the above information in line with the chase.

The cauldron in its initial position above the fire, with its belly full of potential but as yet unmanifested Awen, can be taken to symbolise the dark period of the Brythonic Age and the earlier Iron Age. We sense a profound potentiality to this era but we are unable to give it shape and form. It is as elusive as the steam that rises from the bubbling potion of Awen. It is ethereal, somewhat out of reach, and yet we can taste its delicious romantic appeal on our lips. As time progresses and Celtic society begins to record its progression, the cauldron cracks and spills onto the parchments of the scribes and bards. Time is recorded.

The Hengerdd period of the early bards, with their poems of prophecy and kings, courses across the land in the same manner as the greyhound and hare. They are finding their foundation and their feet. The Gogynfeirdd era expanded on the romanticism of the bards they sought to emulate and dived into the depth of mystery and profundity. They became the otter and the salmon, descending into the furthest recesses of the human spirit and imagination, seeking magic and transformation. The bards of the nobility took to the skies of expression and expansion in the form of the hawk and the wren; having risen above the rest, they forgot that the tiny wren held more magic than the resplendent and proud hawk. They inadvertently became the predators of bardism. As the land fell under the crisis of powerful sociopolitical change, the seed of bardism, its light dimming, was swallowed by the hen of the union and gentrification. Deep within that belly of silence, its light barely burning, it coursed along the waters of change, deep in silent contemplation, forced to question its own identity. A new day arose, and the skin belly was opened once more to reveal a new generation of bards, their brows gleaming with the light of the Awen and the seed of bardism on their lips. These are the bards of the modern-day Gorsedd of Bards, who are literally adorned with an Awen on their foreheads by means of a physical crown decorated with the three rays, and they are also the bards of the new age of modern Paganism and polytheistic practises—the children of Cerridwen. In Welsh they are known as Plant Cerridwen, with *plant* being the designation not only of children, but including progeny, disciples, and followers.[159]

The following table and sigils chart the evolution of Cerridwen and her bards over the last two thousand years. It is compiled to enable you to contemplate the sigils and the different eras in cojunction with the various stages of the birth of Taliesin story.

---

159 Pronounced exactly as the English word *plant*.

Brythonic Era		The deep past and potential for Awen.
Hengerdd Era		Finding foundation. The chase begins. Greyhound and hare.
Gogynfeirdd Era		Journey into wisdom. Delving into the deep. Otter and salmon.
Nobility Era		Flying into expression. Expansion and constriction. Hawk and wren.
Crisis Union Gentry		Decline. Consumption. Sociopolitical restraints. Hen and the seed.
The Silent Era		Contemplation. Journey of the coracle.
The Modern Era		Gorsedd of Bards. Plant Cerridwen. A new birth. Taliesin.

So, where does this leave the modern practitioner of occultism and Paganism?

As I have demonstrated, Cerridwen's ability to survive the turmoil of time, cultures, new religions, and new ways of thinking is testament to the tenacity of her spirit. Throughout my spiritual journey as a modern-day Druid and my travels with Cerridwen and her bards, I am convinced that the spirit we call Cerridwen has reached out from the edge of the cauldron to those who would be inspired by her. For the last 1,500 years of literal history, her prevalence has been promulgated and idealised by the Welsh bardic tradition, but something has changed—there has been a shift of focus in the last couple of centuries, coalescing into a new form and expression of Cerridwen for the modern time.

Whilst the modern bardic tradition of Wales is a treasure to our culture and a part of my life as a Welsh person, it does not serve the hidden, occult spirit of bardism that was present in its ancient form. Times have changed, and the bards have changed. The spirit of Cerridwen has also changed, and her focus is no longer limited to the cultural identity of the Welsh. She has risen like the steam from her cauldron to reach people who would hear her in the furthest regions of the earth. The locality-specific nature of inspiration that was the flavour of medieval bardism has changed, for now we live in a global village. Ideas and new thoughts can be disseminated in an instant with just the tapping of a keyboard. It is, I believe, vitally important to honour those who served to protect this material, but equally as important to know what to do with it in the current time.

Cerridwen's name is rarely uttered within the structure of the Gorsedd of Bards of the Island of Britain, and if it is, it is laden with misconceptions. But something magical is happening: her name now falls from the lips of thousands of people beyond Wales who do not speak the native tongue that preserved her. She has found a new generation of individuals who seek to seed the world with inspiration.

A Different Kind of Altar

The magic hid in all of this is that Cerridwen was not located in the apparent world. It would be centuries before her association with the lake at the edge of the town of Bala entered the bardic imagination. Whilst it is true that no altars or shrines have ever been discovered that were dedicated to Cerridwen, this misses the point and the function of bardism, of which she is undeniably the patron spirit of. The adoration of the bards and their songs in praise of her gifts and powers are a form of reverence to something that is neither visible nor physically present. They attributed their talents and learning to a long lineage of learned bards who acknowledged that at the heart of their tradition and skill was a muse-like being who steered the countenance and power of their expression.

Cerridwen is not understood as a goddess. The medieval bards would have had nothing in their cultural frame of reference to comprehend what a goddess was. This is not to suggest that the Iron Age caste of bards had no understanding of the term. By the time of the Gogynfeirdd bards, over 600 years of Christianisation profoundly affected the way they saw the world. A goddess would have been meaningless to them; people cannot conceptualise what they have no concept of. What we can deduce is that she undeniably existed in their cultural consciousness and the expression of their craft. Arguments continue to burn to this day that for a deity to have any merit and validity, it must be located in the past, with evidence of its worship or reverence. But again, this misses the point. Cerridwen is a goddess appropriate for today, and that is worthy of later exploration, but she also existed in the deep past, just not in the same exact forms. When we go searching for her in the guise that we know her today, we will not find her. The hidden magic of Cerridwen is that she continuously renews herself.

If Cerridwen had a location in the past, she was located on the tongues and lips of the bards. Whilst it is a truism that no structural shrines or altars existed to carry the name of Cerridwen or act as a focal point of worship, I would suggest that there were indeed altars to Cerridwen, thousands of them, and that those altars were the lips of her bards. Her veneration and adoration were in the form of songs that rose like the breath of Awen from the lungs of her bards. Her shrines were the parchment and quill. She has always existed, and if modern occulture and its sceptics can be criticised for anything, it is that they have been looking for her in all the wrong places. We have a preconceived idea of what an altar is—a table of sorts, often held within a structure, building, or space for the purpose of adoration and veneration.

The bards' function was to honour the principles, peoples, archetypes, and situations that were worthy of praise. People, places, battles, and victories were and continue to be immortalised from the lips of the bards. The people listen, and in turn the bards become, to an extent, idolised as the epitome of their craft. We see this occurring to this very day where the Chaired Chief Bard at the National Eisteddfod of Wales becomes a national hero; something magical and transformative happens to the internal psychic constitution of bard and public. Acts of veneration, honour, and respect for the Awen and Cerridwen as its director fall from the lips of bards, and they do so to this day. I claim that these are indeed her altars, and they continue to exist as they have done for centuries. The altars to Cerridwen have been hiding in plain sight.

However, a million circumstances go into the making of one moment, and times were changing. The bards were moving on and could no longer be seen as homespun, worn-out bards desperately clinging to the magic of the old world of yesteryear. They had to change along with the sociopolitical and religious environment of the time.

The last century and the current have given birth to the children of Cerridwen, a new breed of bards that sings the songs of the Goddess of Awen and the mysteries of the cauldron. The altars to Cerridwen exist as much today as they did in the past. They have the potential to exist on your lips in the same manner that they rise to the lips of her bards who understand this function today. Pagan musicians, singers, poets, writers, artists, and teachers the world over speak her name and praise her by means of bardic magic.

She has found you.

The New Bards

I continue to use the term bard, albeit with a different focus to the bards of the Welsh tradition. I use the word bard to describe the individuals whom I refer to collectively as Plant Cerridwen. You do not need to be an accomplished musician or poet to be a bard; remember Cerridwen is the gogyrwen of various seeds. Bardism has numerous forms of expression, each as valid as the other. Whilst an appreciation for the specific crafts of bardism, like the cynghanedd, honours the power of the Welsh bards, it is not a requirement of modern non-Welsh bards to learn that craft—unless, of course, one is particularly and vocationally drawn to do so. Anyone who chooses to develop a relationship with Cerridwen and works as a gogyrwen, who crafts magic with their words and deeds, who strives for knowledge, and who seeks to inspire and evoke the Awen is essentially a bard. When one stirs the cauldron and calls to Cerridwen as a magical ally to guide the direction of the Awen, they are working as a bard. Prayers, song-spells, and incantations that rise in rhyme and are directed in her honour or by means of her name are the crafts of a bard.

The Welsh word for bard—bardd[160]—derives from the proto-Celtic word bardos, meaning "in praise." In the Welsh language it specifically means a bard, a poet, a literary person, an author; figuratively, a prophet, philosopher, or priest.[161] By definition of being an author, I am literally a bard, but figuratively speaking I am also a bard because I class myself as a priest of Cerridwen; I also philosophise and frequently use tools for prophetic means. The craft of bardism is the art and science of creating words that are imbued with power and the subsequent direction of those words. This is a craft that any modern-day witch or Druid will be well versed and practised in. If you are moved to work with Cerridwen and have the integrity to learn and be the best that you can be at your craft, to use words of power and intent, you are essentially acting as a bard and as a member of the children of Cerridwen collective, the Plant Cerridwen.

---

160 This word is pronounced "BARR" followed by the sound one finds in the "th" of the.

161 See online Welsh Dictionary entry (Geiriadur Prifysgol Cymru) under bardd.

18

The Deification of Cerridwen

What has preceded this point in my discourse has mostly focused on history and the evolution of Cerridwen within the bardic tradition. It is now time that we dive into the potion itself, into the heart and belly of Cerridwen's cauldron. It is here where we explore the subtle forces at work in our journey to discover the nature of Cerridwen. It is here where we move slowly away from the mechanics that served to perpetuate her name and her function.

From this point on I shall slightly remove the filter of scholarship, enough so that we may examine the mysteries through visionary eyes. I shall not wholly abandon scholarship in this section, but my primary focus will be on the crafts magical. Therefore, in the following pages there is much in the way of unverified personal gnosis (UPG) and information and inspiration from nearly three decades of Druid practise.

Through our journey into the past, we have glimpsed a tantalising depth to this body of knowledge and wisdom, that something other than history and heritage and tradition lies beneath the surface of all this bardism. We can taste mystery swimming beneath the surface, in the deep, and it is to this depth of profundity, wisdom, and magic that we now dive. We shall discover the nature of what boiled in that potion in Cerridwen's cauldron and how that might be relevant to modern practise.

To begin with, we must explore the nature and evolution of Cerridwen as a goddess, and whether or not this has any merit.

It is highly unlikely that Cerridwen was worshipped as a goddess in antiquity, and to date no evidence of a cult of Cerridwen has been discovered, no statues bear her name, and no temple remains as testament to her worship. But does that actually matter? In my opinion—no. Any obsessive compulsion to find such evidence simply serves to muddy the waters and denigrate the power of apotheosis. For it is by that process that she is now a goddess. There are no hard and fast rules to apotheosis. We did that. We need not look back for validation.

Everything has a beginning, and whilst the persona of Cerridwen has survived for countless centuries in many forms, I reiterate that it should be acknowledged, honourably, that her guise as a goddess is relatively new. This in itself has validity. The New Age traditions, whilst inspired by the distant times, do not need or require to be authenticated by the past; it is a living, breathing spirituality, and the elevation of spirits and archetypes into the rank of deity is perfectly acceptable, and for one good reason—it works. If something works, keep doing it, and the more you do it, the more life you breathe into it.

The archetypes of Celtic myth are strong enough and tough enough to withstand the evolution of modern human spiritual connection. Apotheosis is the glorification of a subject to a divine level, something that we have done in the last one hundred years to the figure of Cerridwen. She is a goddess, but back in the days of the medieval bards, the concept of a goddess was not necessarily a realistic function of the Welsh theological mind. They simply did not exist. People could not conceptualise what they had no concept of. If she had any form, it was that of muse to the bards, and in time, as we have seen, even that function would be ridiculed and wane from history. In a patriarchal society, an ancient and powerful male archetype may well have been perceived as a much larger threat. It would stand to reason that these would be eliminated. And thus, they were denigrated as evil characters in folktales, diminishing their power and hold over the landscape and imagination.

As previously explored, Cerridwen lost her station as muse, as guardian of the cauldron of Awen, and as Europe swooned under the hammer of the witch hunts, slowly but surely Cerridwen became associated as a wits and then as gwrach, a repugnant or repulsive thing. She was rendered harmless, pathetic, a ridiculous character in a harmless folktale. Twentieth-century illustrated depictions of Cerridwen were commonly of the stereotypical broom-riding, hook-nosed Disney villain.

It is not the intent of this book to define what a deity is, but evidently my focus is on Cerridwen as a goddess. And in truth, it does not matter how you define her, whether as a deity with her own agenda and personality or as an aspect of the universe or the human condition. You may consider that she exists only as a psychological construct or a being that emulates an aspect of the divine feminine, however you may define that. As a polytheist, I have my own belief structure, but I work with Druids and witches and other Pagans who have differing views. What unites us and bridges the gaps of difference is relationship. The manner by which we perceive the nature of Cerridwen is irrelevant when one considers what she represents. She is the conduit of Awen.

Deific definitions fall into insignificance when we consider what her role is and how, by connecting to Cerridwen, we drink from a vessel of Awen that has been centuries, if not millennia, in the making. In that manner, as a goddess, she exists; as a thoughtform, she exists. The manner by which you connect or perceive her is irrelevant to anyone else's relationship with her, for the measure of the connection can only be defined by the depth of that relationship. Many have a need for her to be an independent, indi-vidual deity; others are perfectly happy connecting to her as a thoughtform. Either way, Cerridwen's virtues are unaffected. She is a cultural fusion of all that our ancestors found inspirational and magical, and as we have seen, her shape and form was often purposefully changed. But her quiddity—her essence—remains unchanged and unaltered.

It is important that we maintain our gaze on Cerridwen's quiddity as we explore the manner by which she has evolved, whether by her own doing or the agendas of others. Her quiddity is more than her identity, which is often superficially related to the motives of people. We may identify Cerridwen in a number of manners, but they are usually indicative of motivations that suit our need for her. Regardless of how we perceive her, something of her primordial origination remains. In the Welsh language, it is Cerridwen's *anian*[162] that is unchanged by the superficiality of her countenance. Her anian is indicative of her innate nature and quality, and evidently, we have seen that this essentiality of her quiddity has remained unaltered throughout history. Cerridwen's anian is unaffected by her *rhith*,[163] meaning her shape and form. Therefore, regardless of how frequently her outward appearance transforms, her innateness remains unchanged. In Welsh mythology, the term rhith implies that a subject's outward appearance is not wholly stable and can be affected by a number of influences.

By keeping this in mind, we can chart Cerridwen's progression through time and witness her rhith changing to the needs of the four eras of the bardic tradition.

Cerridwen as Muse/Inspirer

In this guise she served as the primary inspirer. By acknowledging and connecting to Cerridwen in this guise, the bard was placing himself in the line of her influence. The term muse in this context is not necessarily utilised to convey a deification, but rather taken as the common English interpretation of "someone who inspires."

Cerridwen as Mam yr Awen (the Mother of Awen)

As the Mother of Awen, her function as a muse transcends from a being that is an agent for the Awen, an inspirer, to an entity whose sole function is to birth the Awen in the apparent world. There is a similarity here to the qualities of the nine Muses of classical mythology, who were perceived as

---

162   Pronounced ANN-yan, meaning quiddity.
163   Pronounced RHEE-th, meaning a thing's ordinary form.

the embodiment and sponsors of metrical speech and defined as goddesses. In her guise as Mam yr Awen, Cerridwen has not attained the level of deity as yet, but she certainly shares a commonality with the nine Muses as being the spiritual embodiment of the Awen itself.

Cerridwen as Gogyrwen, the Separator of Seeds

Her guise as a separator of seeds was an important element to the bards, whose role was to express truth and knowledge. They did this by a constant process of winnowing, a task that can still be found in the bardic arts, where one strives to bring consistency and excellence into one's work, whether that be the creation of a poem, a spell, or a book. This process of elimination is important for the creating of something that one can be proud of, and it speaks to the hearts and spirits of those who stand in the trajectory of that Awen.

Cerridwen as Initiatrix

Whilst many have speculated that the bards performed elaborate initiation rituals, none have survived in writing. We would be foolhardy to dismiss organised initiation by the lack of literal evidence in what was primarily an oral tradition. The later mythology of Cerridwen and Taliesin certainly appears initiatory in nature, and there is much to denote a process of profound challenge, assimilation, and transformation in the poetic material, some of which may contain seeds of actual initiation rituals. As the paddle, or the steerer, of bardism, Cerridwen certainly appears to embody a process of self-development as well as organised development within a collective. In a modern sense she is certainly perceived as an initiatrix, with these ideas stemming from the musings of early twentieth-century academics.

Cerridwen as Gwrach

In my earlier exploration of Cerridwen's denigration, this expression of her countenance was in stark contrast to the wonderous, inspirational being of the early bardic eras. From the mid 1500s onwards, her reputation as the Mother of Awen wanes, and we witness the first stirrings of her transformation into something sinister and ugly. Gone is the beautiful, inspirational woman, replaced by the influence of the stereotypical witch of the English-speaking world. Her guise as a guardian of a cauldron, her casting of spells, and the making of potions lent themselves perfectly to what the English understood as primary symbols of a medieval scorned witch.

Cerridwen as Witch (in a Neopagan Sense)

From the mid-twentieth century onwards, the perception of witches and witchcraft was changing dramatically, and Cerridwen sailed on this wave of change. The new witches, organising into groups with new structures relevant to a new era, were wont to identify with Cerridwen as a witch. Everything about her nature seemingly fit with the new worldview of witchcraft and its practise. Here was a perfectly packaged woman who, to all sense and purposes, represented the new face of witchcraft.

Cerridwen as Goddess

Her rise to the rank of goddess is contentious and one that continues to be challenged. Seemingly, the first written stirrings of Cerridwen as a goddess come from the early nineteenth century and from the pen of the controversial figure Edward "Celtic" Davies, who concluded that Cerridwen had been the presiding goddess of Britain and, indeed, the Great Mother of all creation. His ideas persisted for several decades and influenced other scholars of Welsh Celtic literature. Davies expertly blended fact with fantasy and fiction with agenda, and he did so at the expense of good scholarship. Eventually his conclusions were considered nothing more than conjecture and fantasy.

However, he had kindled a spark in the popular imagination that was to have far-reaching consequences. Professor Ronald Hutton attributes the work of Davies as a catalyst for the modern propensity for identifying Cerridwen as a goddess,[164] whilst simultaneously he admits that literary creations can develop a unique life of their own or channel the powers of the divine.[165] What Hutton is describing is the process of apotheosis—to make or elevate a figure to the status of a deity.

---

164 Hutton, *Pagan Britain*, 369.
165 Ibid., 381–382.

The insistence of influential writers and artists since the time of Edward Davies to the present, that Cerridwen was a goddess in antiquity has certainly muddied the waters. What this book serves to demonstrate is that Cerridwen is magical enough as it is, the attempt to assert her status as a goddess in antiquity does not consider the beauteous relationship the bards of Wales had with her. She was not a goddess simply because there was no need for her to be one. The passionate insistence that she was a goddess in antiquity does not in any way serve her or those who preserved her memory. If anything, it dishonours the magical systems that carried her through time. Finding her in the past as a goddess would not make her any more important or authentic.

Over 200 hundred years have passed since the idea of Cerridwen as a goddess arose. Much has happened in those two centuries. Davies was writing in a time where a million influences were pouring into the cauldron of what was to evolve into modern Pagan practises of various descriptions and traditions. With each one attempting to make sense of their place in the world, the poor scholarship and influences of the nineteenth and early twentieth century served only to further muddy what was already a turbid brew.

To many, myself included, Cerridwen is a goddess today, a rhith that we have placed upon her by the power of apotheosis. She has become a deity for one good reason—because we need her to be a goddess. It is this need that has given rise to her new rhith as divine feminine, and it does so whilst encapsulating and acknowledging her anian. But there is a dichotomy here, for as a Welsh person, whilst I am devoted to a goddess that I identify as Cerridwen, my fellow countryfolk do not necessarily follow suit. If Cerridwen is identified as anything in twenty-first century Wales, she is Mam yr Awen, the Mother of Awen. Generally, in Wales, there isn't a great need or desire for Cerridwen to be a goddess, which is in stark contrast to the needs of Pagan practitioners. Simultaneously, it highlights that these enigmatic figures from the deep Celtic past continue to mould themselves to the needs of the people.

The new Pagan traditions are still finding their feet, with more and more conversations, intellectualism, and inspired works appearing daily to express the growth, development, and need for new Pagan practises. The compulsion to find evidence of deity in the past, to substantiate and justify a deity in the present, is to miss out on the ability of these entities to adapt to a constantly changing world. Our human world is not the same as it was only forty years ago—we have to adapt, and, in the same manner, so have the spirits and archetypes that have journeyed with us.

If there is consistency here, it is in the fact that Cerridwen's rhith changed continuously, yet she remains innately the same as Mam yr Awen, the Mother of Awen. In the same manner, the Celtic-flavoured Paganisms of the twenty-first century bear little, if any, relation to the Paganisms of two thousand years ago, and they do not need to. We are not defined by our beliefs; we are defined by what we do and how we do it. As I touched on previously, the Celts are also a product of today, not simply a relic of yesteryear, and in that spirit, Cerridwen in her guise as goddess is very much a product of modernity.

At one point in time, every deity that is revered by humankind started their lives as a thought, an idea; some would take centuries to solidify into godly form. After a new religious pantheon displaces the old, characters, archetypes, and constructs who were once gods lose some of their divine stature; simultaneously, whole castes of them would vanish out of time. Others existed as spiritual principles or ideas that morphed by a deep need in humanity to becoming deities. Cerridwen demonstrates the tenacity of the spirit of Awen to find those who will carry its seeds and germinate them, and to discover new bards who will dream new myths into being. And so today we find that a female figure from an obscure tradition in ancient manuscripts in an old tongue has risen beyond the confines of parchment and location, and her name is spoken all over the world. It is the power of apotheosis that achieved this.

To a great extent, the ship has sailed—we have made Cerridwen a goddess because we need her to be one. On the surface of things, this may seem overly simplistic or somewhat pedantic. But I firmly believe that it is "need" that has brought about such a well-venerated goddess with what is evidently a global appeal. In my own personal practise, living in the lands that gave birth to these mysteries, I need her in my life. She brings to my life the most inspiration and meaning. Even when I do not feel particularly inspired or inspirational, Cerridwen is there as Mam yr Awen, as mother, as goddess. In the Druid tradition that I follow and by being the inspired ones, the Awenydd, we serve her as goddess of the Awen.

19

Cerridwen and
the Deep Mysteries

Over the next several pages I am going to be exploring four particular forces that are relevant to our deepening relationship with Cerridwen. Namely, they are the Awen, the narrative spirit, the prophetic spirit, and the enchanted spirit, and weaving through all this is Cerridwen herself. In the course of this book, these concepts will naturally appear as separate and sequential, but I ask that you attempt to see beyond the linear limitations of a book in writing and try to connect to the seemingly individual elements, similar to the intricate weaving of Celtic knotwork, where multiple lines meld into one glorious pattern. The beauty expressed by Celtic knotwork is demonstrative of the magic of interconnectivity and relationship, and the same can be said for the concepts that I will be exploring here. But for it to make sense in your imagination, I offer this rationale for you to consider and bring to life in your mind.

Throughout the earlier discourse on the Welsh bardic tradition, we discovered that there is one symbol in particular that denotes Cerridwen and the Awen simultaneously: the cauldron. In popular modern art and writing, poetry and songs, Cerridwen is synonymous with a cauldron. One could easily be forgiven to associate the image of Cerridwen with that of the stereotypical witch from the late medieval period to the present. And as we previously saw, this enigmatic visual was too great a temptation for those with agendas, who took to superimposing that image, conveniently, onto a denigrated Cerridwen in her guise as a scorned witch. The twisted old woman casting herbs and roots and flowers into a gigantic cauldron, changing her shape and form at will, appears to all sense and purposes as the familiar image of the witch with her bubbling cauldron.

The detail that differs and breaks the mould of this stereotype is what Cerridwen is actually doing with the cauldron: she is brewing the potion of Awen. She is bringing that transformative force into the world in order for her target to be transformed. It is an act of profound and powerful magic by a learned and knowledgeable individual. We are informed by the bards of the old world that Cerridwen's cauldron is the source of the Awen in our world and perhaps in all worlds. But for the purposes of this book, it is wise that we focus our gaze on the impact of the Awen on our home planet, whilst appreciating and occasionally delving into its universal component.

As for the Awen itself, I shall explore this in a little more detail later in this section, but for now it is wise to refresh the memory with the description of the Awen that I offered to you earlier in this book:

> *Awen: the creative, transformative force of divine inspiration that*
> *sings in praise of itself. It is an eternal song that sings all things*
> *into existence, and all things call to the Awen inwardly.*

In the Celtic cultural continuum of the islands of Britain, the bards, sensing and articulating the necessity for this force, called it Awen. However, we are unable to conceptualise a force—it is too ethereal, too vague for our little minds to grasp; we need ideas and constructs that enable us to make sense and bring shape and form to the vast forces that create the universe in which we live, and help us make sense of the world and our place within it. The bards questioned what existed to bring the Awen forth before Cerridwen, when the world was in need. It is a visceral description of some primeval chaos into which order was directed, and the world began to sing in harmony rather than as chaotic forces. The conductor of this elaborate creative symphony was and is Cerridwen.

On a macrocosmic level, from the swirling nothingness in the cauldron at the beginning of all things, her potential moved into existence, and in the second the universe became aware of itself, in that exquisite explosion of light, she became the primary song of Awen, and consequently inspiration, transformation, and magic flooded into our universe. This is not to suggest that other divine forces are absent or that Cerridwen is the be-all and end-all; on the contrary, in the tradition of the Anglesey Druids, the potential for all other deities of our universe sprang into existence at the same time, their shapes and form changing and evolving with the growing universe. From this point the deities of sovereignty sprang forth—gods and goddesses of healing, psychopompic divinities, the divine faces of land and sea and sky, and so on ad infinitum.

We can glean further magic when we look at this from a microcosmic perspective, as reflections of the higher mysteries. The Awen in and of itself is too vast for us to grasp; we need to compartmentalise it into little bite-sized pieces so we can make sense of it. But as we do so, we also absorb into our experience the higher mysteries that it emulates. As above, so below; as within, so without. The further down the road of exploration we travel, the deeper our relationship runs.

Into the Cauldron

The cauldron stands centre stage as the holding property that allows the Awen to swirl into tangibility. You could imagine this cauldron as the universe itself, holding within it the potential of all things, from dazzling stars to mysterious quantum forces to swirling galaxies. Or you can imagine it as the myriad expressions of life and the energetic forces of our world. Without the cauldron, the Awen has no form; it is too intangible for us to grasp and fizzles out of existence. In our world the physics of our planet hold the creative forces within the closed circuit of our globe. The same space energetically holds the memory of all things that have existed on our planet. The cauldron's edge allows for the Awen to come into being long enough for it to experience life and living.

What would this cauldron look like? We will begin our exploration in a symbolic manner, before we add the colourful accoutrements of our vivid imaginations. For now, I'd like for you to consider the cauldron as a simple circle; thus:

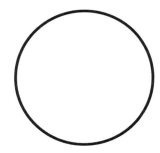

Just like the drawn circle above, the empty space in the centre has the potential to be filled with anything that you can imagine. Pertinent to our journey, this circle represents the rim of the cauldron of the Awen, and swirling in its centre, within the no-thing, is the potential for the great song. The swirling intensifies as the potential creative energy of the Awen brews. Held by the boundary of the cauldron's edge, it swirls into the expression of Cerridwen, its director. Arising from the centre and spiralling out to the very edges, she conducts the great song of Awen, and within that song is memory and knowing and magic. The song finds new lyrics that convey the magic of new life and new forms of expression, bringing the Awen out of chaos and into manifestation. We can symbolise this mystery as a spiralling triskele held within the cauldron:

Look closely at the triskele. It rises from and is indicative of a still point in the centre, and from that point the arms spiral out. They are not separate; the spirals express the centre point that is Cerridwen. In this exploration the triskele arms represent:

The Narrative Spirit (Ysbryd Adroddol)[166]—the force of
   memory and remembering.
The Prophetic Spirit (Ysbryd Proffwydol)[167]—the force of
   knowledge and knowing.
The Enchanted Spirit (Ysbryd Swynol)[168]—the creative force
   of magic and its crafting.

They spiral from the centre, from the point that is Cerridwen, and whilst in constant motion they are inexorable aspects of Cerridwen—they are her and she is them. This is relationship in motion: neither one came before the other; all sprang into existence at the exact same moment. The Awen now has shape and form and direction. All things are remembered within its flowing; nothing is forgotten. Time is an irrelevancy of humankind, and within the currents of Awen blow the wisdom of knowledge and the knowledge of things yet to come. The creative force of Awen sweeps through the universe and into our world, where blades of grass, rocks and trees, clouds and waterfalls, cows and beetles, all things sing inwardly of the Awen, and their expressions are the lyrics of its magic.

All things become windows through which the universe sees itself, but for the Awen to mean anything, it needs expression. As Taliesin said in "The Battle of the Trees":

I have been in many forms,
Until I was set free and wild.

---

166 From *ysbryd*, meaning spirit and breath, and *adroddol*, meaning expressible narrative.
167 From *ysbryd*, meaning spirit and breath, and *proffwydol*, meaning prophesy, prognostication, an inspired poet or author.
168 From *ysbryd*, meaning spirit and breath, and *swynol*, meaning enchanted, magical, bewitchment.

I was a narrow sword,
Made by hand,
I was a droplet in the air,
I was the radiance of stars.
I was a word in a writing,
I was a book in my prime.
I was the light in a lantern,
For a year and a half.

This ubiquitous state of having been in the shape of all manner of existences is indicative of the memory held in the Awen, and Taliesin is able to articulate that as a deep and profound knowing. He is able to achieve this by having moved into the awareness of the triskele and the mother who directs its spinning. The spiralling arms of the triskele contain the potential for the Tal-iesin, the radiant brow, to shine into being, but it needs activating.

As the potential bard/initiate moves into the centre of the triskele and approaches the great mother, they become intimately aware of the triskele spinning within their own being, and its power is transferred and actualised within them. They become a worldly triskele that reflects the supernal triskele of Cerridwen. Relationship ensues, and from that the bard expresses the Awen into his or her world as their brows radiate with glowing, inspired light. It is this mystery that is transmitted to the potential bard during the initiatory components of the later tale, through the journey with land and water and sky, assimilation in the secondary and tertiary cauldrons, and the birthing at the salmon weir.

Having imagined the circle as the rim of the cauldron and the spinning triskele as the expression of the three aspects of Cerridwen, I'd like for you to now look at this next image, which now contains a symbol at its centre: it is the commonly used symbol to represent the Awen.

The symbol occupies the centre, where Cerridwen initiates the triskele's spinning. By moving into this space and standing with Cerridwen, one becomes an active participant in the Awen. But it is one thing to be immersed within the currents of the Awen and it is quite another to be the radiancy of the rays themselves. By positioning oneself in the centre, with Cerridwen at your side or holding your hand or standing behind you with her hands on your shoulders, the spirals of her triskele move into the experience of your living. From this point, your responsibility is to shine—to take the seeds that Cerridwen offers you, plant them, nurture them, and share them with the world. To be the inspiration that this world will always need and want. From the blinding rays of Awen within you, you begin to glow, becoming a representation of the Awen itself.

If you could perceive the triskele occupying a horizontal plane, you would see three gleaming pillars of light radiating from the centre of each spiral thus:

This inverted version of the common symbol for the Awen is a transmitting Awen as opposed to a receiving Awen. It is your Awen in motion being directed out into the world, and within it turns the enchanted, narrative, and prophetic spirit, and their unification is the great song of Awen. When you connect to the Awen and allow it to blow through you, the most appropriate symbol for that would be three downward-radiating rays of light:

/ | \

When the Awen is coursing through you and you subsequently direct it, it is transmitted to the world thus:

\ | /

So now that we have covered some of the theory, let's take to imagination and move that into the experience of being the Awen.

The Great Triskele of Awen

Create a space where you will not be disturbed for a while, and designate the space as sacred in the manner that you are accustomed. If you are unaccustomed to the logistics of ritual, the aim here is to create a space that is delineated as being somehow beyond the ordinary. You may achieve this with candlelight, incense, being in front of or near an altar, or by using words that acknowledge that the forthcoming action is sacred and special.

Centre your presence within this space by doing the following:

- Take one deep and intentional breath in whilst directing your attention to the land beneath you. Breathe out whilst being mindful of that connection.
- Take one deep and intentional breath in whilst directing your attention skyward to the great blue yonder. Breathe out whilst being mindful of that connection.
- Take one deep and intentional breath in, but this time direct your attention to the water courses, lakes, rivers, or sea. Breathe out whilst being mindful of this connection.

Look at the image of the circle, triskele, and Awen combined now that you understand what each represents and their combined meaning, and allow the symbol to float into your mind and remain there for the duration of this exercise.

An effective way of doing this is to stare at the centre of the symbol for at least one full minute, blinking as little as possible. You will notice the spirals will start to glow in your vision, and when you close your eyes, you will continue to see an imprint, almost like a photographic negative of the symbol in the darkness behind your eyelids.

If you are able to stand for this ceremony, do so. If not, ensure you are seated as upright as possible. Recall the image of Cerridwen that you imagined in the first ritual of this book, there upon the shores of Lake Bala / Llyn Tegid. Hold that image in your imagination and call to her. I often find that attempting to learn someone else's words can be tricky and meaningless, for the words need to arise to your lips from your own connection, but as an example of the nature of the call, mine would run something like this:

> Cerridwen, great mother, guardian of the cauldron,
>> goddess of Awen, I call to you.
> Cerridwen, great mother, singer of songs and bard of bards,
>> I call to you.
> Cerridwen, great mother, seed of all seeds, maker of magic, I call to you.
> Hearken to my call, arise and come unto me.
> Cerridwen, mother, maker, let my brow shine!

Allow whatever words or poetry or song to come into your mind, and spend time connecting to the image of Cerridwen that is already nurtured by your imagination. Do not limit yourself to a single verse. Keep going, keep talking, keep connecting. Remember she does so love rhyming poetry, so perhaps as a display of your desire to know her, spend time writing something that rhymes beautifully. If your mind begins to wander to daily chores and the mundane, simply recall the symbol of the three rays within a triskele within a circle. Bring it back to the symbol every time you wander.

Now consider the rays at the centre. This symbol can be mimicked by yourself through standing upright with your arms outstretched, emulating the downward-radiating rays of Awen. The central trunk of your body represents the middle pillar of the symbol, with your arms as the angled rays. With your feet as close together as is comfortable, you can visualise the glowing rays of light flooding through your physical body, radiating its light through you. If you can, recall the butterflies one feels in the pit of the stomach when something exciting is about to happen or that feeling one gets when the first stirrings of love take one over. It is possible to feel those sensations by breathing deeply into the area of your body known as the solar plexus. As you breathe in, you will need to slightly tense your entire body and direct that shiver to the centre of your being. This in essence is a form of emotional energy that magicians, Druids, and witches are accustomed to evoking from within themselves.

Now start breathing in, and with each breath in draw up that sensation in your solar plexus; as you breathe out, imagine that your body glows with light, a radiancy that comes from the Awen itself. See your body as the rays glowing and gleaming with light. Carry on in this manner for as long as you are able to maintain the intensity of breath and the accompanying visuals.

As your breath returns to a normal pattern, bring the symbol back to mind. But this time, imagine that the encircled triskele occupies the centre of your forehead. If it helps you to visualise it, draw the symbol on your forehead and have a mirror nearby to pull your attention to it. Be imaginative—'tis the Awen that we are dealing with here. Imagine the triskele turning, spinning ever faster, becoming brighter and brighter. Swirling within it is the enchanted, the narrative, and the prophetic spirits, and standing behind you is the Mother of Awen, Cerridwen. See it all, like the image from a movie. Breathe again into the centre of your body, drawing more and more emotional energy to the moment.

Now recall the horizontal plane of the triskele with the radiating columns of light shining from the terminus of each spiral. You have embodied the Awen and now it is your turn to shine. From the triskele that is spinning on your forehead, take one enormous breath in, drawing in as much emotional energy with that breath as you possibly can. Hold that breath momentarily as you watch the triskele spin.

Exhale loudly in one single, powerful blast. Keep your eyes closed, and see the glowing rays of Awen transfer from the shape of your body with outstretched arms to the spinning triskele on your forehead. Imagine three blinding rays of light bursting from the centre of your brow. Keep doing it—keep breathing deeply and exhaling loudly.

Affirm to yourself that

> You are light.
>
> You are radiancy.
>
> You are memory.
>
> You are song.
>
> You are magic.
>
> You are Taliesin!
>
> You are the Awen!

Return to the present moment and know that you are inspired. Close your space in a manner that you are accustomed to or simply acknowledge that the task is over and return the space to the ordinary, apparent world.

For ease of reference, the individual stages of this ritual were as follows:

1. Create and delineate a space as sacred to the task at hand.

2. Centre yourself by taking three breaths with the land, sea, and sky.

3. Bring the sacred symbol to mind:

4. Call to Cerridwen.

5. Become the physical embodiment of the rays of light. Breathe in the light.

6. Imagine the sacred symbol spinning on your forehead:

7. Take a deep intense inbreath.

8. Exhale loudly and sharply and project the rays outward.

Having thus explored the nature of Cerridwen in relation to the narrative, prophetic, and enchanted spirits and the Awen, it is pertinent to now look at those elements individually. But whilst we do so, it is vitally important that we maintain a conscious awareness that they are not separate from Cerridwen or the Awen; rather, they are inexorable aspects of them.

20

The Narrative Spirit: Yr Ysbryd Adroddol

In his work on the Welsh bardic tradition, Gwyn Thomas claims that the tradition itself transcends that of personality and rises above individualism owing to its metaphysical foundations. He goes on to elaborate that bardism consists of an ethereal component that is not entirely of this material world, and it cannot be understood by science or reason.[169] Throughout the legendary material that pertains to Cerridwen, the Awen, and the cauldron, Taliesin insists on the magical origin of poetry/bardism; whilst the learning of the craft may have a systematic and almost scientific element, at its core it is a magical craft. It is perhaps indicative of the changing times that this quality of bardism has since diminished in the Welsh bardic tradition, particularly post-industrial revolution, as humankind "grew up" from the fanciful and the enchanted, and yet on so many levels we continue to long for it.

The magical origins of the power inherent in bardism was exemplified in the literary traditions of the medieval period, which placed great emphasis on the power of the spoken word. The magical element of bardism had a

---

169   Thomas, *Y Traddodiad Barddol*, 13–14.

tangible potency that was revered and feared by the populace, in particular those who became the subject of the bards themselves. In his influential work *Ystoria Taliesin*, Patrick Ford eloquently describes the power of the bards as follows:

> [The bard] shaped his material into words and virtually "created" through them, and possessed this power by virtue of some external force that blew through him.[170]

It is evident from the legendary material that the force Ford describes above is a component of the Awen itself. As the bard sings things into existence, in essence the bard is imitating the divine creative energy of the universe, which in turns gives shape and form to the object of his or her attention. From the above descriptions and rationale, there is an implication that something underlies the craft of bardism. I have long coined the phrase "the narrative spirit" to express one of three interconnected and underlying magical forces within the craft and components of the Awen. The narrative spirit is the key to bardic immortality. The bards are the professional guardians of past history—essentially, they are preserving the memory of a craft—and they do this by song.

There is a profound implication here that when the bard, whether new or old, pauses to connect, open their mouths, and start to sing the songs of creation, magic, and inspiration, something else is happening in the subtle realms. In the pauses between the words, within the vibratory quality of the sounds themselves, both the physiology of the singer and the listener are transformed. When the bard sings words and those words are heard, they become independent of the bard and are driven deep into the conscious awareness of both orator and listener. As the words are sung, they become an aspect of the shared cultural collective; they are imbibed with a life of their own whilst simultaneously being expressive of a collective consciousness.[171] This is the narrative spirit—a flowing, ethereal spirit that has not only survived the generations and countless centuries but thrived. The words

---

170   Ford, *Ystoria Taliesin*, 113.
171   Aldhouse-Green in Haeussler and King, *Celtic Religions in the Roman Period*, 331.

of the craft of magic do not exist in a vacuum. The bard consciously moves into the steam that arises from the cauldron of Cerridwen and breathes in its fragrant vapours, drawing in the Awen with every in-breath and expressing their power with every out-breath. The words of the bard invoke the intent of all the words that all the bards before them sang into existence; they are the cauldron's kin. It is all related.

The narrative spirit thrives in the popular imagination, it lives in the words of authors and the songs of singers, it is crafted and sung, and it carries within its currents the magic of the bardic tradition in its entirety. The narrative spirit carried on the breath of song blows through each bard, and with each singing, recitation, and expression, it grows in intensity and power. There was a time when it was limited by geography to the western flanks of the British Isles, in the regions now known as Wales, Cornwall, and Cumbria (the northwest of modern-day England). But the breath of the narrative spirit has blown far and wide. Its power now blows through bards, Druids, magicians, and witches in every corner of our planet. And those who feel its inspired winds blow over them can be inspired to take up those songs and add to them. With each breath, in and out, the narrative spirit journeys far from its home in the regions of the British and Welsh bards. It finds voice in your being, your expression.

This wondrous, divine aspect of Cerridwen's direction of the Awen is reciprocal, for when one moves into the current of the narrative spirit and is thus inclined to sing the songs of Awen, those who are moved by your actions are equally transformed. Recall from earlier in this book how the bardic tradition has an oral and aural component to it. For the Awen to effectively transform, it must be reciprocal; it cannot be selfishly held as a possession that is not shared with the world.

In line with the exercise that you performed earlier, the bard receives the Awen by a power akin to invocation, their mouths open, and words fall from their lips. The rays radiate outwards and are transmitted to the aural component, the ears of those who listen. Equally inspired, the audience receives the Awen and may go on to transmit it themselves, and so continues the process of receiving / | \ and transmitting \ | / the Awen.

Held within the narrative spirit is the power of sum totality. Within its currents the overtly human fascination and often obsession with genetics and what one can and cannot connect to depending on the colour of one's skin or the place of one's birth pale into insignificance. Our spiritual culture is not a possession; we do not own it, it may have originated and been given shape and form in these lands that I occupy, but how can we not celebrate and be joyful in its sharing? For in that sharing the narrative spirit thrives. Within that thriving the ancestors are remembered and honoured, and their wisdom germinated to seed the future with Awen.

In a workshop given to the modern Druids of Anglesey, eminent scholar Dr. Gwilym Morus-Baird offered a beautiful description of what happens to one's internal constitution when one moves into the currents of Welsh bardism. In his lesson to the Druids, Gwilym described this process as "speaking with the voices of the dead"—a simple statement that contains all the beauty and wonder of the narrative spirit, for that is precisely what one does in reciting the words of the old bards. Their inclusion in this book is not for unnecessary padding or to show off words in an arcane language for their apparent antiquity. On the contrary, they are included—and you are encouraged to connect with them—for they hold within them the keys one requires to more easily access the power of the narrative spirit. You may live a thousand miles or more away from the shores of Wales or might never have visited this corner of the world. You may not have a single drop of Welsh blood running through your veins, not an echo of genetics, but I tell you that that means naught. For within the currents of the narrative spirit you become the descendent of the bards and they your ancestors in Awen. Honouring a culture and its idiosyncrasies is important, yes, as is striving to develop non-appropriative practises. But please do not be led to believe that you are unable to work with the magic of these lands, for that magic transcends location.

For so many people in far-flung corners of the world, there is something within all this Celtic stuff that feels and tastes familiar, almost a déjà vu that sings to a part of you that you are unable to ignore. It pulls on the heartstrings and catches the breath. The narrative spirit does not sing through culture and blood alone: it works through a third channel, that of the psychic constitution. This is a deep, profound calling that one feels, and it causes an attraction to systems and traditions that may be far removed from your physicality and familial history, yet those who sense the calling are unable to ignore it.

The bardic material that retains the memory of Cerridwen and the narrative spirit literally are words that the ancestors spoke, sang, recited, and brought to life. Within this book there are several examples of old verses, poems, and stanzas from ancient books of poetry and mythological tales. But it is vitally important to not consider these as relics of an old language, but as living entities in and of themselves. Whilst the examples that you will find scattered through this book are on paper, they contain only the potential for the narrative spirit to sing through them, but it is not a given. For them to transcend into the currents of the narrative, they must be lifted from the paper or screen and, with intent, connected to and sung. The exercises in this book will encourage you to do just that, and within the original language if you can, for they literally are the words of the ancestors. But that is not to say that an English version or indeed any other language is not imbibed with the narrative spirit, for to say that would be to limit its power. Energy flows where intention goes. When you take to retelling the tale of Cerridwen and her cauldron, in whatever setting, keep this in mind: remember that you are engaged in memory. Pause to purposefully step into the currents.

Quill and parchment preserved the old poetry and myths for posterity, but gods forbid that they remain only as smudges of ink on paper. In their written form, the power within them cannot be sensed or felt; for that to occur they must arise to the lips—your lips are the altars, the shrines to Cerridwen, and it is upon them that the spinning triskele can be tasted. As words fall from your lips, you are actively engaged in the function of bardic memory and, reciprocally, those who hear your words will remember. The power hid in the words is indicative of the narrative spirit, and their spinning is woven by the magic of Cerridwen as she perpetually draws it from the cauldron.

Consider the above discourse, and focus your mind and imagination on the sigil that appears below. Held within its pattern is the ever-flowing motion of the narrative spirit. It is a sigil of memory and remembering, veneration and intent. Woven into it are the ancestors and their struggles and joys in maintaining a tradition that would seed the present with wisdom. Included within it is the hum of the enchanted and the prophetic spirit and Cerridwen, whose voices sing in unison with it, inexorably connected. The three dots in the centre, unbound and immersed, represent you in the here and now. Re-read this chapter, cast your eyes on the sigil, allow it to burn into your mind's eye, and take to contemplation. Whenever you need your intent to move into the streams of the narrative spirit, simply recall the sigil below and bring it to mind.

21

The Prophetic Spirit: Yr Ysbryd Proffwydol

Dygogan Awen dygobryssyn,

The Awen predicts, beckon.

Maraned a meued a hed genhyn,

We have our treasured possessions and peace,

A phennaeth ehelaeth a ffraet vnbyn,

The supreme chief is ready to give,

A gwedy dyhed anhed ym pop mehyn.

And after the war, we shall have settlement in every place.[172]

The bardic systems and traditions endowed the bards of Wales with significant and transformative occult powers. Whilst the term "occult" is no doubt problematic in a historical sense, I do feel it is an appropriate designation to describe the powers imbibed and expressed by the bards, inasmuch as their abilities arise from a system of teaching that we might equate today as a mystery school. The bards were privy to secrets that were hidden from the

---

172 *Armes Prydein Mawr, The Prophesy of Britain,* translated by the author from the text of *Armes Prydein o Lyfr Taliesin,* edited by Ifor Williams.

general populace, so in this respect I consider their talents and abilities to have had an argel (occult, hidden, or concealed) quality to them, and we shall explore what some of that means in this section.

However, the mere hint that elements of the tradition might have expressed an occult quality is evidently problematic for conservative minds, and this is demonstrated in the manner by which translators have connected with the material through time. Whilst I do not believe that the more conservative of translators have an agenda to remove or disguise anything that may be perceived as occult in nature, I do believe that they possess and express a bias based on their inability to conceptualise the necessity or validity of that which is occult in nature.

Examples of this can be seen in modern translations of material from the Book of Taliesin. In the psychopompic poem "Mabgyfreu Taliesin (The Tales of the Juvenile Taliesin)," the Taliesin persona is entreating a great parent to consider what it was that brought forth the Awen before Cerridwen at the very beginning of the world, a world that needed the divine spirit of inspiration to sing its potential into being. The poem asks the listener to consider the nature of the world and the necessity of Awen whilst also considering the nature of death. In this section Taliesin asks:

A wdosti ti peth wyt,

pan vych yn kyscwyt:

Ae corf ae eneit,

Ae argel canhwyt?

Do you know what you are,

When you are sleeping:

Are you a body or a soul?

Or an occult radiance?[173]

---

173   Translated by the author from J. Gwenogvryn Evans's *The Facsimile and Text of the Book of Taliesin.*

In modern translations the final line of that stanza is altered so that in the version by Celtic academic Marged Haycock, the line reads "Or a pale and mysterious thing."[174]

In the latest version by Gwyneth Lewis and Rowan Williams, it reflects another meaning: "Or a shining angel."[175]

W. F. Skene, translating the work in his 1868 classic *The Four Ancient Books of Wales*, took a slightly different approach with "Or a secrecy of perception."[176]

The above demonstrates a striking difference in the translation of three words, ae argel canhwyt, which seems somewhat remarkable. On first glance this may appear inconsequential, but it is the nature of the Awen and the inspiration that it invokes that is being addressed here, and that the function of Awen, Cerridwen, and her ability to bring it forth that is pressing on the bard's audience. The seemingly innocent manner by which the above stanza is translated diminishes the subtle, magical connotations that are being expressed by the bard.

The first word, ae, implies an interjection that in and of itself is emotive and expresses a feeling; the second word, argel, means something that is secret, hidden, concealed, and occult[177]; whilst the third word, canhwyt, is borrowed from the Latin cantela, meaning candle or luminary, and in a figurative sense it implies something that is light, bright, and radiant.[178] We are by now accustomed to the adjective "radiant" being synonymous with the Taliesin persona and the shining brow of Awen, therefore it is no coincidence that the term is used here in a figurative sense to denote the internal, hidden radiancy of an individual. In the oral tradition this would have been understood as an inner radiancy originating from the Awen itself, with the statement carrying an emotional connotation that the listener would have felt. And this is an important function of not only the bardic tradition, but of

---

174   Haycock, *Legendary Poems from the Book of Taliesin*, 243.
175   Lewis & Williams, *The Book of Taliesin*, 64.
176   Skene, *The Four Ancient Books of Wales*, 543.
177   Bevan, *Geiriadur Prifysgol Cymru*, 197.
178   Ibid., 410, 414.

the Awen—it is emotive, something one feels deep within the core of one's being. The Awen is not a concept. It is tangible; it can be directed. And all of this arises from the hidden, concealed, occult attributes of the Awen; it is a magical force.

However, occult associations can be challenging to those who are not comfortable with such subjects or who do not have a personal relationship with its potentiality and potency. Yet the material itself begs one to consider what is concealed from plain sight and the nature of the Awen as a profoundly magical force. Whilst the literal tradition has preserved the beauty of the bard's words, they are also subject to mistranslations and agendas, and perhaps the most significant component that is missing in the literal sense is emotion and feeling.

These qualities run hand in hand with the Welsh language, where certain phrases, poetry, and even individual words can invoke a profound emotional response in the listener. A fine example of this would be the Welsh word "Hiraeth," which is poorly translated to mean a deep longing, nostalgia, or profound homesickness, often described as a longing for Wales that only a Welsh person can feel. The reason I claim that it is poorly translated is owing to the fact that, in essence, it *cannot* be translated, for the word conveys a feeling rather than the ordinary articulation of language. To hear someone say they are in sufferance of hiraeth is to sense some of the pain they are enduring. One single word contains the potential to punch you in the stomach and cause one to recoil from the emotion it carries. Words have power. Words of such nature can often be found in the literal tradition, but what we cannot sense is the emotion expressed during the singing of the material. And this is key, for not only might the audience have been stirred into an emotional frenzy, it is apparent that the bards themselves often entered ecstatic states during their singing. The most famous account of this comes from the pen of Giraldus Cambrensis in his twelfth-century work *The Journey Through Wales and the Description of Wales*:

> Among the Welsh there are certain individuals called Awenyddion who behave as they were possessed by devils. When you consult them about a problem, they immediately go into a trance and lose

control of their senses, as if they are possessed. They do not answer the question put to them in any logical way. Words stream forth from their mouths, incoherently and apparently meaningless and without sense at all, but all the same well expressed, and if you listen carefully to what they will say you will receive the solution to your problem. When it is all over, they will recover from their trance as if they were ordinary people waking from a heavy sleep, but you will have to give them a good shake before they regain control of themselves. When they do come around they can remember nothing of what was said in the interval. They seem to receive the gift of divination through visions which they see in their dreams. Some of them have the impression that honey or sugary milk is being smeared in their mouths.[179]

We might initially dismiss the above account of frenzied individuals were it not for the fact that the Welsh bardic tradition is teeming with poetry that is expressed in perplexing and nonsensical verse. Giraldus's account is the first mention we have in the literal tradition of a caste of people called Awenyddion, a term composed of *Awenydd*, meaning an inspired bard, with the suffix *ion*, pertaining to "those of." It appears that Giraldus was made aware of the centrality of Awen in the function of a caste of individuals who possessed what appear to be occult or supernatural abilities. On balance, having explored the myriad of attributes within the technical element of the bardic tradition, it is evident that the tradition also expressed, maintained, and taught an ecstatic function. Developing an understanding of the science behind the composition of poetry was one thing, but the skills of shapeshifting, spiritual transmutation, and the inhabiting of living expressions and life forms other than one's own were also essential skills of the bards—skills that can be understood by students of the occult traditions of the twenty-first century.

In their introductory material to the new translation of the Book of Taliesin, Gwyneth Lewis and Rowan Williams state that translating the Awen as a form of inspired muse is misleading and that one should perceive

---

179   Giraldus Cambrensis, *The Journey Through Wales and the Description of Wales*.

the Awen more as an altered state of consciousness.[180] Within this state the bard may demonstrate extreme and ecstatic behaviour akin to spirit possession, where they appear to not be fully in control of their own senses, sensibilities, or physical forms. Within this state the bard would often prophesise the outcome of battle or matters of kingship and politics. One might conclude from this that moving into the currents of Awen is not necessarily a sublime and gentle experience, but also a potentially ecstatic one. I find this particularly interesting and compelling as a twenty-first-century occultist, for it tells me that my ancestors' understanding of magical practise and techniques far surpassed what ordinary historical education would have one believe.

Something else is bubbling under the surface: the function of possession. In this case, the bard is not only moving into the currents of Awen and therefore assuming a state of omnipresence and omnipotence, they are simultaneously being possessed by the narrative, enchanted, and prophetic spirits. They are essentially becoming Taliesin, or the radiant brow, by the power of possession. Celtic academia accepts the likelihood of a historical Taliesin, who upon his death was venerated as Prifardd (Chief Bard) and thus emulated and mimicked by future bards, several of whom either adopted the title of Taliesin or made claims that their poetic works originated from a legendary Taliesin figure. This tradition continued for centuries, with the identity or identities of the originators of the Book of Taliesin poems remaining anonymous, associating themselves instead with the persona of Taliesin.

Scholar Will Parker claims:

> In the midst of the sequences, the poet enacts a state of possession by the spirit of Taliesin, and conducts the audience on a panoramic journey through time and space, as seen through the omniscient eye of the mythical bard.[181]

Taliesin affirms that he has been a myriad of shapes and experienced a baffling array of incarnations and life forms, giving permission to the bards

---

180   Lewis and Williams, *The Book of Taliesin*, xxiv–xxv.
181   Parker, *The Four Branches of the Mabinogi*, 97.

to be thus endowed by occult and supernatural abilities indicative of a mystery school rather than a simple sojourn into frivolous poetry for the sake of entertainment. The Taliesin figure claims to have been at the beginning of all things and to have existed through an impossible span of time, to not have mortal parents, to have experienced many different forms of life and expression, and to have sat in the courts of the ancient Celtic gods.[182] Everything within the tradition suggests a body of wisdom and knowledge that far surpasses modern assumptions of the bardic schools, and this all hinges on the Awen.

In an occult sense, the Taliesin spirit is that which is expressed by the bard. Whilst Parker implies the possibility of Taliesin being a separate entity, I believe that the Taliesin spirit is a coalescence of the collective memory of the ancestors, the enchanted spirit, the narrative spirit, the prophetic spirit, and Cerridwen swimming in unison within the bard, resulting in the expression of the radiant brow, Taliesin. In Geoffrey of Monmouth's *Vita Merlini* and the account of a conversation between Taliesin and Merlin, we are offered the following account, indicative of a supernatural bardic ability to inhabit life forms and concepts other than one's own:

> I was carried away from myself and I was like a spirit, I knew the acts
> of past peoples and could predict the future. Then since I knew the
> secrets of things and the flights of birds and the wandering motions
> of the stars and the way fish glide.[183]

The above, when taken into consideration with the vast corpus of Taliesin wisdom, encourages the modern practitioner to access the visionary, and I would go so far as to claim that Cerridwen insists on developing one's visionary and occult skills. I do not, however, believe that the Taliesin spirit is the disembodied essence of an actual living person who now swans about in some Celtic afterlife waiting to inspire folk. My own personal gnosis is inclined to consider that the persona of Taliesin gives life and meaning to the narrative, enchanted, and prophetic spirits, and was thus enhanced

---

182 Haycock, *Legendary Poems from the Book of Taliesin*, 9–10.
183 Parry, *The Life of Merlin*, 33.

and empowered by subsequent bards who claimed they were expressions of the genius of Taliesin. In essence, they created a thoughtform, and one so powerful that the Taliesin figure, embodying the qualities of Cerridwen, swam through them. Essentially it evolved into an ethereal force that transcended locality and time and, in effect, developed a life of its own for the promulgation of wisdom. Bards continued to identify themselves as Taliesin, not necessarily as an individual who had once lived, but as an ideal and a radiancy that comes from being the Awen. To modern occultists this is not a far-fetched conclusion, but for the primary influencers of Celtic academia it was an alien concept from the offset.

Giraldus's account of the Awenyddion and Geoffrey of Monmouth's *Vita Merlini,* together with the bardic tradition, provide a compelling corpus of material that pertains to the magical, occult function of Awen. This in itself reaches back into the distant past and to a primitive form of Indo-European magic. Much of this concerned the making of kings and the satirising of chieftains and leaders. Whilst the magical prowess and expression of the tradition waxed and waned through the countless centuries, it is apparent that a consistency of magical thought associated with Awen persisted unto the modern era.[184] Which begs the question—how did such a thing survive the centuries, and can one tap into it in the twenty-first century?

The answer to that question is a resounding yes. We are quite capable of tapping into its currents.

Whilst this is not the appropriate section to discuss the crafting of magic by materials of the earth in union with the power of sound, it is pertinent that I give pause to the essentiality of occult powers and abilities. Cerridwen boldly informs us that she is the most knowledgeable one to have existed, and her admirations are for a gifted and talented magician. In the twenty-first century, she has evidently become synonymous with the positive and empowering aspect of the witch, which is in stark contrast to her denigration as a repulsive witch figure of the late medieval era. Whilst often it is the enigmatic and mysterious material of the bardic tradition that appeals to the

---

184   Conran, *Welsh Verse*, 18.

masses, for they tantalisingly offer the seeker a taste of mystery, it can be at the expense of the prophetic material. It is within them we can deduce that the bards excelled not only at immortalisation and the preservation of memory and tradition, but were accomplished magicians who excelled at the arts magical. It is the demoting of magic within the tradition that has weakened the bardic tradition today to a point where it is devoid of profound mystery and mostly expressive of the science of language.

The same danger faces modern populist occulture. Everything within this particular system and tradition is magical in nature, and we shall explore this further a little later. But for now, suffice to say that even in twenty-first-century Paganism, there is a danger that in our attempts to glean respect of our peers and acceptance within secular society, we risk diluting the necessity for occult talent. Cerridwen is skilled in magic and expects her children to be equally proficient. It would be a disservice to the entire continuum of the bardic tradition for us to nurture occult practitioners who have not been encouraged to develop their occult abilities.

Consider the above discourse and how or if occult gifts and abilities are important to your practise. The sigil presented below captures the essence and mystery of the prophetic spirit:

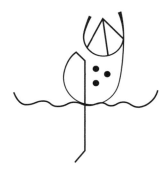

22

The Enchanted Spirit: Yr Ysbryd Swynol

Swirling within the supernal triskele of Cerridwen as the director of Awen is the spiral of the enchanted spirit, or Yr Ysbryd Swynol. This spirit represents the hands-on approach to magic that would stereotypically be associated with the modern practises of spellcrafting, Druid magic, and witchcraft, where one utilises materials of the earth for the crafting of magic. It is apparent throughout the later tale of Cerridwen that she just so happened to emulate the function of what the late medieval world was identifying as a witch, with her gathering of herbs and the iconic cauldron atop a blazing fire. The symbology within the later tales lent themselves perfectly to the vision of the witch. But, before I explore the nature of Cerridwen and her connection to the modern world of witchcraft, it is important to spend a moment looking at the enchanted spirit that courses through the expression of Cerridwen.

In her role as the maker of the brew of Awen, Cerridwen is knowledgeable enough to take on the identification of various plant allies to prepare the potion. Her fascination and association with the family of Dôn give further credence to her position as a crafter of magic. They get their hands dirty in the material of the earth, they can summon great things from plants and change the shape of things and people. Cerridwen herself is able to change her shape and form at will, and there is an implication through all this that she and members of the family of Dôn understand the nuts and bolts of how magic works—the science of magic.

She knew which plants to collect, as did Gwydion and his uncle Math when they created a woman of flowers, as did Aranrhod when she created the sound of the three fates that she placed on her son, and as did Math when he took to his wand to cause great change in the physical world. They are all skilled and proficient magicians. They do not use the power of sound alone but also take to their allies in the natural world. This must come from learning and relationship. It is this understanding that I perceive as that which swirls within the enchanted spirit, the science of magic.

There is a simple and good reason why modern practitioners of the occult arts practise magic: it works. If it didn't work, we would not take to wasting our time. Whilst it may on the surface appear whimsical to those who stand on the outside looking in, it cannot be said that the majority of magical practitioners are whimsical or deluded. There is deep intelligence and analytical filters that modern-day magicians utilise in the crafting of their magic, including a profound understanding of how the magical universe works. This does not come from a seat of ignorance or fantasy; it comes from a place of knowledge. The harnessing of magical forces requires attention, concentration, and skill. It employs all the senses of the magician in the making of magic—qualities expressed by Cerridwen in the "Cadair Cerridwen" poem.

The enchanted spirit teaches us that all things are connected by invisible, subtle webs of relationship. Quantum and particle physicists have employed imaginative names for the forces that they perceive to be acting on the universe, from quantum foam to quarks to string theories and dark matter. Magic, perhaps, is the science that we have yet to quantify and compartmentalise. It is the understanding that not all things in the heavens and on earth can be seen and studied in a manner that would satisfy the scientific community. Magical practitioners comprehend that all things that exist and have expression in our world are microcosmic representations of the greater universe. Within this we understand that there are sympathetic forces that form correspondences between the physical and nonphysical, or spiritual, worlds.

We exist in a world where physicality is our primary point of reference, and yet science itself informs us that to an extent this is merely an illusion. Our world consists of atoms and particles held together by forces, only long enough for them to appear existent. Human eyes can only perceive a small fraction of the electromagnetic field, and if we were capable of seeing all the spectrums of existence all at once, we would surely lose our sanity. The distances between the nuclei of our atoms and cells and their perimeters are vast, consisting mostly of empty space. This emptiness of space encompasses and permeates all things. This space is the fairy mound, the hollow hills, the cauldron, and it exists within you.

All things are connected by forces that defy rationality and entertain and maintain the scientific community in their perpetual search for the key to it all. Magicians, witches, and Druids have long since understood this concept of interconnection and utilised it for magic. When we consciously reach into this space between spaces, we are reaching into the place of our origination, to the mystery that brought all things into being. It is within this space between space that the breath of Awen blows.

We are able to influence the quality and flow of this space between space and its impact on the physical world by a variety of means: spellcasting, conjuration, sorcery, divination, sigil and talismanic magic, to name but a few. In sympathetic magic we search for correspondences in the natural world that imitate the object of our desire or wish. For example, if one was wont to perform a healing spell on an individual with a chest infection or breathing disorder, one might employ the qualities of the plant lungwort. The surface of its leaves looks quite similar to the patterns inside the human lung; it is this correspondence that is reached for to activate the magic. If someone needed strength and tenacity, one might call to the properties of the oak. Hawthorn and its berries might be called on for assistance in helping someone overcome and make sense of emotional heartbreak or a heart condition on a physiological level.

The efficacy of magic and its outcome is dependent on the magician's ability to observe the world through subtle eyes, to see the in-between places, to read between the lines. For this to occur, our focus must be slightly different from that of the ordinary waking state, which can be dense and reactionary. We rarely take note of what is actually going on around us and observe that our human community is only one amongst a million other communities, and in combination we are the collective community of this planet. We are not separate.

This is partly why a study of the Wheel of the Year in one's tentative exploration of modern Pagan practise is essential, for it causes us to stop, take heed, and observe a world that we believe we are familiar with. To those who fully engage, they begin to sense more to the world than first meets the eye. Their world begins to glow in brighter colours as they shift their awareness from the humancentric approach that is practically taught to us by being a member of a global community, of which we are only a small and temporary aspect of. This is a form of initiation into a new awareness, and it is essential for the practise of magic. To sense the subtle and perceive the space between spaces that connects all things, we must learn to be still and identify that space within our own beings. In my tradition we have a name for this process: we call it finding one's taw.

In the Welsh language, the term taw can be seen as a component of a myriad of words that express its spirit such as distawrwydd (quietness) and tawelwch (tranquillity). Taw allows us the opportunity to be still, to find an inner silence where eventually the busy chatter of the human mind is hushed temporarily. It is a process by which we consciously stop, settle, and disengage with the humdrum of ordinary life, and step into the extraordinary. In taw we start by observing our surroundings and flooding our senses with all the available data that bombards us, both internally and externally.

The sounds of the elements, the whispering of trees, the rise and fall of your breath, distant traffic, the light of stars, the sound of crashing waves; we permit it all to infiltrate the senses like a symphony, attempting as we do so to not isolate any particular sound or instrument. In taw we stop; we are not actively listening to the gods or to the spirits of place, we are not offering prayer but rather moving into a state of simply being, of finding stillness. It is within this stillness that we sense the quality of the space between spaces and the edges of our assumed perimeters become unclear.

As the state of taw progresses, we cease to know where we end and the ground beneath us begins. In taw we find the stillness and peace of our centre, of our origination, of our place within the river of Awen. We take time out to be, not to do. Doing can happen later, doing is what we ordinarily do; taw allows us to return to our factory settings if only for a short while. To be refreshed by the flowing rivers of interconnection. Taw is not something we do together with our communities and groups, but something we do for ourselves. Spirituality is not all about expression, but also about being at home with oneself, to know oneself. The insights from being in the state of taw arrive in hindsight, and they can be profoundly transformative and enriching.

Taw instils within me a state of tranquillity amidst the drama of my life, a time out of time, a place to find the peace within myself, to engage with the space within me that connects me to every expression of the universe. Taw is when I sit in the woods or on the edge of my local beach with starlight painting dreams in the night sky. Within it I sit in the delicious currents of Awen and allow it to flow through me.

It is an awareness of this space that facilitates effective magic, and from that awareness a further three skills are necessary for the crafting of magic. They are:

Intention

Imagination   **Application**

Holding one's intention throughout a magical working is essential, for it directs the mind, the body, and the spirit to the task at hand. Simultaneously, it informs whatever forces or spirits you have called upon as your allies of your objectives.

Imagination is key to this, of holding in your mind the subject or object of your intentions. Holding a full-blown cinematic image in your head is quite the task, and for some nay on impossible. If you struggle with this, I suggest you use what I find most effective in my own magical practise and is scattered throughout this book: a sigil. And from all this, we apply the magic. Usually this will take the form of a ritualised action that further informs the ordinary mind and world that something extraordinary is taking place. This might be the crafting of a potion or unguent or the making of an herb bunch or smudge. It may be the shaping of a poppet or the crafting of artwork or the oration of magical verse. Either way, the application of the magic will invariably have a physical aspect to it.

Ritual is key to setting the space and informing the mind that something extraordinary is occurring. In essence, ritual is the act of stopping, of delineating an act or space as being sacred or sublime, and the utilisation of symbols and objects that correspond with the desired outcome. In ritual the magician is engaged with three aspects that are vital to a successful outcome:

Visualisation

Gesticulation   **Vocalisation**

Visualisation is akin to imagination: it is the seeing of an image, symbol, or sigil within the mind and maintaining a hold on it. Gesticulation is the actions one performs with one's body, and these can be exaggerated and often dramatic movements that appear beyond the ordinary. They are determined, pronounced, and wilful, and often involve tools. Vocalisation is the accompanying verse, chant, englyn, or prose that one has devised or prepared prior to commencement of the ritual. Combined, they form the triskele of ritual practise. They are not sequential nor linear but occur all at once.

These qualities of magic and ritual are imbibed into the enchanted spirit that spirals from the Great Song of Awen under the direction of Cerridwen. These attributes are captured in the sigil below. Contemplate this as you consider the enchanted spirit:

To recap:

- The magic of the narrative spirit sings through the tripartite function of blood, culture, and psychic constitution. It is the power of memory and continuation.
- The prophetic spirit embodies prophesy, divination, prognostication, and the sight.
- The enchanted spirit teaches us the skills and the science of magic by moving into relationship with the natural world and the magical allies therein.

These magical, occult abilities are muscles in the fine body of Awen, but if they are not exercised, they atrophy and weaken. The combining of all three elements deepens our relationship with our own magical and psychic constitution.

23

The Awen

To a lesser extent, the discourse thus far has touched upon the Awen on several occasions, but based mostly on the brief description that I offered to you in the first section of this book, which is worth revisiting here:

> *Awen: the creative, transformative force of divine inspiration that*
> *sings in praise of itself. It is an eternal song that sings all things*
> *into existence, and all things call to the Awen inwardly.*

However, the Awen has a complex and varied history that arises from the countless generations that have explored it. Whilst its actual origins are unknown to us, there is much that we can learn by a study of the word itself, the concepts hid within it, and the relatively new symbol that was appropriated to it. The journey thus far has touched on the Awen in several ways, for in truth, it runs through the entire discourse of this book. But it is most appropriate that we cast an eye onto the mechanisms that carried the Awen through time and why it holds such appeal and enigma today, as it did over a thousand years ago. To do so is to perceive it within the cultural context of its creation and expression, and by doing so, we simultaneously glimpse not only its enormous importance and relevance to the bards, but also the being attributed as its guardian and primary director, Cerridwen. The Awen and Cerridwen cannot be separated; they are inexorably entwined.

On closer examination, it will become apparent that there is significantly more to the Awen than first meets the eyes, so in order for us to understand and appreciate its function, we must attempt to dissect it in a manner that we can reconstruct without causing enormous damage to its vital internal structure. This is the danger of any form of literal analysis, that we might strip something of its inherent magic, so whilst it was essential for me to explore the bard's relationship to the Awen in the first section of this book, it is equally important that in this part we maintain a conscious awareness that the Awen is fundamentally magical in nature. Yes, we are able to explore it as a concept, but we would be foolhardy to not maintain our vision of the ethereal nature of Awen. In essence, the history and scholarly examination is all good and well, but unless the Awen can be connected to as an actual magical force, it is simply armchair philosophy and a concept of literal and linguistic beauty alone. This would be a disservice to the Awen and to Cerridwen. I ask that you keep this in mind as we progress through this section.

One of the earliest written references we have to the Awen is from the pen of Nennius and his naming of a bard called Talhaearn Tad Awen (Iron or Strong Forehead, Father of Awen), which I briefly touched upon in chapter 6. Nennius is also tenuously associated with being the inspirer of the later symbol that has since become associated with the Awen, the three pillars of light which appear thus: / | \. However, there is no concrete evidence to suggest that this is so, but there is no doubt that in the 700s the term Awen was widely used and probably understood. Whilst dozens of examples of the use of the word Awen can be seen throughout the poetry of the bardic tradition, this discussion does not afford the time or space for exploring them all. It is, however, important from a visionary perspective that I focus on the poems that concern the Awen, Cerridwen, and her cauldron.

The majority of these come from the mouthpiece of the legendary aspect of the Taliesin persona. There are a handful of references to the Awen in the Black Book of Carmarthen, but the most pertinent comes to us from the fifteen references in the Book of Taliesin, and as I previously explored several of these directly reference Cerridwen. In a nutshell, the references to the Awen are praising in expression and allude to the Awen's magical origins and nature. Taliesin insists that bardic knowledge originates and rises from the cauldron of Cerridwen and that it has been to the far-flung regions of the otherworld that are connected with the Awen. It implies that the Awen causes it to know and to have experienced multiple life forms and experiences.

The first part of this book explored several poems in relation to the Awen, but there is one stanza in particular that I wish to share with you that I believe perfectly exemplifies the Awen's function and power. It comes to us in the epic poem "Angar Kyfundawt," which might be translated as the "hostile confederacy" or "the unfriendly crowd." This poem is over 265 lines in length and riddled with mysteries that I only wish I had the time and space to share with you. Within the poem we encounter Cerridwen's son Afagddu, Gwion Bach is also present, as is the cauldron, and Taliesin claims knowledge of a myriad of things and of having been in the guise of a multitude of forms. Alas, owing the restrictions of space and time, we must focus our gaze on what Taliesin says about the nature of Awen:

> *Yr Awen a ganaf,*
> *O dwfyn ys dygaf,*
> *Auon kyt beryt:*
> *Gogwn y gwrhyt,*
> *Gogwn pan dyueinw,*
> *Gogwn pan dyleinw,*
> *Gogwn pan dillyd,*
> *Gogwn pan wescryd,*
> *Gogwn py pegor,*
> *Yssyd y dan vor.*

> *The Awen I sing,*
> *From the deep I bring it,*
> *It is a world-encircling river,*
> *I know its size,*

I know how it ebbs,
I know how it flows,
I know its course,
I know its retreat,
I know what creatures
Are under the sea.[185]

I will presently recommend that you read the above out loud in both languages. Yes, regardless of your knowledge of the Welsh language, I encourage you to have a go. There is power in the movement of words, and as I have previously explored, the reciting of the words moves one into the currents of the narrative spirit.

If we examine the above stanza, we can learn a little more about the nature of Awen:

The Awen I sing, from the deep I bring it.

Here Taliesin is referring to the Awen as a song, a trait that will be familiar to you by now, but it also hints at the origin of the song, that it comes from a region called the *dwfn,* or the deep. This is a reference to the indigenous Celtic otherworld known as Annwfn.

It is a connected river that flows.

In this line Taliesin is equating the Awen with water, a common trait throughout the bardic tradition, where it is often associated with rivers, streams, and the wind. In the original language, it is composed of only three words—*auon,* meaning river; *kyt,* which is a noun to mean something that is circling in union and communion[186]; and *beryt,* meaning to flow. You can recite this quite easily yourself by saying *AV-on kit BER-it,* and you will immediately get a feel for the internal rhyming structure of rudimentary cynghanedd within just that little line. Say it over and over a few times.

---

185   Translated by the author from the original Peniarth Manuscript 2, designated the title Llyfr Taliesin and held at the National Library of Wales.

186   Haycock, *Legendary Poems from the Book of Taliesin,* 156.

By doing this, you will be emulating the sentiment that Taliesin is attempting to transmit to you about the Awen being a connective current that unifies all things in our world and in our known universe. By stepping into its currents, we fall into communion with it. The Awen allows for you to become the window through which the universe looks at and experiences itself. Everything exists within this field, which I frivolously refer to as "The A Field." It is owing to the connective nature of Awen that Taliesin is able to experience the life and expression of a plethora of shapes and forms other than his own.

> *I know its might, I know how it ebbs, I know how it flows.*
> *I know when it overflows, I know when it shrinks.*

Here Taliesin is exemplifying the experience of being in the Awen. This is not armchair philosophy or a mental exercise. It is experiential. It comes from having experienced something, not imagined it on a whim. Taliesin has direct knowledge of the Awen, and because Awen permeates all things, Taliesin is able to move in and out of experience, a process that we could quite correctly call shapeshifting.

> *I know what creatures there are under the sea.*

Regardless of something being hidden from sight, Taliesin has the ability to perceive it. He displays an omnipresence that is tantamount to godliness, but he does so with delicacy and beauty. Whilst in English it may come across as slightly arrogant, there is a subtle and yet profoundly empowering flavour to it in the Welsh language that alludes to a hidden meaning, with the secret being "I can do this, listen to what I am saying, for I say that you can do this also." This is essentially what swims beneath the lines and in between the words. We witnessed earlier the account in *Vita Merlini* where he seemingly knows the manner by which fish glide, and here we are again, peering into the depths of the ocean and knowing what mysteries lie there, physically and metaphorically.

Herein lies the importance of singing these songs, of actually allowing the words to fall from your lips and moving into the current of Awen, where performance becomes an act of creative magic. The attainment of Awen produces not only a profound depth of poetic inspiration, but it brings about this immense sense of oneness with all things. There is a sense here that those who move within the streams of Awen have attained a degree of illumination that is akin to godhood, or at the very least implies a transcendence.

EXERCISE

Singing from the Deep

We purposefully and with intent moved into the glowing light of the Awen when we explored the triskele, but now I would like for you to engage another one of your faculties to move into the experience of Awen: sound. If you will, please indulge my fancy for a few moments and take what I have said above quite literally and bardically (if such a word exists). Look at the original and phonetic version of the first four lines of the above stanza; do not fear the sounds that may be quite unfamiliar to you, but rather be excited by them, for they potentially carry the power of the narrative spirit, and by singing them, it will shine through you, a quality that I consider to be a rather wondrous and amazing thing.

Now, do not overanalyse the structure of the sentences; keep in mind that these are sounds. If you attempt to rationalise the various use and placements of letters in the written form, much of which has changed over the centuries, you will serve only to confound yourself. Re-read the above descriptions of the lines, which will compliment what you have already learnt about the Awen. I would like for you to repeat the stanza over and over until you are quite familiar with the way it sounds. Once you are familiar with it, take to gazing at the sigil on page 214, which represents the qualities of the Awen as captured in the verses.

So, with that, throw yourself into the sound of this particular stanza, with the trick being to let go of expectations or a sense of doing something correctly or not, as the case may be, but rather to enjoy the sounds and words spoken by ancestors long since taken to dust. There is magic here, for not only are the words themselves as old as the parchment that first took them to writing, but their sounds contain the sum totality of all those who sang them before. They hold and embrace the narrative spirit. Look at the structure of the words below—there is a pattern to the stanza, which comes from the magic of cynghanedd.

Original Middle Welsh	Phonetic Version
Yr Awen a ganaf	Urr AH-wen Ah GAN-av
O dwfyn ys dygaf	Awe DOO-vun Ur DUG-av
Auon kyt beryt	AV-on kit BER-it
Gogwn y gwrhyt	GOG-oon Ur GOOR-it[187]

The trick to the vocalisation or singing of these stanzas is to chant them in a mantra-like fashion long enough for your mind to stop analysing what is going on. A few minutes will not be sufficient, whereas 20–30 minutes or longer will cause a shift in your consciousness that will enable the deeper meaning of the poem to flood through you. Recall the qualities that Cerridwen expects in her children: commitment, learning, and devotion. In a quick-and-easy, have-it-now world, we are often reticent to spend time on a practise, but I ask that you do so—to really have a go, to deepen not only your connection and understanding of the Awen, but also, by proxy, your relationship to Cerridwen.

In this exercise, it is the Awen that YOU sing, and it is from the deep that YOU bring it, not Mrs. Jones who lives down the street or some ancient unknown Welsh bard, but you. For the Awen to be anything other than a delightful concept, we must bring it forth from the deep and into the here and now, the result being that one has moved into the currents of the blessed holy breath of inspiration; one becomes Awenydd, one who is inspired. Nobody can do that for us. We must do it ourselves.

As you sing the stanzas, consider the image of Cerridwen as you perceived her in the ritual you undertook to meet her at the start of this book. Hold that image in your imagination; if you like, use words of invitation to ask Cerridwen to be present during your exploration of the Awen. Consider the

---

187   A soundfile of this stanza can be found at the suggested Youtube channel listing in the resources section.

magical, occult qualities of the Awen as embodied by the prophetic spirit. With all this in mind, make yourself comfortable in a space that will afford you some privacy and peace.

The stanza contains a natural four-beat rhythm per couplet, with eight beats in total. If you are thus inclined to fancy additional auditory and sensory input, I suggest a small drum, the palm of your hand against your thigh, or a small twig onto which you have wrapped a ribbon strung with small silver bells, the type you might purchase for midwinter decorations. If this proves too distracting, omit it from the practise.

Moving into the current of Awen can potentially be an intense experience and one that may well affect your short-term memory. When we let go and we are as spirit, much can occur that may evade memory. Therefore, a tip: use the basic sound recorder app of an electronic smart device to record the entire session. The image of the triskele held in a circle should also be brought to mind and imagined as a glowing light in the centre of your forehead. Don't worry if you get carried away by the sounds alone; having previously visualised the triskele glowing upon you, it will be there nonetheless, but if you can, periodically bring it to mind as you progress through this exercise.

And with that, contemplate the sigil below and begin. Keep singing for as long as you possibly can.

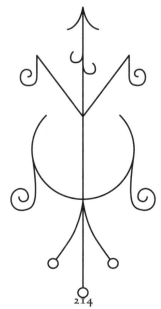

The above exercise is recapped in the following steps—

1. Create and delineate a space as sacred to the task at hand.

2. Centre yourself by taking three breaths with the land, sea, and sky.

3. Call to Cerridwen to assist you.

4. Recall the qualities of commitment and devotion expected by Cerridwen.

5. Drum or tap out four beats per couplet, eight in total.

6. Begin to sing the stanza whilst imagining the sigil on page 214.

7. Imagine this symbol upon your forehead:

8. Allow session to end, have a snack, and record your thoughts.

Occupying the stream or current of Awen cannot be maintained for hours on end, and therefore the experience will naturally conclude. As it does so, allow your senses to return to the here and now. Breathe deeply. Have a little snack and a drink, and turn your thoughts into writing or journaling.

This exercise can be repeated in various degrees of intensity as often as possible or whenever one feels the need for inspiration.

◆ ◆ ◆

The Awen was considered incredibly holy and blessed, and from my previous explorations it is evident that this was the case in both Pagan and Christian traditions. The ability to shift into its currents and express it was a spiritual treasure and one that daren't be abused. Questions would remain and debates would burn hotly as to whether the Awen was a gift from the Holy Spirit of the Christian god or from the cauldron of Cerridwen. I like to think that the beauty of the Awen is in the fact that it can be either or both.

Evidence of manuscript tampering has come to light in recent years, and whilst I covered this subject more fully in my book *From the Cauldron Born*, there is one example worthy of revisiting. Peniarth Manuscript 111, which records a version of the tale of Cerridwen and Taliesin, informs the reader that the Awen is not only *bendigedig* (blessed) but that it *rat yr ysbryd glan* (comes from the Holy Spirit). However, when the manuscripts were examined in the later decades of the twentieth century, it was discovered that things were not quite as they appeared. The words "rat yr ysbryd glan" had been added by a different hand at a different time over an erasure in the text. Technology enabled the experts to peer beneath the words and discover the indentation of the original script. Whilst it maintained that the Awen was indeed blessed, the indentations beneath the erasure read "ysbryd proffwydoliaeth," the prophetic spirit.[188] Whilst the change is small, its impact would have been enormous and indicates that there were intelligences present who were purposefully altering the texts. We will never truly know the motivations for this, but what is clear is that someone went to enormous efforts to disguise a previous entry.

As the world changed and the bardic schools moved from one era to the next, it was not wholly appropriate for the figure of Taliesin, whom the bards loved so much, to remain as a figure of an ancient past. It was important for the bards that the concept of Taliesin and the Awen evolved into the new era and to what they perceived to be an enlightened age. With this in mind, elements that perpetuated the Awen, including the persona of Taliesin, continued into the Christian traditions, and as Marged Haycock so eloquently states, "absorbed the latest elements of learning as well as retaining the key to the mysteries of the old world."[189]

---

188   Ford, *Ystoria Taliesin*, 35.
189   Haycock, "Preiddeu Annwn and the Figure of Taliesin," 58.

24

What's in a Word?
The Meaning of Awen

We have looked at the magical connotations of the Awen in the old world, but as yet we have not taken a good look at the word itself. As you already may have deduced, there is much hidden in the Welsh language that can reveal a tremendous amount as to what is being conveyed. By the twenty-first century there were countless books that examine this little Welsh word. The majority, through no fault of the authors, are reliant on what is often taken as gospel but which invariably comes from a seat of mistranslation and misunderstanding.

According to the *Dictionary of the Welsh Language*, the Awen is described thus:[190]

> **Awen**—Celtic *aue-n*, o'r gwr *au(e)*—chwythu. (Celtic aue-n, from the root word au(e), meaning to blow.
> 1. (Ffynhonnell) Dawn, athrylith neu ysbrydoliaeth farddonol.
>   (The source of poetic gift, genius of inspiration, the muse.)

---

190   Bevan, *Geiriadur Prifysgol Cymru*, 240–241.

2. Awydd, tuedd, meddwl, athrylith. (Desire, inclination, mind, genius.)

If we examine the word closely, we will see that it consists of two syllabic sounds—AW and EN. The *Dictionary of the Welsh Language* offers this explanation:

> AW—Gwreddair tybiedig I awel, awen, ewyllys, ac hefyd hylif, neu nwy. (Root word putative to breeze, awen, will, and also fluid or gas.)[191]

> EN—Gwreiddair enaid, y rhan ysbrydol o ddyn sy'n teimlio, deall, cofio, ystyried. (The root word for soul, the spiritual component of man that feels, understands, remembers and considers).[192]

In addition, there has been some arguments over the syllabic sounds themselves, and that another possible order would be AH-WEN. In this manner, the ah sound would refer to breath or wind, and the wen, in a similar fashion to the same suffix in Cerridwen, would denote something as being holy or blessed. Therefore, its translation would be blessed holy breath. In truth, nobody can wholly agree which is correct, but I do believe that there is truth to be found not only in the various meanings attributed to the manner by which the word is constructed, but also in the concepts that arbitrarily surround the Awen within the bardic tradition. *Celtic Culture* offers a beautifully articulated description of the Awen that not only captures the complexity of a single word but also its supernatural origins within the cauldron of Cerridwen:

> Awen is a Welsh word meaning poetic gift, genius or inspiration, the muse. Belonging to the same Proto-Celtic and Indo-European root as Old Irish ai (< *aui) poetic art and the Welsh awel (breeze), it is also related to the English wind. Ultimately awen belongs to the same root as that of Welsh gwawd, Irish fâth (prophecy) and Fâith (prophet). The etymological sense of awen is a "breathing in" of a

---

191   Bevan, *Geiriadur Prifysgol Cymru*, 237.
192   Ibid., 1211.

gift or genius bestowed by a supernatural force, for example pair Cerridwen (Cerridwen's Cauldron) in the Taliesin legend.[193]

If we look to modern occulture and twenty-first-century writing on the subject of Awen, it is usually translated as "flowing spirit" or simply as "inspiration." Whilst neither of these are wholly incorrect, they also miss out on something profoundly magical. Now that I have explored the various elements of the Awen within the bardic material, we can deduce that it is imbibed with certain qualities that, in hindsight, will afford us a different connection to the word.

To recap, the function of the Awen that we have explored thus far can be listed thus:

- The Awen is a steadfast and powerful song.
- The function of a bard was to bring Awen forth.
- Its singing or utterance literally and magically brings things into being/existence.
- The Awen is a transformative force.
- The Awen is simultaneously ecstatic and sublime.
- Cerridwen's song of Awen is the most dignified of them all.
- The Awen transmits itself through time in the form of seeds that pass from lips to ear, ear to heart, and heart to spirit.
- The Awen originates as a pure sound.
- It originates from the cauldron of Cerridwen.
- It is described as a current and a breath.
- It is a river that flows and unifies.

Running through those themes is a common thread: all of the associations with the Awen from the past pertain to the Awen as something that carries or transmits a sound and something that is moving by means of the breath of song or the fluidity of water. It is not stationary—quite the opposite, in fact, as for it to become stationary would result in the stagnation of

---

193   Koch, *Celtic Culture*, 148–149.

Awen. Energy flows where intention goes. The wonder of this small word is that it captures the essence and energy of so many qualities essential to the transmission of inspiration and the seeding, gestation, and expression of wisdom. Let's look at the array of meanings attributed to the word in the form of a list.

Awen:

- source
- genius
- inspiration
- desire
- inclination
- breeze / wind
- breath
- will
- fluid
- gas
- soul / spirit
- blessed
- holy

It is tempting, of course, to attempt to capture the essence of the word and translate it into something that would be useful within the English language. In truth, this is almost impossible, for the structure of the Welsh language is such that the utterance of one word is enough to impart meaning through feeling. Personally, I am rather fond of considering the Awen as "blessed and holy breath" mostly because the power of the sound within the bardic material is ingrained within my life experience—it is an inexorable aspect of my cultural identity and awareness. The magic of my language and its traditions are carried on the breath by means of words, and it is this that I inherently feel when I utter the word Awen. And yet, I sense a flowing, an ethereal, almost gaseous quality all at the same time. But the key here is a term I use almost fleetingly—*feel*.

The Awen is felt. We cannot help but analyse and dissect something in an attempt to discover its inner mechanism, and gods only know I am as guilty as this as any other individual. On some level, this in and of itself is tremendously satisfying, even if it does miss the point. Therefore, rather than trying to define what the Awen is linguistically, I suggest you shift your awareness of it to connect to it emotionally, and the word itself will be more than adequate to express that relationship. It is by connecting to the Awen that its song is kindled within the heart and spirit, and articulated emotionally as it traverses from within to without, on the currents of breath.

The Power of Awen

Primarily the Awen is a transformative force. It induces deep and profound change in those who are moving in its currents and those who gaze at it from a slight distance. Consider for a moment the references to the Awen as a river, as something that is flowing eternally. As we imagine this river, we find ourselves in a peculiar position: we can either take off our metaphorical shoes and socks and enter the river or we can bask in its beauty from the banks. Either way, the Awen will affect us. The majority of people's interaction with the Awen is by proxy of one who is moving in and out of its currents—in essence, one catches the Awen. I frivolously describe this condition as a DTI, or a Druid-Transmitted Infection (Inspiration), where the stream of Awen moves from the experience of one individual to others who get caught in its flow.

If you can, recall a time where you heard someone speak or address a group of individuals, either in person or by other technologies, that moved you immensely. Whether to tears or laughter or to action, recall that sense right here in this moment. On a physical level, nothing extraordinary happened; sound waves travelled through air to reach your auditory canals, you perceived them, and your brain assimilated them into relevant experience within you. But of course we are aware, emotionally and psychically, that there is significantly more to the world than simple waves and transmission of energetic principles into experience. There is Awen: a force so powerful that it is given names in other spiritual cultures and expressions that attempt to define an ethereal, supernatural energy that transforms. Great preachers move in its currents, inspirational speakers swim in its ebb and flow, teachers of traditions and systems consciously move into its tides, and those who listen feel its power course through them.

The experience of being human can, at times, be dense; disconnection is almost taught to us, programmed into us during our upbringing. Peer pressure and other social obligations can cause many to suffer a form of separation anxiety. The antithesis of the Awen is what I refer to as the Big Lie, the great hoax that is perpetuated in modern living. We are taught that one day we will arrive at a state of utopian perfection, having achieved all we can in life, worked for the new car and the new house, saved our pennies for that rainy day, struggled through school, graduation, and employment for that elusive dream that people keep telling us about. It's just around the corner, keep going, you will get there.

And so we hustle and we bustle and we work for that retirement package, and that golden finish line comes closer and closer—and then so many of us will die or, if we get there, we will find ourselves too exhausted and disillusioned to know what to do with our golden age. Swathes of humanity become institutionalised and secure in their insecurity: stay where you are, it matters not if it does not fulfil you. The Big Lie tells us what is important: financial success, material gain, professional development. It does not address the subtle qualities in life that bring profound meaning. Magical practitioners are not immune to this state either. Cerridwen herself fell into this trap of wanting her son to fit in, regardless of the cost. Did she ask him? No. She made the decision for him, the ugly duckling compensated by great intellectual skills, so that he would be accepted amongst the great and the good. The beauty in the legendary material is that even those identified as divine or otherworldly seemingly make human mistakes.

It is a double-edged sword, for we require the learned professionals and the architects and successful folk of the world that Afagddu might have blended in with, but perhaps we feel that these qualities supersede or are superior in some way to the subtle traits of the human experience. They can often lead to immense pressures and stresses on individuals that can very often lead to their undoing. In my professional life, I work for the coroner service, and I can no longer count the number of individuals I have dealt with who took their own lives because of financial stresses. Money, the necessary evil of the human world, and yet it only exists as an abstract concept that the majority of us cannot grasp. It is energy in motion that for a while appears in a steadfast form as coins or paper or digits on a screen. Yet the energy behind it is intangible, fickle. And with that, the modern world pays little credence to other influences that are equally as intangible—wisdom, inspiration, magic.

Cerridwen took to her skills of magic to compensate for her son's profound ugliness and brew a cauldron of Awen that would raise him to the ranks of or above those nameless, faceless individuals whose acceptance she wanted for her son. And yet, in truth, there were peers. Cerridwen displayed a quandary that afflicts so many people, a state where one is fearful of a fear that is as yet intangible. Turning to magic should not be a knee-jerk reaction. Cerridwen is not demonstrating a weakness here, but a lesson in the fundamental use of magic and Awen. They are gifts, and ones that should not be abused. And yet we often see examples of the abuse of Awen, where one uses one's ability to inspire for ulterior motives and unwholesome agendas. In a similar ilk to magic, the Awen is a neutral force. It is how one utilises it that defines the quality of the action.

The pressures of modern living can cause us to cease to see the magic and the awe in the world, and so often one can fall into a spiralling descent of frustration, anger, and contempt. Within that state we no longer fulfil nature's intention of being aware of itself, but the Awen heals this condition to a great extent and activates a different form of lucidity that sees beyond the structures our world would have us hold as supremely significant.

The individuals who are drawn to the magical have all experienced a significant moment of lucidity, almost as if Cerridwen herself silently walked up to you, leaned towards your left ear, and whispered, "Pssssst—wake up, you're dreaming." To have that wow moment, to see beyond the veil of ordinary and perceive the extraordinary that one is an inexorable aspect of, this moment of wild awakening often changes folk forever. They become transformed by some power or force that only a second before they were not consciously aware of. In my tradition this is the voice of Cerridwen and the song of the narrative, enchanted, and prophetic spirits calling one into wisdom.

The Awen facilitates the transformation of anxiety into joy. This statement is one that I hold dear to my own experience of this life. The Awen expresses itself through my life in a number of ways, through my vocation as a writer, in my professional life, in my role as an actor, and it does so in a manner that evokes great joy within me. I often found myself in states of anxiety, and when one raises one's head above the parapet, as is often the case, especially when you write books—anxiety is almost an expected state. Combine this with imposter syndrome and endless cycles of self-sabotage, where seemingly that fickle inner voice of the self-saboteur is the loudest and boldest. It is easy to become addicted to the anxiety and perpetuate its vicious cycles. In my own life, I needed to find a way to offset that anxious state and transform it into something more constructive—joy. It hasn't been easy, but to see the Awen in what you do and consciously move into its stream certainly helps me to take a step back from the anxieties in my life and consciously transform them into joy.

25

The Awen-Filled Legacy of Iolo Morganwg

As I have demonstrated on several occasions thus far, the Awen has been offered a symbol that captures its energy and essence. Often referred to as the pillars or columns of light, they are drawn thus:

/ | \

There is little evidence to suggest that our bardic ancestors utilised this symbol, albeit there is a tenuous description in Nennius's alphabet that may hint at a symbol appropriate for the powers of inspiration. The symbol as it appears today is mostly inspired by the efforts of one individual, a Welsh bard of the late eighteenth and early nineteenth century called Edward Williams, who took the bardic name of Iolo Morganwg. Whilst this discourse does not afford the space I feel would be necessary to do him justice, it is important that I touch briefly on the Awen-filled story of this remarkable individual, for it sings loudly of the power of Awen to transform, not just an individual, but the future. His symbol for the Awen has become directly associated in Neopaganism with Cerridwen, making an exploration of his influence a valuable exercise in our understanding of Awen in the modern world.

Iolo Morganwg was a stonemason from South Wales, an imaginative, poetic genius who made elaborate claims of ancient documents and wisdom that he had discovered and preserved for the world to see. Blighted with ill health, he was addicted to the narcotic laudanum for over fifty years of his life, spending most of his days in a drug-induced state, and yet poems in their thousands fell from his frenzied mind onto scraps of parchment. He composed elaborate poetry, inspired prose, but falsely claimed that some of the poems were written by ancient bards. It would be decades before anyone realised that some of his works were not quite what they seemed. And yet, through all of the accusations of forgery and deception, Iolo dreamed something into being that those in the different streams of Celtic spirituality today, both monotheistic and polytheistic, are descendants of. He dreamed a new mythology into a being and planted seeds that would gestate a profound wisdom in the future.

In a time of great social crisis, he dreamed an identity for the Welsh that took as its foundation that the bardic tradition of Wales was a direct line to the ancient Druids of Britain, who he perceived as the true ancestors of the Welsh. He longed for his people to connect to the might and power that the Romantic movement imagined the Druids to express. And in doing so, he deliciously imagined a new identity that the Welsh could be proud of: he blended fact with fiction, legend with history, myth with reality. His bewildering array of notes and journals continue to baffle modern academics who strive to make sense of this enigmatic figure. He claimed that the language of the Welsh intimately connected them to the language of primitive Britain and to the secrets of the Druids. As we have seen in our exploration of the Welsh bardic tradition, he was not wholly incorrect, albeit a Romanticist; there were pearls of truth that coursed through his work.[194] His love for Taliesin as the epitome of the expression of Awen is evident in his work, although he rarely focuses on Cerridwen; the Awen and the radiant brow

---

194   Jenkins, *A Rattleskull Genius*, 262.

were certainly elements that tickled his bardic imagination. He even called his son Taliesin.

In a profoundly logocentric world, where new thoughts and ideas were expected to be substantiated by manuscripts, Iolo simply invented a past that we, as the Welsh, could be proud of. In doing so, he posthumously opened the memory of himself to enormous criticism and accusations of forgery that are barely understood or articulated beyond the borders of Welsh academia. And yet, he carried the seeds of Awen and profoundly influenced a future that he could not have imagined. In the twenty-first century, those drawn to the Cerridwen and Taliesenic mysteries who may artistically express, understand, or wear the symbol of the Awen all carry the dream of Iolo Morganwg. He is testament to the Awen's consistent stream and how it too changed its countenance to meet the needs of different people at different times. The period he occupied was a cauldron of new ideas, with the new era of the bardic tradition in its infancy and occult fascination among the learned of the time increasing in popularity.

Iolo Morgannwg was a controversial figure who scorned the snobbery of academia. He was irritable, poorly, and argumentative, yet simultaneously enormous fun, who relished in what he considered the business of serious frivolity.[195] Afforded the nickname "Whimsical Ned," which he seemingly delighted in, he amused, angered, and frustrated those who made his acquaintance. Yet, underneath the various masks he portrayed to the world was a sensitive and humane man who was deeply committed to benevolence, justice, and freedom. He wrote:

> No idea can be more grievous to me than that of quitting this life without having been in some degree the benefactor of mankind.[196]

Alas, he was not to gain nor glean any great kudos or recognition during his lifetime. Confused and bewildered, no longer able to identify which of his own works were genuinely inspired or hid another peer-pressured agenda, he met the end of his life. At the age of 79, on the morning of

---

195   Jenkins, *A Rattleskull Genius*, 1.
196   Ibid., 25.

Sunday, 18 December 1826, in desperate poverty, he died. His remains were buried in the floor of Trefflemin (Flemingston) Church with barely any mourners present. No marker identifies the spot of his burial. But, perhaps if an epitaph to Iolo can be said to exist, it does so in the shape and form of the symbol that represents the Awen:

/ | \

This primary symbol of the Awen today can be seen adorning books, insignia, and symbols, statuary of Cerridwen and her cauldron, robes and cloaks and jewellery; it has become synonymous with the Druid tradition and of the significance and power of the Awen, worn by Druids and non-Druids alike. It is a symbol that transcends cultural differences and tradition-specific symbology. It is not a symbol that exclusively belongs to the Druids, albeit it is frequently utilised as an identifier for modern Druids, but rather it is one that is shared by them. A general search through the internet will result in three specific forms of the common symbol for Awen. They are:

- encircled with three dots above the rays; variations might include three circles surrounding the rays:

- un-encircled with three dots above the rays:

• original as devised by Iolo Morganwg:

Attributed to Ross Nichols, the founder of the Order of Bards, Ovates and Druids, the addition of the three dots above the rays is relatively modern. It also serves a useful reference point as to which school of thought is connecting to and expressing the Awen. The third example, which omits the dots, can still be seen today within the organisation of the Gorsedd of Bards of the Island of Britain and the National Eisteddfod movement. It adorns their garments and ritualised tools, proclamation scrolls, the official banner, crowns, and chair. Generally, the symbol with the three dots is indicative of a Neopagan Druidism and spirituality, and it can be seen to represent the three drops of Awen that burst forth from the cauldron of Cerridwen.

Iolo's dream, although never realised during his lifetime, birthed the glowing rays of a new Awen, one appropriate and applicable to a new age. The three rays, or columns as Iolo referred to them, carry the light and stream of the Awen. He wrote extensively about the symbol and its function, and whilst much elaboration has occurred since, it is important to honour the seeds of his Awen, for those seeds are now intimately connected with Cerridwen. Here is his description of the symbol:

> Thus are they made; the first of the signs is a small cutting or line inclining with the sun at eventide, thus /; the second is another cutting, in the form of a perpendicular, upright post, thus |; and the third is a cutting of the same amount of inclination as the first, but in an opposite direction, that is against the sun, thus \ ; and the three placed together, thus / | \.[197]

---

197   Williams, *The Barddas of Iolo Morganwg*, 21.

This association with the position of the sun can be further exemplified by observing the play of shadow on a single monolith standing against the line of the horizon. Whilst standing before the stone, we would see the position of the sun's zenith at noon during the four solar stations of the year casting long shadows from the base of the monolith thus:

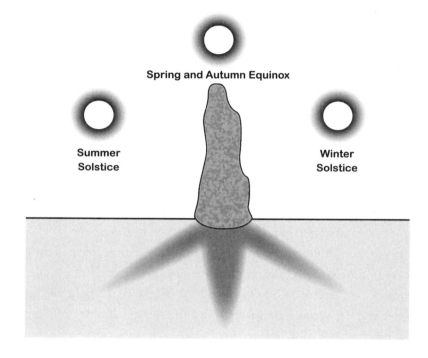

You will note that the shadows over the course of a solar year will cast the symbol of the Awen onto the ground. We continue to demonstrate this phenomenon artificially during the Anglesey Druid Order's open events using a partially sealed box and a small stone positioned so that three torches shine upon it from the back of the box. This rationale for the symbol cannot be ascertained to have been fathomed in ancient times, but it is a beautiful way of demonstrating the symbol's association with the natural world and the light of our sun.

Bewilderment and Inspiration

In his often-bewildering work, Iolo goes on to describe the manner by which the rays of light were first perceived, albeit his only cultural reference at the time was a Christianised religious expression. At first sight the references to a monotheistic God can be jarring, but it is important to consider the religious climate in which he lived.

> His name was pronounced, and with the utterance was the spring- ing of light and vitality, and man, and every other living thing; that is to say, each and all sprang together. And Menw the Aged, son of Menwyd, beheld the springing of the light and its form and appear- ance, not otherwise than thus / | \, in three columns, and in the rays of light the vocalisation, for one were the hearing and seeing, one unitedly the form and sound, and one unitedly with these three was power.[198]

Hidden within this paragraph is a subtle mystery, that of the name of the apparent individual who first perceived the rays or columns of light: Menw the Aged, son of Menwyd. "Menw" is the shortened term for understand- ing, intellect, and mind, and we are told that this mind or intellect is aged or ancient. The "son of Menwyd" means the primary intellect or mind. How- ever, the term Menw is also related to benyw, meaning woman. The title can be translated in a number of perplexing ways:

Ancient mind, the son of mind.

or

Ancient Woman, the son of Woman.

Alas, neither make a whole lot of sense, but they belie a complexity to Iolo's perception of the universe, that on one level was locked into a logo- centric, Judeo-Christian mindset, but on another his ideas broke the mould of religious conformity. What he offers is a somewhat contradictory descrip- tion of something being observant of the Awen that transcends gender

---

198   Williams, *The Barddas of Iolo Morganwg*, 17.

norms and is not an individual per se. In no chronological or systemic order, his exploration of the Awen covered hundreds of parchments, in disarray and confusion, and yet consistently he wrote and spoke of its profound qualities. As to the symbol itself, he often referred to it as "Yr Arwydd Glân," meaning the pure or holy sign, and the "Tair Colofn," the three columns:

> / | \. That is to say, they are called the three columns, and the three columns of truth, because there can be no knowledge of the truth, but from the light thrown upon it; and the three columns of sciences, because there can be no sciences, but from the light and truth.[199]

Throughout his work on the Awen, he touches on elements pertinent to the bardic tradition, and whilst we cannot be wholly assured that he was privy to the secret of the bards, he certainly demonstrated a genius for poetry and strict meter. The new system of the bardic tradition was yet to find its feet fully under the table of bardism, and ironically, it would be Iolo's inspiration that would go on to cement the values of the new bardism. His ideas and pseudo-Druidic philosophies would form the central pillar upon which all the ceremonies and rituals of the Gorsedd of Bards of the Isle of Britain would be adorned. These same rituals would go on to be included in Pagan Neo-Druid traditions and systems. He no doubt understood on some level the secret of the bards, and his work frequently refers to a "cyfrinach," a secret that only those within the ranks of the bardic tradition would have understood. Central to this secret is the power and nature of sound and its ability to transform. This element is clearly demonstrated in the works of Iolo in the manner by which he describes the quality of the symbol.

At face value they appear as three simple strikes to represent various stations of the sun and are erroneously attributed the title of Awen. However, the symbol is not the Awen per se, but rather an indication of its quality: sound. Iolo elaborates that, upon pronouncing the name of God, Menw, or the intellect and mind, understood that it

> was on hearing the sound of the voice, which had in it the kind of utterance of three notes, that he obtained the three letters, and

---

199   Williams, *The Barddas of Iolo Morganwg*, 67.

knew the sign that was suitable to one and other of them…Thus was the voice, that was heard, placed on record in the symbol, and meaning attached to each of the three notes:—the sense of O was given to the first column, sense of I to the second or middle column, and the sense of W to the thirds, whence the word OIW. That is to say, it was by means of this word that God declared his existence, life, knowledge, power, eternity and universality.[200]

What Iolo is articulating is that each column represents a letter, which in turn carries a sound, primarily the vowel sounds O, I, and W, pronounced Oh, Ee, and Oo. In combination they represent a word that he attributed to the name of the creative force of the universe itself. Inevitably, the only concept that Iolo had for this overarching power was that of the Christian god, and throughout his work he references this deity, and yet he does so in a way that subtly implies that he delighted in other non-Christian philosophies. Iolo was well-versed in world religions and occult traditions, and it is likely that his concept of the divine did not conform to the status quo, yet he hid his understanding of the divine within acceptable terminology. To those of the modern occult movements this can be problematic, for it can be incredibly difficult to see past the seemingly Christianised references. And yet we must, for in doing so, we can glimpse a mystery beneath the terminology indicative of his time spent between the worlds and in his intellectual study of other systems.

Combined, the vowel sounds O, I, and W represent the creative energy of the universe, by whichever name one is comfortable using: Great Spirit, God, Goddess, the One, the All. Iolo consistently used the Welsh term for God, Duw, albeit his definition of that term was not wholly explained. Instead he explored what can be seen in his work as the seven divisions of the divine, each one afforded a name and a task and a purpose. They express a pantheistic ideology rather than a strictly monotheistic principle. And through all this coursed the song of Awen, being manifest in all things in existence—the sea, the land, the earth itself, and the air around and within it. All of the

---

200   Williams, *The Barddas of Iolo Morganwg*, 19.

visible and invisibles of the world, whether on the earth or in the sky, all the worlds, of all the celestials and terrestrials, every single intellectual being and existence, everything animate and inanimate sings inwardly of the Awen.[201] The thing we have in common with every single expression of existence in our universe is the song of Awen. The Awen is attracted to itself, so when sung, the Awen cannot help but sing in unison with the voice of the singer. We have already learnt that the Awen is a sound, and Iolo perpetuated this principle. But one could ask, why? What for? Why was Iolo compelled to explore new ideas about the Awen?

In all likelihood he was responding on several levels to the huge socio-political and cultural climate at the time. He lived in a melting pot of ideas, in an enlightened age. The majority of his time was spent between the worlds in a narcotic-induced haze, and whilst I do not condone the use of narcotics for spiritual illumination, it is certainly a tool that has been used and continues to be used. In my musings, I fancy that Iolo spent more time between the worlds and in the currents of Awen than he did in the mundane. Whilst unable to conceptualise a world wherein the divine feminine existed as an element of worship or reverence, his poetic works expressed a longing for the muse of Awen. There is no evidence to suggest that he identified this muse with the name of Cerridwen, but perhaps she is there, just hiding beneath the surface of late eighteenth-century peculiarities. It is tempting with all his talk of Awen and Taliesin that his "Ode to the British Muse" certainly invokes a spirit that emulates that of Cerridwen:

> Muse of Britannia's favour'd land,
> Still blooming in immortal youth,
> O! Let me join thy glorious band,
> Thou guardian of celestial truth.
> Enthron'd amid the source of light,
> In wisdom's robe divinely bright,
> Unveil to me thy peerless charms,
> Whilst, Walia's rural shades along,

---

201 Williams, *The Barddas of Iolo Morganwg*, 23.

The native grandeur of thy song,
My soul intensely warms.[202]

Iolo longed for a world that was deeply inspired and evocative of ancient secrets; perhaps those romantic notions made his often-harsh reality an easier pill to swallow. Regardless of his motivations and his achievements, which were in all reality not recognised during his lifetime, his seeds of Awen have flourished into a new tree of tradition that captures some of the qualities of the ancient bardic traditions. Without a doubt, the Celtic-inspired Pagan traditions of the twentieth and twenty-first century contain blossoms and leaves that have grown from the seeds that he planted over 250 years ago. His austere, poverty-stricken existence was made bearable by his profound imagination and his daily sojourns to laudanum-filled worlds between worlds, where the current of the Awen ran uninhibited by the sensibilities of the ordinary world.

---

202   Williams, *Poems Lyric and Pastoral*, 1–2.

26

The Song of the Awen

In the modern bardic tradition of Wales, and expanding on the ideas initially explored by Iolo Morganwg, the symbol of the Awen carries a name, and one which beautifully and profoundly articulates its nature. Now herein lies one of the secrets of the Awen as it has evolved to fit and suit the needs of modernity. One of its secrets is held in the fact that the symbol is erroneously called the Awen, for it has an actual name—it is called Y Nod Cyfrin, simplistically translated as "the mystic mark." This title beautifully articulates the mystical nature of the Awen: it invokes the past and the secrets that the bards insisted they were privy to. It does all of this whilst being pertinently modern. It was important for the Awen to move on in modern terms, and it did so, for it continued to hold great meaning and relevance to the people of Wales.

In keeping with the various bardic examples explored earlier in this book, it was apparent that the ancient bards maintained that their skill had an element of secrecy to it. This sentiment continues to this day whereby the majority of New Age occult traditions that are initiatory in nature contain teachings that only those initiated are privy to. It is fitting that the Awen's trajectory bifurcated and took a new path into the new world. Whilst still a vital component of the current Welsh bardic tradition, the Awen has found its voice being sung within new traditions that would be unrecognisable to the early bards and inspirers. Its song can be heard far and wide, on every continent and falling from the lips of the new altars of Cerridwen.

But what is this song, and how do we sing it?

In almost every reference to the Awen in the bardic material, there is an allusion to a song, quite often described as being steadfast, pure, and strong. Its utterance can bring about incredible things and cause things to spring into being by power of its song. Through all this, we are informed by the early bards that it is Cerridwen's song that is the most dignified of them all, perhaps indicative of her position as primary conduit for the power of the Awen. So how do we sing it, and what, if anything, will that actually do to the singer?

I have pressed upon you, I hope, the necessity for the internalisation of the Awen so that one can move steadily and surely into its currents and feel its power blow through you. Thus far we have envisioned the origin of the Awen and the triskele that represents the three aspects of the Awen. We then moved onto the power of rhyme, lyric, metre, and the magic of sound that originates from the breath of the ancestors themselves. But there is a third component that is now necessary for us to internalise and experience, which is the flow of Awen's song through us in a manner that brings the previous exercises together and allows us to feel and be the Awen as it blows through this world. But before we do this, we must explore the quality of the song itself.

Thus far, you will understand the complexity held within that tiny four-letter word *Awen*, and that it encapsulates will, spirit, breath, holiness, soul, song, etc., etc. We have also learnt that everything in the universe sings the Awen inwardly and in praise of itself. Iolo consciously chose vowel sounds to capture the energy of the song as it courses through our world, and it is particularly relevant to our experience here on this planet.

Vowel sounds perfectly capture the vitality of breath. Whenever we sing them, they are carried exquisitely on waves of breath in a manner that is quite different to consonants. The function of a consonant is to shut or change the shape of the airways and almost clap their sound into existence. A vowel will continue for as long as the breath is capable of directing it. Some of the softer consonants, for instance an N or an M sound, do not harshly snap the airways shut, but they certainly moderate and affect the quality of the air as it flows from your lungs. It is for this reason that the singing of the word Awen alone is peculiar and often jarring to a native Welsh person, for we are subtly programmed to understand that the Awen is an adjective to describe a sound—it is not the sound per se, but a bridge that crosses the chasm of sound. The N sound at the end of Awen is particularly odd to a native tongue when in the process of chanting the word alone. Whilst the concept of the sound being vowels is a new articulation, attributed mostly to Iolo Morganwg, it certainly invokes the bardic tradition and their philosophy of the Awen in a beautiful and magical manner. We are no longer privy to all the secrets of the old bards. What Iolo did was create new secrets based on his inspiration—one might even suggest that a process of channelling was involved in his work.

If we consider that the most appropriate meaning for the word Awen is blessed or holy breath, we can play with this in a way that can bring about profound connection and transformation. If you will indulge me, I would like for you to now sing the vowel sound O, pronounced like "oh." Take a deep inbreath, and on the outbreath vocalise the vowel loudly. Do this in any key that is comfortable, but make it musical, make it a glorious sound. Acknowledge a point within the sound where you are aware of the breath nearing its end, and then make the sound for a hard C as in *cat*. Do this now...

Ohhhhhhhhhhhhhhhh.........C.

You will note that the C is particularly jarring within the glorious vowel sound, as the shape of the mid portion of your mouth and tongue, and in particular the topmost part of your throat around the point of your epiglottis, changes dramatically. Your airway is snapped shut, preventing breath from escaping your lungs. Consonantal sounds do not employ the breath in the same manner as vowels, and it is vowel sounds in particular that connect us to the divine quality of breath.

In Western languages, the words for breath, spirit, and soul are intimately connected. The word "spirit" evolved from the Latin word *spiritus*, meaning vital breath. Both the Latin words for soul and spirit, *anima* and *animus*, are derived from the word *anemo*, meaning breath or wind. In Hebrew, the term for wind and breath, *ruach*, is also taken to mean spirit.[203] In the Welsh language, the term *ysbryd*, meaning spirit, also implies breath.

When we open our mouths and sing, the sound that is produced is audible breath; it carries within it the essence of spirit. Here, within the closed circuit of our blue planet, sound has a unique quality indicative of the properties of our world. We have an atmosphere unlike any other planet in our solar system, and whilst there may well exist other worlds with similar atmospheres to our own, for us, here, on Earth, the quality of sound produced by breath is unique to this experience.

We can survive without food or water for extended periods of time, but without breath we die within the space of a few short minutes. Robert Gass describes the power of breath as "the immediate, palpable projection of our life force into the world."[204] The mysteries of life itself are hidden in the power of breath, and through breath we are able to express our experience of being present in this world. Life and consciousness are connected by the power of breath. Our ability to be inspirational is equally connected to breath, derived from the Latin *inspirare*, meaning to blow into or breathe upon, or the breathing of life into creative pursuits.

Whilst Awen can mean blessed and holy breath, the message here is that your breath is equally as holy and blessed. And when you use your breath with intention and move into the currents of Awen, everything around you will be compelled to rise up and sing in unison, for everything sings the Awen inwardly. It is by this method that we teach our students of Druidry how one communicates and connects with our nonhuman kin. It is all very well to say

---

203 Gass, *Chanting*, 53–54.
204 Ibid., 53.

that Druids communicate or speak with trees or witches speak to plants, but what does that actually mean?

Finding a Voice

I remember the very first time I came across that concept in my early days of exploring Paganism. I was left a little bewildered and confused, and I could not help but feel somewhat inferior to my peers because I could not hear the trees speak to me. I was quite familiar with the tasks that Cerridwen undertook in gathering the herbs and plants of the land to brew the Awen, and it was made clear by my earlier peers that it was her ability to communicate with the plant kingdom that enabled her to select the appropriate allies. This made the entire situation quite dreadful. Why could I not hear the plant kingdom speak? Trees do not have vocal cords, and neither do they have ears; their entire nerve systems are different to ours, so how on earth does one actually communicate with someone so different?

We do so by means of the song that we all share within us: the song of Awen.

I recall quite vividly a workshop where I was given the task to go and speak to a tree and glean any wisdom from it or anything indicative of communication. I failed miserably. I must have sat with the tree for over an hour and felt nothing other than ridiculous—there were no voices, audible or otherwise, just a beautiful tree. On returning to the class, I was staggered to hear others claiming to have had full-blown conversations with their trees. They reeled off whole lists of properties and impressions, none of which I had had any sense of whatsoever. I left feeling that I had failed on my first tentative steps into Paganism. How could I be a Pagan if I couldn't speak to trees?

It took one sentence from someone completely unrelated to trees or Paganism to transform the way I perceived communication. It was a Welsh language documentary about bardism, and within it, one of the interviewees casually said that regardless of how different we may perceive ourselves to be from any other life form, we all have one thing common: we all sing the song of Awen. The Awen's music is the same in everyone and everything, it is the lyrics that differ according to one's experience. The resulting song is unique, and it is the tool by which the Awen and, in turn, the universe experiences itself through the countless windows of expression. So I took to thinking that if I contain the music of Awen, then so would that rowan tree I was desperately attempting to communicate with. The lyrics, of course, would be different, mine based on the fact that I am a human being and the tree, that of being a rowan, or mountain ash. But we have something in common, a shared musicality.

But how on earth would I hear her song? It still didn't make a lot of sense to me. I needed to do something that would bridge that logical side of my mind with the subtle, invisible spectrum. And the answer to that was to sing.

What Iolo Morganwg inadvertently offered was a method by which one could connect to everything in existence, by acknowledging and then expressing a commonality that we share with all things: sound. This statement will by now not seem at all new or peculiar to you, having read many examples of this state of all-being and all-knowing in the various poems I have shared from the mouthpiece of Taliesin. We too can participate in this, and the method for doing just that is, in essence, quite simple, although it will require some effort on your part to maintain a consistency of song.

EXERCISE

Singing the Awen

Play with the sound quality of the three vowels that we explored earlier, designated by the letters O, I, and W.

Worry not about the order in which they are presented to you; you may sing them in any order that you like, changing that order as often as you feel. It is the sound that matters, not the order in which they are placed. Armed with the sounds themselves and the knowledge of the power of sound and the vitality of breath, take yourself to meet a nonhuman being. It may be a plant on a windowsill of your home or a tree in a park or a garden, it may be a babbling brook or a raging waterfall. You decide. Whilst your chosen kin may well not be in possession of vocal cords, they interact with the atmosphere around them nonetheless. A tree and a plant breathe in a similar fashion to you; a body of water evaporates and rises into the breath of sky to condense and eventually fall back to earth. All things interact with their environment to a lesser or greater extent, and all things sing. For the purpose of this exploration, I shall focus on our subject being a tree.

Key to this exercise is to focus only on the quality of the sound and not on forcing any kind of communication. If you attempt to force communication, you will be subjected to the influence of your assumptions and expectations. It is best not to have any at all. Just sing the sounds. There is no need to close your eyes, but instead focus on your chosen new friend and sing to them. And keep on singing to them. Aim to spend at least 45 minutes to one full hour singing.

Consequently, several things will happen on a number of levels. On a physiological level, something particularly magical happens within the systems of your body. Song and singing profoundly affects almost all of our senses, and the vibratory quality of the sound is particularly affecting, having direct action on the cells of your body.

Regardless of whether or not you consider yourself a good, poor, or adequate singer, the energetic power of your voice will directly affect you and all things within energetic reach. The power of singing will release a torrent of hormones through your body, particularly if you keep at it consistently for a decent duration of time. It is within this task that we begin to feel the tantalising magic of mind, body, and spirit working in harmony, neither separate from the other but interwoven like fine fabric.

Flooding through your body will be the hormone oxytocin, also known as the cuddle hormone for its ability in facilitating feelings of bonding and connectedness. It is particularly present during singing and profoundly present in group singing. In small group-controlled tests, blood drawn before singing and after showed an increase in oxytocin levels and a decrease in the stress-inducing compound adrenocorticotrophic hormone.[205] In addition,

---

205 Study published online by the US National Library of Medicine, www.ncbi.nlm.nih
.org/pubmed/16362985.

blood levels in tested individuals demonstrated elevated levels of the secretory hormone immunoglobin A, which is significant in developing robust and effective immune systems. The implication here is that singing strengthens your immunity.

These profound physiological changes are not restricted or limited to the physiology of the singer alone; they directly affect anyone or anything that is receptive of the sound waves produced. In human beings, hormone levels can be profoundly affected by the act of listening. There are numerous studies available in the public domain demonstrating that plants possess mechano-sensory machinery that enable them to produce and perceive sound in order to make sense of their environment. Whilst no sensory organ has been identified in the plant kingdom, the effects of sound upon our plant kin has been well attested and is generally accepted within the scientific community.[206]

Whilst research in this area is not as yet advanced, there is evidence to demonstrate that tree roots produce crackling sounds at a consistent frequency of 220 hertz that causes the tips of the roots of other trees and plants around them to orientate themselves in the direction of the sound.[207] Mystics and occultists would no doubt be unsurprised by these recent findings. However, UPG aside, there is enough scientific evidence to suggest that our kin in the plant kingdom can sense, produce, and be affected by sounds.

Whilst the physiology of singer and recipient is affected, so is the physical body in its entirety, which responds reciprocally. Local physical structures, i.e., the body of the singer and the body of the tree, are influenced by the combined physiological forces that act within and upon them. These result in several beneficial influences on the body, which can lead to a general sense of well-being and connectedness. The third principle is that of the spiritual and the unquantifiable; whilst this cannot be subjected to laboratory testing, the results are tangible. It is this principle that allows for a sense of communication to seep through logic and rationality. It is within this spiritual space

---

206   See study published online by the Frontiers Institute, www.fronitiersin.org/
        articles/10.3389/fpls.2018.00025/full.
207   Wohlleben, *The Hidden Life of Trees*, 12–13.

that usually, in hindsight, one gleans a sense of having intimately been in the presence of another individual.

When one's conscious awareness is engaged in an act of singing, it allows for the mind to wander unimpeded by its sometimes restrictive sensibilities. The key to this exercise is to not aim for conversation, but to strive for connectedness by the quality we have in common—sound. The hormones that rush about your body will activate your emotions in ways that are quite different to your ordinary experience, and many of them are the same hormones that you release during sexual engagement. There is ecstasy, contentment, connection, rapture, and joy all paradoxically vying for your attention, and the same can be said for the tree. Do not force conversation, but engage in connection.

The Awen floods through the sound of your voice, and in turn, the tree cannot help but raise its song to meet that of yours. It is compelled to do so. The Awen is attracted to itself.

Physicality, physiology, and the spirit are all engaged in this exercise, and now that we have explored the nature of what is happening during the act of singing the Awen, we can begin.

The various steps of the above exercise are recapped thus:

1. Having chosen a location, take yourself to it.

2. Set aside 45–60 minutes for this exercise.

3. Centre yourself by taking three breaths with the land, sea, and sky.

4. Call to Cerridwen to assist you, and state your intention.

5. Introduce yourself to your chosen plant kingdom ally.

6. Begin to sing the vowel sounds.

7. Allow the session to peacefully conclude, and offer thanks before departing.

This exercise shifts one's perspective from how we usually communicate to the potential of new methods of communication. Record how the exercise made you feel and what impressions you gleaned by performing it.

It would help if you did this as a creative task, allowing the subtlety of com-munication to bleed through the experience.

The Awen is active, and to sense its blowing through us, we must actively vocalise and energetically move into its power. We live on a unique world, a place where expression is facilitated by the atmosphere that surrounds and imbibes us. Breath is the bridge between the density of the physical and the lightness of spirit.

27

Cerridwen, Annwfn, and the Andedion

In the tradition of the Anglesey Druid Order, the gods are categorised as the powers of four distinct realms of existence. The first three, land, sea, and sky, are indicative of the natural realms of the apparent world and the gods that empower these regions. They are namely the House of Llŷr (ocean), the House of Dôn (land), and the House of Beli Mawr (sky). Whilst these embody a macrocosmic value in the same manner that we do, their apparent qualities will end when our world is destroyed by the swelling of our sun. This gives the gods of our tradition a delicious finite value as expressions of our apparent world. It is a quality that we have in common with them. Whilst we accept that they have an immortal aspect or spiritual element, just like we do, they are also informed and giving expression by the idiosyncratic elements of this world. The fourth category, the House of Annwfn,[208] are in our tradition referred to as the Andedion, and they are quite different.

---

208   Annwfn is also commonly spelled Annwn and is a term given to the indigenous Celtic otherworld.

Our experience with the deities of land, sea, and sky are a part of our everyday secular and spiritual pursuits and activities. We are accustomed to working with and connecting to the spirits that are said to inhabit the natural world. They reflect qualities and properties inherent within the apparent world, and very often many of these powers are directly associated with natural phenomena or natural forces. Others appear to have their own agenda and agency. Rivers, hills, and mountains might be perceived as having characteristics of the divine and be named as such, for these tutelary landscapes take on a personality. Every aspect of living expression on our planet can be conceptualised as a microcosm containing sympathies and correspondences that connect the lower planes of existence to that of the higher—as above, so below, a common philosophy in occulture.[209]

However, the fourth category of the Andedion is directly associated with what is commonly referred to as the indigenous Celtic otherworld, and Cerridwen ranks as a member of this caste of beings. It is often and erroneously spelled Annwn. In its original form, Annwfn is more correct and captures the mystery held within the word. Several of the poems that allude to or name Cerridwen directly also contain within them references to Annwfn. Before I commence with the reminder of this discourse, it is apt to explore some of the function of what Annwfn is, where it might be located, and any associations Cerridwen has with it.

The earlier exercises of this book will have demonstrated that the cauldron can be seen as a metaphor for the holding properties of the universe and of inspiration, transformation, creation, and Awen. It has become evident to us that the Awen and its font are under the guardianship of Cerridwen, for it is she that by some hidden means brings the Awen into our world for its expression by her bards. Therefore, if Cerridwen is the guardian of these forces, and Taliesin claims that it lies in the deep (*dwfn*), it is logical to assume that Cerridwen is also associated with or familiar with the realm of Annwfn, the indigenous Celtic otherworld. However, the term "otherworld" must be addressed, for I fear that the word is loaded with misconceptions.

---

209   Radin, *Real Magic*, 60.

In translation, it is tempting to identify Annwfn as either an otherworld or an underworld. The latter has infernal associations and is loaded with Christianised imagery of a hell-like dimension, whereas the former term brings to mind a land or kingdom of the dead. Neither is wholly correct. Within the descriptions of Annwfn, the dead are blatantly absent. Whilst populated with human-like beings, their abilities appear heightened from ours, and yet they portray vulnerabilities that we do not possess or that humans can easily overcome. The inhabitants of Annwfn can converse with the humans of our world and seemingly interact with our dimension with relative ease. Unlike the ideas of the lands of the dead, humans are able to access Annwfn and also leave at their own volition, a quality not so readily available to the spirits of the dead. Likewise, the inhabitants of Annwfn do not appear as spirits but as biological beings that the races of our world, human and animal, can interact with and, in many instances, mate and breed with. The inhabitants of Annwfn also age, die, and can be killed, albeit at a pace that is different to our world. One of the kings of Annwfn, Gwyn ap Nudd, is said to ride out on the eve of Calan Gaeaf (Hallowe'en) and collect the souls of the dead. Whilst he assumes a psychopompic role, it is not stated that those souls are taken to Annwfn, and whilst those who reside in Annwfn have some abilities and powers that defy the physics of our reality, they are not the spirits of disembodied, deceased human beings.

The word Annwfn has two significant meanings.

Annwfn consists of two syllables, an and the mutation of dwfn (wfn). The "an" prefix is fickle; as an intensifying prefix, it offers a suggestion that the location of the "dwfn," which itself can be taken to mean the deep and also the world, is impossibly deep and would be translated as "the very deep place." However, as a negating prefix, the meaning is quite different: an + dwfn, in this case taken to mean the world, would be rendered in English as "the not world." Essentially, Annwfn can be one of two things: not this world or the impossibly deep.

The term Annwfn not only has a double meaning, it is also bilocated, meaning it appears to have two aspects to it, one being an "otherworldly" landscape that is separate to the reality that we inhabit, whilst the other is located within us, essentially as our "deepness." And within that deepness, we are connected to the primordial forces that brought everything into existence. Annwfn within and Annwfn without, meaning we may reach inwards to find and connect with the forces of Annwfn.

Within the deep place, we perceive the existence of beings or deities that bring into manifestation the potential of Annwfn, the underlying energetic principle that breathes life into our universe. They do so in order to direct that potential in a form that maintains its structure, albeit for a limited time. They act as facilitators whereby we can grasp the unmanifest in a manner that does not result in insanity. To delve into the cauldron of potential with no structure to hold that experience, with no point of reference, would tear our perceptive abilities into a billion pieces. The vast, unknowable nature of Annwfn is embodied in the qualities of the Andedion, who help us negotiate the pools of eternity without being undone by the experience.

In its other guise as "not this world," the physical location of a realm called Annwfn can be imagined as a world that inhabits another universe that is not our own. And yet these universes, like a child's soap bubbles in a fairground, bump into one another, and at these junctions one can directly access that other realm, and likewise. My Welsh ancestors conceived and continue to believe that liminal places such as hills, streams, caves, and groves hold the potential for accessing other worlds, and at these locations two worlds can collide.

Our reference for the term Andedion comes from our siblings in ancient Gaul, found on lead tablets, the most famous being the Tablet of Chamalîeres, which says:

> *Andedion uediiumi diiiuion risu naritu Maponon, Aruernatin: lotites sni eooic sos brixtia Anderon.*
>
> *I beseech the Andedion, the divine Maponos Avernatis, by means of this magic tablet: quicken those names below by the magic of the underworld spirits.*[210]

---

210   Koch, *The Celtic Heroic Age*, 2–3.

According to scholar Will Parker, the second word on the tablet, uediiumi, is related to the Welsh word gweddio, meaning to pray or invoke. It appears that the creator of the tablet is imploring the assistance of a caste of spirits identified as the Andedion to assist in their magic. Usually translated as the "underworld gods" or the "infernal ones," the etymology of Andedion and its cognates in both Welsh and Irish imply that the term was used to refer to gods of the deep, or the "not world," synonymous with the Welsh Annwfn.[211] It appears that the caste of gods collectively assigned the term Andedion were a group of supernatural entities in their own right, with their own agenda, and do not exist within the physical restrictions and limitations of our universe.

Tegid Foel, Cerridwen, Gwyn ap Nudd, Rhiannon, and a host of other archetypes stand at this position, poised between the apparent world and its realms of land and sea and sky. They funnel the energies of the unknowable universe into a form by which we can understand and move into relationship with. They are, just as their home is described, within, upon, and inside, interwoven, neither in our world nor fully in the other, but somewhere between. Guardians of Annwfn.

In this position Cerridwen is the conduit by which we can break down the mysteries into a form that is more readily digestible by the human mind, without overwhelming us to the point of insanity. It is she and her great cauldron that stabilises the inspirational forces of the universe long enough for them to come into being and to be held in experience by you and, by proxy, the universe itself, for you are a window through which the universe perceives and experiences itself.

The Taliesin persona in its bardic expressions claims to reach into Annwfn to pull the potential of Awen from the deep by the power of his voice.

Yr Awen a ganaf, o dwfn y dygaf.

The Awen I sing, from the deep I bring it.

---

211   Parker, *The Four Branches of the Mabinogi*, 644.

To recap:

- Annwfn is bilocated.

- It exists as its own reality, but it is accessible to this world and vice versa.

- It exists as the deep place, the creative furnace that brings our universe and perhaps others into being.

- As the deep place, we can access it internally through the deep spaces within us that connect us to all things.

- The currents of Awen originate in the deep Annwfn.

- A caste of beings / deities are assigned as the directors of its forces and are afforded the rank of Andedion.

28

Cerridwen and the Bardic Mysteries

The skills of bardism are a necessary requirement for adherents of Cerridwen, for there is an aspect of her nature that loves and adores the play of words and the beauty of sound and its transformative power. Cerridwen is the prototypic Chief Bard: she nurtures and encourages her Plant to develop and promulgate their abilities until their brows glow brightly. As Mam yr Awen, her role as caring mother is clear within the bardic tradition, and yet her strict approach is quite apparent. She is not a parent that allows her children to literally get away with anything.

Cerridwen forms the centre of the bardic tradition, and, as such, her *cadair* (chair) is the best of them, and when they come to be judged, no other chair will equal hers. Those words sing out from the stanzas of the "Cadair Cerridwen" poem, as we saw earlier, and whilst we explored that poem in some depth, there is yet more mystery that we may glean from it.

An element of the excellency of her chair can be seen within the modern Welsh bardic tradition and the competitions of the National Eisteddfod, the main prize of which is the chair, a physical chair made of wood that is local to the location of the annual Eisteddfod. The bards who submit their works to be examined by the Gorsedd of bards are essentially judged for their competency and ability to express the Awen. What is of note is that even Cerridwen's chair was subject to a form of examination and judgement, albeit we are not informed who, or perhaps what, will be judging. This critical evaluation of the skills of the bard is not performed so that just reward or punishment is dished out to the bard, but to evaluate the quality of the Awen that is being received and transmitted. The fact that Cerridwen claims that her own chair is judged informs her Plant that even the quality of her expressive Awen is subject to examination, and that we must not fear criticism or judgement, but we must strive for excellence and purity of Awen.

The Awen can be abused, and inspiration can be used for ulterior motives that do not have the creative processes of the Awen at their heart. Many in positions of power can and will abuse that power for their own needs. Others can appear so inspired and so great that they may present as aloof and standoffish, unquestionable and unchallenged. Cerridwen's lessons for her bards, her Plant, is to always be open to challenge, be confident and radiant, and trust the Awen and your connection to it to bring about a great chair so that when yours is judged, it will be seen as the best of them.

But what of this elusive chair—what is it and what does it do? As usual, the Welsh word for chair, cadair, has several layers of meaning, and pertinent to this discourse, there are three of particular note. On one hand the term cadair can imply an actual physical chair, usually constructed of wood and used for sitting. The second meaning brings the bardic tradition into light, for the chair is the symbol of the pencerdd, or chaired bard of the National Eisteddfod of Wales. The *pencerdd*, meaning "chief crafter of song and poetry," once chaired within the structure of the Gorsedd of bards becomes the *prif fardd*, the Chief Bard.

In this position, the bard is ritually subjected to a change of identity and undergoes a complex ritual of transformation. In his or her role as the prif fardd, they lose their name and are identified by their bardic name. In essence, the bard is now the epitome of the distillation of Awen that has bubbled up through the collective of bards to be expressed in them. For the remaining year they will be identified as the nation's Chief Bard, but on a magical level, with the physical chair in their possession, they are immortalised, forever to be identified as prifardd, Chief Bard. They become subjects of legend and myth; they are revered and honoured by the people as the outward expression of Awen in this world. In old customs, before the advent of the annual physical chair as a prize and status symbol, the Chief Bard would wear a miniature silver chair upon the garments of their left shoulder, thus enabling them to be identified as such. Upon the death of the chaired bard, the physical chair will remain, and indeed, several of these ancient chairs continue to exist as museum pieces, further immortalising the bard in the imagination of the people.

The grandeur of the National Eisteddfod rituals is a visual treat and a treasure of our culture, but this is not the only system that acknowledges the power of the bard. Throughout the world, the new bards in modern Pagan Druid circles, groves, and orders will present their Awen to that group and then be judged. The one deemed most inspired is awarded the title of Chief Bard for the forthcoming year. The judging is often emotive, taking great account of how the bard made the judges feel inspired. To many outside of the cultural bardic continuum of Wales, the element of judging can seem harsh and perhaps unnecessary. But one must remember that the Awen is a gift, and the Chief Bard is the physical representation of the power of Awen within the organised structure of a bardic circle, grove, order, or coven. They act as a reminder of the creative and transformative forces of Awen. They serve to epitomise Cerridwen's qualities as prototypic Chief Bard and her expectation that her children should be learned and excellent. They bring things into being; they serve as educators and inspirers. They exist today as they have done for countless centuries.

A good and consistent example of this is performed annually by the Druids of the Anderida Gorsedd in the English southern county of East Sussex.[212] The Anderida Gorsedd, and many other examples, perfectly capture

---

212   See list of their Chief Bards on their website www.anderidagorsedd
     .org/the-bardic-chair/.

the quality and necessity of the bard as central to the structure of their spiritual expression. In many cases, modern Pagan circles and groves who acknowledge a Chief Bard may not be able to articulate why this came about, with several claiming that something about it simply "feels right." Inadvertently they are emulating and mimicking a ritual that is centuries old and perhaps over two millennia in the making. However, what they are emulating is reminiscent of the practises of the Welsh bardic tradition, with words and terminology directly inspired from that system. In my musings, this gives further credence to the tenacity of the spirit of Cerridwen in finding those who would be the seeds of Awen in the world.

The third meaning for the term cadair is the principle of bardic metre and the quality of sound in verse, an attribute that we have extensively explored. One small word not only expresses a myriad of meanings, but is intimately connected to the tradition that ensured Cerridwen's survival into the future.[213]

But what of the present? What mystery and meaning can we glean from this today?

The bards, as Plant Cerridwen, emulate her function as the prototypic Chief Bard, and now that you have explored and experienced what it means to move into the centre and swim in the currents of the narrative, enchanted, and prophetic spirits, you will have a sense of the power of the centre. The cadair (chair) represents the still point at the centre of the universe where the bard is witness to creation. The triskele of the great song of Awen spins out from that position. With their brows radiant and gleaming, the bard sings and makes magic. In this position the bard loses their personal human names and is gifted with a bardic name; often this name will be discovered by the bard itself or perhaps channelled. At other times the name is given to them by another bard. This magical name is not a new concept to modern Pagan practitioners, where the adopting of pseudonyms that reflect an inner quality or an alliance is quite common. The bardic tradition demonstrates a

---

213   Bevan, *Geiriadur Prifysgol Cymru*, 375.

consistency of this practise over centuries of time, indicating a sense that this process was important.

The taking of a bardic name is a sacred act that implies the bard has undergone profound transformation. It transcends the cult of personality and is indicative of a relationship that the bard has with their locale, their history, and heritage; they are not names plucked from the ether simply because they sound enigmatic or mysterious. The Chief or prominent bards of Wales do not have Facebook accounts under their bardic names, and yet the names are not a secret. They have profound meaning to the bards' expression of being the centre and the triskele spinning within them and the Awen that blows through them.

Before the world of social media, television, and the internet, one might never have discovered the personality that lay behind the bard, for it transcended the ego. Whilst to a degree the bards of the old world attained celebrity status, the actual persona remained mostly hidden. When one gets caught up in the ego, one becomes trapped in the mundane. We are liable to be ensnared by illusions when we fall into the belief that everything revolves around the ego. The bardic system prevented much of this by acknowledging the bard as one that had transcended personality and become a quality of the Awen collective. This sense of mystery and transcendence is the beating, expressive heart of the bardic tradition.

However, the element of transcendence requires an additional note, for in the twenty-first century, the Great Song of Awen has transcended the Welsh bardic tradition and can be seen around the world. In a time that is sensitive to issues of cultural appropriation, it is, I believe, imperative that one acknowledges and honours the seeds of the tradition that perpetuated the survival of Awen, Cerridwen, and bardic magic. As the children of Cerridwen, we have a responsibility to seed the future with Awen, and with that responsibility comes the ability to respond to changing times and a world that is facing newer challenges and crisis. The role of the bard in today's magical traditions is to instil in others the spirit of inspiration. Anger does not inspire, hatred and resentment do not inspire; in a disenchanted world, it is the role of the enchanters, the Plant Cerridwen, to transcend anger and powerless hatred to inspire through love, knowledge, and truth.

As a bard, your role is to sing the Awen into being and for others to be transformed by that connection. In a modern setting, whenever a Druid, a witch, or a practitioner by any other name stands in the centre of the circle and brings forth the Great Song of Awen, they are a bard. In the centre, their rightful position, they bring forth the song of Cerridwen and swirl the powers of the narrative, enchanted, and prophetic spirit into the circle. In rhyme, verse, or prose, the bard sings of that connection and kickstarts the process of magical transformation. A bard transcends modern titles and designations of roles and traditions, for bardism is a function: it is something that you actively do. A bard is the mouthpiece for the Awen, for Cerridwen; a bard is the radiant brow, the Tal-iesin. A Druid can work as a bard, and equally so can a witch, a warlock, and a priest or priestess of the divine. Regardless of what you define your spiritual path to be, the function of the bard and your position as one is a wondrous and magical addition to any system. It brings a spiritual heritage that is older than we can imagine into the circles of today. It is ancient and modern all at the same time.

It would be appropriate that I offer you my definition of how I identify as a bard as a way to exemplify that one does not need to be a great metred poet to be one. I am a writer. I express my connection to what inspires me in the hope that others are thus inspired. I occasionally sing, and whilst I am not the world's best singer by any stretch of the imagination, the act of singing, of writing, and of my other work as a comedian transforms my anxieties into joy. I do this consciously and with intent, holding my awareness of bardic magic in mind as I perform this work, whether as words on paper or face to face with other people. In turn, my hope is that the transformation happening within my being transforms others and helps turn their anxieties into joy. It is an act of magic.

Stirring the Cauldron

❖ ❖ ❖

RITUAL & PRACTISE

◆ ◆ ◆

This section is about finding expression in one's devotion to Cerridwen with invocations, offerings, and rituals to connect to the mother of Awen. We'll cover how to be inspired and how to maintain one's inspiration with daily practises, meditations, and inner journeys. Here you'll find practical techniques for being the Awen in the world and discovering new ways of moving into relationship with Cerridwen. We will use old and new songs to find our bardic voice and expression. Spells and charms are also included within the following pages.

Appropriate Appropriation

There is a strong possibility that you, reading this book right now, may not be Welsh or even have a connection to Wales. But somehow, by some means, you have found your way to reading this particular book. Cerridwen has found a way to seed within you the spark of Awen. You are the sum totality of all things that went before you, including the magic of the Welsh bardic tradition, which is held somewhere deep in the recesses of our species memory. By all means, learn a little Welsh or at least strive to understand the complexities of the history that brought Cerridwen into the light of twenty-first-century Paganism. Know that you are equally expressive of the Plant Cerridwen and have as much right to claim that title as any Welsh person.

Whilst it is important to develop honest, nonappropriative practise, do not ever think that you don't have the right to claim Cerridwen as a goddess that is valid for you. Our modern world has given her a new form of expression that is changing and inspiring the lives of countless individuals throughout the world. With songs, articles, poetry, books, art, statuary, rituals, and workshops crafted and offered in honour of Cerridwen, she is more alive today than she has been for the last four hundred years. It is the Plant

Cerridwen that have brought about this staggering attention to a spirit that for countless generations was only known to the people of Wales.

If the current Welsh bardic tradition does not perpetuate the mystical qualities of Cerridwen's crafts and her magical attributes, then she will find those who do. Having been limited to the experience of the Welsh bards for centuries, she now flies on the blessed breeze of Awen and is reaching out to a new and different world.

Developing a Nonappropriative Practise

We live in times where the sensitivities of cultural appropriation are at the fore of public concern, with people striving to be sensitive to other cultures whilst simultaneously feeling drawn to work with said cultures. The same can be said for the Welsh Celtic material. As a native Welsh person, I am fiercely proud of the efforts of my ancestors to preserve the wisdom that I am able to enjoy and work with today. These did not arise in a vacuum. The deities, spirits, archetypes, and constructs that occupy the vast landscape of Celtic-inspired Paganism today are products of the cultural cauldron that stirred them into being. It is important to honour the inspired source of the material without claiming possession of them. The issue of cultural appropriation has to some extent been blown out of all proportion to fulfil the sensitivities and agendas of individuals who feel that they are speaking on behalf of a culture that is not theirs and consequently laying down the law, as it were, as to what you should or should not be doing. Invariably the individuals who shout the loudest are not members of the culture or community to which they appear to be defending. Human beings have always borrowed ideas and new thoughts from one another, appropriating them into their own cultures and communities; not all appropriative traits are negative. Being inspired by a culture is quite different than claiming ownership of its culturally specific expressions.

The Welsh have long been vilified for just being Welsh, our language ridiculed, our rights compromised, our land taken from us. Yet with all this, we adore and take pride in discovering people who are moving into relationship with our language, our culture. Know also that we do not claim direct ownership of the material either; we have served only as its guardians. The roots of the material and the traditions that connect to it channel deep into the soil of Britain and were here long before the political delineation of Wales and its manmade border. There was a time when the myths, spirits, and gods by whatever names they were known were purely Brittonic, but today they are Welsh, preserved by and in that language. Appropriation is an issue, but there are ways to develop relationship with the wisdom of the Welsh Celts in manners that are honourable and have integrity of spirit. In simple terms, please don't steal our culture's treasures, but rather attempt, as hard as you can, to develop a genuine and sacred relationship with them. Remember, Cerridwen admires those who commit to learn.

To achieve this, I offer these suggestions:

- Honour the history of the people that preserved the material that you now work with.
- Honour the bards that strived to learn and perpetuate the material you can easily access today.
- Strive to understand the history, development, and evolution of the language. Our language is a complex and living thing that works on multiple levels of meaning.
- Learn a little of the language—you don't need to be fluent, but have a go. The sense of achievement from being able to offer a simple song of praise, a prayer, or an invocation will truly move you. Words have power.
- Honour the magic the bards applied to sound. Sound is a conduit of magical intent. Learn to pronounce words of power, especially names.
- Understand and honour that the Welsh Celtic material is also of the present as a living tradition; we are here today, right now. Speak to us, we don't bite, we can help. We love the fact our gods and goddesses and myths have spread their wings to inspire the world.
- Read the myths and engage with them as reflections of your internal mythological landscape.

- If you are able, pilgrimage to the lands that gave rise to the myths. Whilst Cerridwen is accessible throughout the world, there is something about being in her waters that will change you forever.
- Speak to local people about their homeland.
- Honour the Welsh bardic tradition and its strict, complex system of bardic metre by creating and vocalising prayers, incantations, and vocal offerings in rhyme. This takes effort and dedication.
- Honour the river of continuation that you step into when you take the above into account. Be a part of it, not just an observer.
- Develop sacred relationship that comes from a place of deep honour.
- Work from a platform of love, wisdom, and integrity.

Creating a Cerridwen Altar

Anyone who visits my home cannot help but notice the rather large space I have in my office that is dedicated to Cerridwen. It is an integral part of my home, my office, and my life as a Druid and a writer. It forms a focus point where I can stop each day and perform tasks, ceremonies, rituals, spells, and musings. Nobody sees any of these actions; they are mine to make in solitude and in the company of Cerridwen. My altar did not suddenly appear overnight, albeit there was a moment in time that I decided on its location. Instead it has grown organically as I have deepened my relationship with Cerridwen. My friends and family can read into the symbols, objects, and items on the altar and see the passage of my life within them. They can deduce meaning from the space because they are in relationship with me.

I cannot see Cerridwen physically—she does not possess a carbon-based physical body—so the manner by which I develop my relationship with her must somehow address these limitations. Nothing beats heading over to Bala for an afternoon spent at her lake, for there is a sense there that is different to anywhere else on earth—there is a tangibility to her presence in that location, as if the landscape holds a different kind of lyric. However, Bala is just over an hour from my home, and my schedule does not permit me the luxury of going there every day. Therefore, I have re-created a sense of what I feel at Bala at home, and it is centred around my altar. The space covers the top of two fairly wide bookcases placed side by side. In central position is a large and treasured statue of Cerridwen and her cauldron that I purchased from a sculptor friend in 2001. Included on the altar are objects, images, and items that remind me of something inspirational or somehow relay the qualities of Cerridwen. As I am wont to do, I placed the necessary components of an altar onto a triskele and drew up a list of appropriate items.

Representations

Colours   **Offerings**

In usual triskele fashion, the arms spiral out from the centre point, which I perceive as Cerridwen herself. The task then is to consider the three qualities stated and play with them in an exploratory fashion. Here is an extract from my own notes from 1999:

> **Representations:** Physical cauldron or images of cauldrons. Flowers and herbs that represent light and vitality. Images of greyhound, otter, hawk, hen, and pig. Natural seeds and grains. Bowl or chalice of water. Symbols or representations of the Awen. A small sieve. Foraging tools, sickle, etc. Poetry and songs on paper. Candles.
>
> **Offerings:** Lights. Songs. Fresh flowers. Candles and incense. Foraged seeds and berries.
>
> **Colours:** White, blue, silver, deep greens, red, black.

My personal Cerridwen altar also acts as my ancestor altar. I have depictions of some of Wales's most famous bards upon it, some of their words, and a copy of *The Facsimile and Text of the Book of Taliesin* sits upon it. In addition, I have included photographs of my own dead who have inspired me. When I perform my daily Awen affirmation and devotional to Cerridwen, my ancestors are also there to watch over me. They are a comforting presence in my creative life.

The key to an effective altar is relationship. It acts as the focal point in my home where I am able to capture a clear sense of Cerridwen's vitality. It has also been two decades in the making, so energetically it is imbibed with my wishes and prayers and intent. When you create your altar, keep the three qualities stated above in mind, and expand upon them to express the relationship you have with Cerridwen.

Cerridwen's Three Crafts

The old tales inform us that Cerridwen was learned in three crafts—but, as we previously explored, there is no way to fathom exactly what they were. In a modern sense, deducing what we can from the bardic tradition and utilising UPG, Cerridwen's crafts can be seen to reflect the three realms of land, sea, and sky as placed on a triskele. This does a number of things: it allows us to categorise her skillset in a manner that we can view objectively, it enables us to utilise a map of sorts to define what her crafts represent, and it deepens our relationship to her.

Depicted on a triskele, each arm corresponds to attributes that we have already explored and are familiar with, and I present them to you thus:

Cerridwen's Crafts in the Spiral of Sky

Equates to the narrative spirit. Here we can glean a sense of the power inherent in sound, song, poems, artwork, words, dance, and movement.

Cerridwen's Crafts in the Spiral of Sea

Equates to the prophetic spirit. In this spiral we see the skills of prophesy, divination, and the sight. The tools of this spiral may be Ogham staves, tarot and oracle cards, palmistry, astrology, etc.

Cerridwen's Crafts in the Spiral of Land

This spiral equates with the enchanted spirit. Here we encounter crafts of the materials of the earth and spellcasting using tools and equipment such as candles, poppets, talismans, wands, swords, and sacred knives.

The Spiral of Sky—Bardism

**The Spiral of Land—
Swyn/Spellcasting**

**The Spiral of Sea—
Prophesy & Divination**

Draw the above triskele in a journal or notepad and consider your skills in each category. Make a list beneath each triskele designation that highlights your skillset.

- How do they express themselves in your life and spiritual practise?
- How do they contribute to and inspire your community?

Devote yourself to the learned qualities of Cerridwen by choosing one subject to study intensely for an entire year. Make this an offering to Cerridwen. Begin by choosing a point in the year (most useful would be a seasonal festival) and aim to study until the festival returns the following year.

A CONTEMPLATIVE JOURNEY OF INITIATION

Becoming Gwion Bach, Part 1

Diversity of opinion about the mythologies shows that the work at hand is continuously renewed and made current, complex, and vital. The allegory of initiation within the tale of Cerridwen remains static if one does not engage with it on a profoundly personal level. In order to bring the tale into motion, we must develop a relationship with it. Recall the earlier references to Ifor Williams's claim that the later tale of Cerridwen and the chase with Gwion Bach is key to understanding the mysteries. That key is engagement with the material as an inherent aspect and experience of your internal mythological landscape. The most effective way of doing this is by perceiving the story as something that is happening to you and then ritualising it.

Taking this in mind, begin the process by meditating and rewriting the tale of Cerridwen from the experience of yourself in the position of Gwion

Bach, the initiate. In essence, this must be an experience that you perform alone; if the Celtic scholars are correct, the name Gwion translates as supernatural venom.[214] Collateral damage from attempting to ride the tailcoats of somebody else's experience will lead only to toxicity. The experience must be yours and yours alone. Within the tale, as the cauldron spills its contents, its venom kills a herd of horses drinking from a nearby river. Horses are common symbols of sovereignty in Celtic traditions. In this sequence we see the result of gate-crashing someone else's initiatory journey. The collateral damage from that incurs a blow to your inner sovereignty.

Placing yourself in central position as Gwion Bach, imagine the story unfolding around you. This is best done in a bardic manner: imagine it, then write about it—bring it to life in verse or song or art. In my experience of living the tale, I wrote about it in the first person. It is the creative expression of your engagement with the tale that will cement the experience as being yours. What new perspectives can you glean from this, from being central to the story? Consider the following statements before you reimagine the tale as your journey with Cerridwen and the cauldron of Awen.

- Gwion did not call to Cerridwen; it was she who summoned him to do her bidding, and he was not intended to receive the Awen. What does that mean to the narrative and to your experience of it? Why did the Awen choose someone for whom it was not intended?

- If Cerridwen called to Gwion, does this imply that deity seeks us out? Consider the nature of a "calling" and how that might be applicable to your experience.

- Gwion is paired with another figure in the tale, a blind man. This companion represents the function of liminality, of being betwixt and between. What is the nature of the relationship between Gwion and the blind man? Why is liminality necessary?

- Stirring and tending to a cauldron for a year and a day is an enormous commitment to the request of

---

214   Hamp, "Varia II," 149–154.

another being. What does this task tell you about the nature of commitment and devotion?

- Three blessed drops erupt from the cauldron to land on Gwion's thumb, which are then ingested. What would that moment of clear wisdom and knowledge feel like?

- Within the chase sequence, what can you learn from being in the guise of the animals? What mystery or message do they relay?

- Gwion is finally absorbed into the body of Cerridwen and transferred from her belly to her womb as a seed. What happens to Gwion during this bizarre conception?

Set aside a minimum of three hours to consider and reimagine the tale as your experience.

A RITUAL OF INITIATION

Becoming Gwion Bach, Part 2

Now that you have spent some time contemplating and reimagining the tale as an aspect of your own journey, it is time to shift this inner landscape into the apparent world. The ingredients necessary for the brewing of Awen can be seen as attributes of the individual. The correct recipe requires the distilling of one's inherent qualities for the Awen to reach a boil, and for this to occur one must journey into the dwfn, the depth of oneself. "Know thyself" is a fundamental tenet in any spiritual exploration.[215]

Preparation

For this ritual, you will need:

- your Cerridwen cauldron

- water

- a small round mirror, small enough to place at the bottom of your cauldron

- rice paper and a nontoxic or food-grade pen

---

215 For a comprehensive exploration of the neccessary ingredients as aspects of oneself, see my previous publication *From the Cauldron Born*.

- a disc of cardstock, paper, or any other suitable
  material upon which to draw a triskele (it should be
  large enough for your cauldron to stand upon)

Once more, reach for the triskele as a symbol to map out your inherent qualities that correspond to the realms of land, sea, and sky:

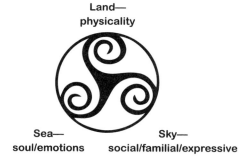

**Land—
physicality**

**Sea—
soul/emotions**   **Sky—
social/familial/expressive**

As part of the preparation, spend considerable time contemplating your qualities—the good, the not so good, and the indifferent—that correspond to each realm. For example, in land, consider your physical body, the manner by which you impact, influence, and affect your physical world. How does the physical world impact you? What support structures exist in your world, and how do you contribute to them?

In the realm of sea, consider the seat of your emotions and their impact on you and the world around you. Contemplate the manner by which you react to situations energetically. In this realm it is important to consider mystery, spirituality, and religion and that which nourishes and feeds your soul.

In sky, move onto considering all the expressive qualities that affect your life in social interactions, domesticity, and familial relations. Consider how and why you express yourself in certain situations and circumstances. This is the realm where we are judged the most and where we judge both ourselves and others.

Be honest with the above exploration, and keep in mind that the cauldron will not boil the food of a coward, therefore one must be painfully honest with oneself. Remember: this is her cauldron, and these are her rules. Consider this entire ritual as therapy in a cauldron, with Cerridwen being your therapist. Integrity, honesty, and intent will ensure the cauldron's boiling. At the conclusion of exploring each realm, devise a sigil to emulate those qualities. This sigil needs to be unique to you and your living.[216] Once you are content with the sigils, draw them on squares of rice paper. The paper should be small enough to lie fully on the water's surface within your cauldron, but not too large as to require folding.

On a piece of stiff cardstock or any other material that you are creatively called to utilise, draw, carve, or paint upon its surface a triskele. For this ritual, it is pertinent to consider the spiralling arms as your qualities of land, sea, and sky.

The Ritual

Create and delineate your chosen space as sacred in a manner by which you are accustomed. Position your cauldron in a manner by which you can easily and comfortably peer into it. Take three deep breaths, one with the land beneath you, one with the sky above you, and one with the seas that surround you. Call to Cerridwen to assist you, using words that are reflective of your relationship with her, and imagine a glowing light upon your forehead.

Take your triskele disc and position it beneath your cauldron, then recite these words or similar in verse:

> *Sea, sky, and land*
> *Foundations of the cauldron stand.*
> *Sky, land, and sea*
> *Imbibe within my virtues three.*
> *Land, sea, and sky*
> *My Awen bright from these shall fly.*

Take a moment to imagine your triskele spinning slowly, increasing in speed, gaining heat and warming the cauldron's belly.

---

216   For a modern guide to creating sigils, see Laura Tempest Zakroff's *Sigil Witchery*.

Next, take the mirror disc and gaze upon your reflection whilst you bring the sigils you have drawn to mind. Consider them one by one, then position the mirror inside your cauldron reflective side up.

Take your water and pour it into the cauldron to approximately three-fourths full. Know the mystery that there is no new water on earth, and water holds the memory of all waters that have ever existed. The memory of the ancestors, of Lake Bala, of the initial cauldron, of the river and sea upon which the potential Taliesin journeyed—all of this is contained within the water that you pour. Honour and acknowledge the power of water as a conduit of memory, the giver of life.

Position yourself so you can peer into the cauldron and see your own reflection deep in its belly. Water, shadow, and darkness will play on the clarity of your reflection, but gaze upon it intently. Your qualities warm the cauldron from beneath. From the dwfn, the depth of the cauldron, your shape and form arise, and yet it is obscure, unclear, but full of potential.

Now take the index finger of your dominant hand and begin to swirl the water within the cauldron. Take the sigil on rice paper that represents your qualities of land, consider them for a moment, and drop the paper onto the water's surface. Vocalise these qualities:

> I acknowledge, accept, and honour my qualities of land,
> which are _____. Cerridwen, Mam yr Awen,
> accept these, my offering to the cauldron. I am your
> child, I am light, I am radiant, I am Awen!

Stir the paper into the water and watch as it begins to dissolve, releasing the energy of your sigil into the water. Sing this englyn of distillation in multiples of three:

> *Cauldron fill, soon to spill,*
> *Awen bright shall burn.*
> *Here distil and until*
> *Awen's gifts I learn.*

Repeat the process with the sigil for the realms of sea and sky in the exact same manner as above. When all three paper sigils have been offered to the cauldron, contemplate the nature of what you have just performed.

- The cauldron is warmed from below by your qualities.
- The potential of your shape and form is held in the belly of the cauldron.
- The cauldron's brew is imbibed with your qualities from above.

You may continue to stir the cauldron with your index finger for as long as you please, but keep bringing to mind the image of Cerridwen and the light upon your forehead. Take to the englyn once more and continue to sing it for as long as you feel is required:

Cauldron fill, soon to spill,
Awen bright shall burn.
Here distil and until
Awen's gifts I learn.

As the energy of the ritual concludes naturally, peer into the cauldron once more. Watch the paper as it dissolves (this may take minutes to several hours to occur) and see your reflection within. This is your cauldron, these are your rules, this is your Awen. Your past, present, and future collide in its belly. Conclude this ritual by giving thanks to Cerridwen. The cauldron's cracking and releasing of the drops of Awen occurs at the point where your Awen spills from your imagination into your reality. In truth, the Awen's divine drops rise and fall continuously. At times when the Awen feels distant, repeat this ritual.

Conclude this ritual by giving thanks to Cerridwen.

Close your space in the manner by which you are accustomed.

You may retain the water and dissolved rice paper within the cauldron for as long as you deem necessary. When you feel it has done its work, discard the water sensibly and place the mirror on your Cerridwen altar. Repeat this ritual whenever you feel the need for deeper connection to the source of the Awen.

The individual steps for this ritual are recapped as follows:

1. Contemplate your qualities of land, sea, and sky.

2. Devise a sigil for each quality of land, sea, and sky.

3. Draw sigils onto individual squares of rice paper.

4. Create a triskele on cardstock or other material.

5. Create and delineate your space as sacred.

6. Take three breaths with the land, sea, and sky.

7. Call to Cerridwen to assist you.

8. With accompanying words, position the triskele beneath the cauldron.

9. Contemplate with the mirror and then place into the cauldron.

10. Add water to the cauldron.

11. Gaze into the cauldron's belly and see your reflection.

12. Whilst contemplating, swirl each rice paper sigil into the water accompanied by the song.

13. Bring the ritual to its conclusion.

SPELL

A Swyn to Glean Poetic Inspiration from the Cauldron of Awen

There are times when we do not always feel particularly inspired or we struggle to create rituals, invocations, or prayers. One might need to perform ritual in public or be called to write an invocation. Whenever you are struggling to create something inspired in the form of words, then take to this simple ceremony. The words used therein are ancient; recall my previous discussion on the power of words and of moving into the narrative spirit. The beauty of this particular spell is its ability to tap into the enchanted and prophetic spirit as well.

For this spell, you will need:

- your Cerridwen cauldron (make sure it is watertight)
- a small candle of any colour that pleases you
- matches
- a small jug of water

Create and delineate your chosen space as sacred in a manner by which you are accustomed. Take three deep breaths, one with the land beneath you, one with the sky above you, and one with the seas that surround you. Call to Cerridwen to assist you, and imagine a glowing light upon your forehead.

With your cauldron in the centre of your space, light the candle and position it to the right of your cauldron. Take the jug of water and fill the cauldron until three-quarters full. If you are able to collect the water from a source other than your kitchen, then do so, being mindful and in the moment. Focus on your breath, in and out, and continue to imagine your brow glowing. Gaze into the cauldron in this manner for several minutes.

Now take your dominant hand's index finger and swirl it in the water, creating a small vortex within. Next take the candle and purposefully drip the melting wax onto the water's spiralling surface. Look at the patterns of wax that form, and glean any meaning from the shapes that may explain your need, desire, or the reason why you might feel blocked or uninspired.

Begin to chant "Gair fy ngair o'r pair yn perthyn," pronounced GUY-rh VU NG-aeer OH'rr PIE-rh UN PAIR-thin. If you prefer to say it in English, or perhaps in both languages, "Word of my word, kin of the cauldron rise."

As you chant, begin to stir the water once more with your dominant index finger and maintain as much as possible the glowing light on your brow. Lose yourself in the sound of the chant; its internal rhyming structure is impeccably created in the original language. Trust the words and sing them.

Chant for as long as you are able. When the time feels right, stop chanting and sit in silence for some minutes.

Conclude the spell by offering thanks to the ancestors for their words, to Cerridwen, and then close your space by the manner that you are accustomed to doing.

A Swyn for Clarity

This winnowing spell will help you to filter truths from untruths, fact from fiction, or any other issue that you may require clarity for. Use this particular spell when you are unsure of what course of action you should take, or to deduce or determine if a situation is right for you. In essence, this is an act of divination. Use whatever divination system you are most comfortable or familiar with.

In my own practises, I am partial to using the tarot. With my cauldron in a central position within my chosen space, I shuffle and remove two cards and place one on the left of the cauldron and one on the right. The card on the left represents the matter at hand and its underlying energies that you may not be conscious of. The card on the right represents the answer to the question.

In the bardic material we are told that there are a number of *gogyrwens* in the Awen, those who sieve for the truth. This stanza connects to the principle action of the gogyrwen, but in this case, you will be acting as the gogyrwen, winnowing for clarity.

Create and delineate your chosen space as sacred in a manner by which you are accustomed. Take three deep breaths, one with the land beneath you, one with the sky above you, and one with the seas that surround you. Call to Cerridwen to assist you, and imagine a glowing light upon your forehead.

Position your cards or other divination tool on either side of your cauldron. Bring to mind the issue at hand. Hold both your hands, palms downwards, above the cauldron. Imagine your brow beginning to glow brightly, and sing:

Seith ugein ogyrwen a sydd yn yr Awen.
(phonetic) *SIGH-th IG-ain OGRE-wen AH SEETH un Uhrr Awen.*
There are seven-score gogyrwens in the Awen.

The trick is to maintain your grasp on the song, the glowing light on your brow, and the question at hand. Keep singing for as long as you can or until at least seven minutes have passed, after which you then reveal the card or divination device on the left, followed by the right.

Record the session in your journal, and close your space in your usual manner.

Daily Awen Affirmation

Consistency is key to effective affirmations. Brushing your teeth once does nothing for your oral hygiene, but brushing twice a day every day maintains their well-being. Going for a run once a month will do nothing for your fitness, but a thirty-minute jog every day will result in transformation. The same can be said for spiritual practises: the more consistent we are, the better the results.

I perform this simple affirmation every morning at my personal Cerridwen altar. Regardless of whether I am spending the day writing or in my ordinary job, I find this affirmation useful. I perform this simple spell in the time it takes my kettle to boil for my morning coffee; in turn it has become routine. It helps ground me in Awen and keeps me mindful throughout the day that I can be inspired and be inspirational. You will be familiar with this verse from an earlier exercise with the Awen. The verse can be used in a multiple of manners. In the public rituals of the Anglesey Druid Order, this verse is used within our ritual liturgy to instil the proceedings with Awen.

Take three deep breaths, one with the land beneath you, one with the sky above you, and one with the seas that surround you. Call to Cerridwen to assist you, and imagine a glowing light upon your forehead. At your altar, shrine, or space devoted to Cerridwen and her mysteries, hold your hands over your cauldron and sing the following either in Welsh, English, or in both:

Yr Awen a ganaf,

O dwfyn ys dygaf.

(phonetic) *Urr AH-wen Ah GAN-av,*

Awe DOO-vun Ur DUG-av.

The Awen I sing, from the deep I bring it.

Chant the stanza in multiples of three until you feel centred and can clearly imagine your brow glowing brightly. At which point, I stop, take a further three deep breaths with land and sea and sky, and then go about my business.

DEVOTIONAL

Daily Devotional to Cerridwen

My altar is a constant reminder of the gifts of Cerridwen, and it is at this space that I call to her daily to instil within me her nourishing gifts and remind me of her constant presence in my life. I recite the stanza below as I light candles in her honour and leave whatever offerings I have selected for that day. More often than not, the physical offerings I leave take the form of incense, but energetically the verse itself, sung, also acts as an offering. Rhyming verse is traditionally used when working with Cerridwen, but recall the function and magic of bardism from my earlier discourse, and the fact that a verse is essentially a song. Now, one can either recite this in plain speech in a mantra-like fashion or you can be creative and add harmony and rhythm to it. I tend to use both techniques and find that what harmony I select within the moment often reflects my mood and state of mind. The words are consistent, but the harmony and rhythm are not, and I believe that this in itself builds relationship with Cerridwen. I am not always stable and happy and content, and it is important to me that my relationship with Cerridwen should reflect that. The tone I use tells her what is happening in my life and how I am feeling. This is one of the few verses that I use in the English language in my own daily practise.

Recall the images and emotions from the introductory ritual in the first part of this book where you met Cerridwen at Lake Bala, and keep expanding on these. That particular ritual should work in addition to this daily devotional, where you constantly work on the inner planes to strengthen your relationship with Cerridwen.

At my altar I take my usual three breaths with land and sea and sky, and whilst focusing my gaze on the cauldron and the image of Cerridwen in mind, I sing the following englyn:

Come now, Mother Divine,
Guard now this cauldron mine,
Make now my world all thine,
Awen's light within me shine.

I do not limit the time taken to perform this devotional. It is important for me to be fully in the moment, present and aware. I allow the quality of sound to be dictated by my mind and body, which further enhance the sense of being fully present.

Once the song has concluded naturally, I finish with a prayer that I shared in the opening pages of this book:

O Cerridwen,
Duwies yr Awen,
Ceidwad y Pair,
Rho dy Awenyddiaeth
A'r fy siwrne
Ac ar fy ngwaith.[217]

O Cerridwen,
Goddess of Awen,
Keeper of the Cauldron,
Bless me with the light of Awen
On my journey
And on my work.

---

217 Search YouTube for my channel—Kristoffer Hughes—for sound files of all Welsh entries in this book.

The Power of Three

The Awen initiates the transference of Celtic wisdom in a tripartite manner. The conception of the rays lent themselves beautifully to triadic wisdom. In modern-day Welsh Druidry, the three rays represent the qualities of:

Cariad—Gwybodaeth—Gwirionedd

Love—Knowledge—Truth

Triads allow one to remember and recall various teachings and philosophies in a manner that can be easily assimilated by the human mind. The Y Nod Cyfrin symbol can be utilised to chart and map the qualities of your Awen by contemplating and considering the nature of one's seeds in relation to the above triad and the manner by which they are expressed. This exercise can be ritualised, if need be, and performed alone or as an aspect of a group activity or ceremony.

It calls for those present to contemplate the symbol of the Y Nod Cyfrin for several minutes, by gazing intently at the symbol below:

The rays and drops of Awen are positioned within a circle to represent the cauldron itself.

Consider:

First Drop—Define love; what does it mean to you?
Second Drop—What is the foundation of your knowledge?
Third Drop—What is the primary truth of your life?

The drops act as the seeds, the foundations of your Awen's expression. They are nurtured by your life and living and have the potential to radiate as the glowing rays of Awen. Now consider them one by one as the seeds germinate and grow:

First Ray—How does your perception of love present itself into the world? What function and quality does it take? How does it impact?

Second Ray—What is it that you do best? What are your primary skills that arise from a platform of knowledge and experience? How does it express itself and what quality does it take? How does that impact your world and those within it?

Third Ray—To know truth, to love truth, and to maintain truths are perhaps the most difficult of tasks. Your truths might not be the truths of others. How do you express your perception of truth through your living and into the world?

From the above exercise, condense those qualities down to a triad that expresses the song of your life. For example:

> The three gifts of my life are to love myself as much as I love others, to know the limitations of my abilities, and to speak my truth with integrity, even if that truth is unpopular.

Retain the triad, for it will capture a moment in time. A million circumstances go into the making of one situation. In a month's time or a year, the qualities will have changed. This is a good exercise to stop and evaluate the quality of the things that drive us.

The Cauldrons of Land, Sea, and Sky

What follows is a short discourse to enable you to contemplate and digest the information contained within this book. Contemplating the themes that follow summarises the contents of this book, whilst the ritual function of this contemplative exercise feeds your primary cauldron, moving the information from this book into your experience of Cerridwen. For this exercise, you will need your cauldron, placed on a flat surface, and three smaller cauldrons or vessels that will hold a tealight candle. Place a candle in each vessel and postion in front of your cauldron thus:

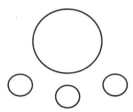

In addition, you will need three incense cones of your choosing. Assume that the small vessel on the right represents the cauldron in the realm of land, the central one the realm of sea, and the left one the realm of sky. Take to sitting comfortably, and if you so wish, delineate the space as sacred in the manner by which you are accustomed.

Approaching the Cauldron in the Realm of Land

Light the candle in the cauldron of land and contemplate the following. A sigil is offered to you at the conclusion of each realm to enable you to capture the essence of this discourse.

The cauldron in the realm of land contains the potential for inspiration and also defines the quality of that inspiration. This is Awen in its formative stages. It is the very idea of Awen as it takes shape and form in the apparent world. Here we see the trials, efforts, tribulations, and achievements of humankind in this world. Whilst deliciously connected to the other two realms, this is the realm that we are most in touch with, and whether justifiably or otherwise, it is the one that we place the greatest significance upon.

Throughout this book we have seen how the ancient bardic tradition of Wales moved steadily from Celtic Britain to a Celto-Romano society. They persisted through the decline of the common Brittonic languages and into the early development and evolution of what was to become the Welsh language. The cauldron boiled, its steam rose into the air, times changed, and the bardic tradition found its feet and moved through four significant ages to the present. There is a message of consistency here, and sustainability of practise and tradition—traits that we may see in our own lives, our own families, and our spiritual development and progression. Knowing where we came from, where our traditions came from, and venerating them is an important aspect of orthopraxy.

Whilst the cauldron in the realm of land is full of potential, it also contains the potential for all things—not all is love and light, not in the worldly affairs of humankind. The cauldron is potentially hazardous, and collateral damage is a real risk to those who would venture to its rim. As we saw with the dealing of bards, regardless of the work, humankind has always had the ability to justify its own shortcomings and its bigotry and self-fulfilling desires. The fire beneath the cauldron is intense; its potential is immense. The brew within its belly contains the wisdom, creative force, and knowledge of all the worlds.

The cauldron does not, however, stand in isolation. It is the product of hard work, commitment to learning, and devotion to one's craft. It represents the physical qualities that surround your work today. It is indicative of the holding attributes that give your life the shape and form you require to shine. None of us exist in a vacuum. We are a product of connectivity, and we all share in community, human and nonhuman. This deep connectivity can be utilised to serve one's hidden agendas or it can be utilised to serve the primary function of Awen—to inspire, to be inspiration, and to be inspired. But the path to inspiration is fraught with struggles and difficulties, and yet these too contribute to the quality of the material that forms the cauldron itself.

The cauldron in the realm of land symbolises the nourishing and sustaining qualities of the vessel. Without the power of Awen in the physical world, we become starved of inspiration and fall into ever-increasing traps of apathy and despondency. Without inspiration, the world dulls; its colours fade, or at least they appear thus to the eyes who fail to be the Awen in the world. Disenchantment ensues, and yet the Plant Cerridwen are the enchanters. This is our gift, to become the enchanters of the world and to fulfil nature's prime directive of being aware of itself.

Cerridwen asks you to acknowledge the suffering and sorrows of the world and to know that you cannot cure them all, but you have the ability to live with joy. Joy comes from immersion in the streams of Awen. It changes your world, and by proxy it has the potential to change the world. It is so easy to become disenchanted by the things that occur around us. We can be overwhelmed by the tribulations of the world. Cerridwen asks that you stop, take heed, and take note of the immediate world around you. Consider the actions of the old bards, who influenced their entire world by working locally and creating a web of inspiration. We can do the same. Share your Awen within your square mile, and if you have the ability to stretch beyond that mile without being overwhelmed, then do so. Inspiration is contagious; it spreads—never underestimate the power of your Awen.

The act of learning, of becoming learned and imbibed with knowledge and having the sagacity to use that knowledge in the world, sustains not only the spirit and the soul, but has a profound effect on the human body. These qualities taught to us by Cerridwen are self-perpetuating. The more one practises, the more one feels a connection, and a great sense of achievement leads us to feel good, and to feel good about our place in the world. One cannot inspire if one does not feel inspired. Whilst the materials of mystery are sustaining on many levels, we must also learn to support ourselves within our tasks, to stand in the power of our inspiration, whilst simultaneously acknowledging that we are a part of a greater whole. This is the process of transcendence.

One way of achieving this is to share another trait that is held by the cauldron of land, that of hospitality. This famed trait of the Celts is one that we continue to hold with pride in the modern world. When we give of ourselves, we ultimately give to ourselves, for we are all connected on so many levels—everybody is a winner. Share what you know, share what you do. The mysteries of the cauldron are not possessions, and they shine their brightest when we share them with others. When we share of our vulnerability, we give of our body and spirit. Cerridwen is not possessive of the mysteries and neither does she hinder one's access to the stream and currents of Awen. She in an encouraging mother and simultaneously a taskmaster. She asks that you emulate those traits to share of your Awen with integrity and good intentions.

Recall the function of the seeds. Cerridwen is the gogyrwen of various seeds, but know the mystery: an acorn may be the seed of an oak, but it only holds the *potential* for becoming that great oak; it is not a given right. A lot can happen between planting and seedling, growth and maturity. As we stand next to the cauldron of land, Cerridwen offers you a handful of seeds but asks that you become the sieve that winnows the potential from them. Each seed must undergo a winnowing of your own doing, and it is your responsibility to find the fertile ground in which to plant them. Your seeds are not matured by accident, like a bramble seed dropped from the beak of a passing bird. On the contrary, you must sustain them, nourish them, and nurture them. We do not all hold a fistful of seeds that will rise to become mighty oaks, and in the metaphysical world of Awen, size really is not everything. A humble nettle is equally as valid as a giant sequoia. If your neighbours' seeds shoot up to be gigantic trees and you have a garden of flowers, tend to your flowers; do not be dismayed by the show of another, for they are not your seeds to nurture. Cerridwen is the gogyrwen of various seeds, each one as valid as the other.

This is the message of the cauldron in the realm of land: to understand the factors in your life that support you and how you support them, to acknowledge the power of symbiosis and the quality of nourishment. It is often tempting to focus only on the spiritual, to rise above the mouth of the cauldron in the fragrant, ethereal steam, to be mysterious and enigmatic. And yet, we can neglect the material from which the cauldron is formed, for it too requires our attention. Each of your actions has a consequence.

Whatever you cast into the cauldron's belly, however transformed, will ultimately bubble to the surface.

As you consider the cauldron in the realm of land, contemplate the sigil below and the potential for inspiration in your world, and how you might bring it to life:

Light an incense cone from the flame and position the cone within the belly of your cauldron.

Approaching the Cauldron in the Realm of Sea

Light the candle in the cauldron of sea and contemplate the following:

The sea connects all things on earth, and as a metaphor its connectivity can be perceived as the vast ocean of the universe where all parts are in relationship. The cauldron in the realm of sea allows us to peer beneath what is happening on the surface and discover the nature of the bubbling processes of distillation. We are compelled by the nature of the sea to hide, contain, and give meaning to mystery. Beneath the crafting of magic, the singing of songs, and the rituals blows a force and a power that compels us and intrigues us. More and more deep thinkers are rising to the challenges that modern Paganism faces to explore the nature of what we do, why we do it, and perhaps why it works.

Faith is not a requirement, but knowledge and knowing is. We experience; therefore, we know. The new face of the Pagan traditions does not require one to believe in anything, but rather to move into deep relationship with the principles of our traditions and experience them. This lucidity is essential to transformation. The cauldron in the realm of sea is what we feel and inherently sense. Passing something off as genuine practise and knowledge is all very well if we can substantiate those claims, but here in the realm of sea we are permitted to utilise our occult talents and our unverified personal gnosis, so long as we make those sources clear.

It is beneath the waves of the sea that we are reminded of the magical quality inherent within modern traditions. We must not lose sight of the magical. The sea serves to remind us of the undifferentiated state of the universe and of our origin and the origins of all things. It is the place of pure emotion. In the experience of our planet, the sea is made tangible by our oceans and seascape. It ebbs and flows in the same manner as our internal emotional landscape. All the waters of the earth originate from and are given meaning by the sea, and yet the mystery within this is that they often contain shapes and forms that appear as separate existences. This illusion is seen in the many aspects of water, tears, fountains, springs, raindrops, and snowflakes. All appear as individual, yet all originated from the same source and return to it.

The vice of the realm of sea is the danger of liminality and of becoming permanently liminal. It is essential that one keeps oneself rooted in land whilst swimming in mystery. We must hold to the knowledge that whilst ethereal and magical, even the sea is constructed from particles of matter; in turn, they express the mystery of land and rise to the secrets of sky.

Consider the cauldron in the realm of sea and the function of mystery as you contemplate the sigil below:

Light an incense cone from the flame and position the cone within the belly of your cauldron.

Approaching the Cauldron in the Realm of Sky

Light the candle in the cauldron of sky and contemplate the following:

The journey into expression begins in earnest now. I have strived to provide you with a comprehensive background to where Cerridwen came from and how and why she has survived the ages. Having done this and armed with you the tools required to deepen your relationship with her, the next task is yours to take. The seeds of Awen in this book take on much of my personality and journey; they are my wish to dream a new mythology into being, one where you are a part of it. Your part in this dream is the promulgation and promotion of Cerridwen and the radiant forces of Awen—to be the inspiration that this world so eagerly needs and deserves. But for this to occur, we cannot be bound or form allegiance with one realm over another. Land will keep us grounded, the sea will transmit its teachings of deep mystery, but it is the realm of sky where we express ourselves. It is a combination of all three realms within us that move us from armchair philosophy to a platform of doing.

Strive to acknowledge and honour the other seeds of Awen that surround you, but know that it is the germination and nourishment of *your* seeds that are of utmost importance. Take time to care for your own inspiration. Do not be led to believe that another's expression is somehow better or superior to yours. Find your strengths and commit to them. Be the best that you can be in this life. Glow brightly, with integrity for what you do and why you do it. Be inspired by the efforts of others, but do not be unhinged by them or succumb to feelings of inferiority. Your role in this world is to shine your light, but know that there are people out there who will want *your* light to reflect *their* values. Pay them no heed. There are also people who thrive in the shady places where satisfaction is gleaned by dimming another person's light. Do not ever let anyone dim your light. If they accuse you of burning too brightly or not shining for the right cause, offer them some sunglasses instead. Let your Awen beam from your brow. Be defined by what you do, not by what you believe.

Only those who are inspired can inspire others; strive for inspiration. Consistency is the key to expressing the cauldron in the realm of sky. Spiritual theory, philosophy, and deep thinking are valuable traits, but without practise they are errant. It is daily and consistent practise that nurtures relationship and strengthens the bonds between yourself and the principles, archetypes, spirits, or deities that you are allied to. These are the tasks that one performs alone, in solitude, and whilst elements of them can be shared with community, their effectiveness lies in their ability to transform you.

As an author I am compelled to share the words, chants, spells, and vocalisations that I have found the most useful in my practise. This invariably limits the material to my experience. The key with the cauldron in the realm of sky is to be inspired by shared words, not enslaved to them. Cerridwen delights in the sound of rhyme and verse or recitation and song. Your best and most effective offerings will come from the edges of your own creativity. Delve deep.

The universe is constantly reaching out and experiencing itself through the myriad of expressions and experiences available to it. When the universe wants to experience inspiration, it extends itself as you, the reader. When we are the expression of Awen in the world, the world will be inspired, even if that world is limited to your immediate surroundings and those closest to you. Rise above anger and bitterness, resentment and envy. Be reliant on your own inner light to shine. Consider the above, which is captured in the essence of the sigil below:

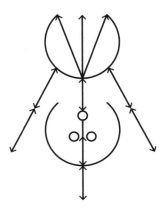

Light an incense cone from the flame and position the cone within the belly of your cauldron.

Watch as the fragrant smoke from the three cones swirls and rises from your primary cauldron. The smoke contains your potential to rise as a child of Cerridwen, radiant and inspired.

Close this exercise in a manner that you are accustomed, and allow the candles to burn out of their own accord.

Conclusion

My sincerest hope, throughout the pages of this book, is to offer you a snap-shot of Cerridwen through time and demonstrate the manner by which she was preserved and how she survived the ages. Her history is complex and fraught with crisis and inspiration; it is simultaneously the history of a people, my people, and their dreams and aspirations. This is history of the heart just as much as it is the history of a culture and its expressions. There is much that I have not been able to cover in this tome, but this work may well plough a new ground in which others will plant their seeds in her honour.

Cerridwen instils within us the necessity for Awen and the virtue of the radiant brow. There was a time when even the radiancy of Taliesin was in jeopardy. At the turn of the twentieth century, J. Gweongvryn Evans in his introductory material to *The Book of Taliesin* said the following:

> Delphi is deserted and Taliesin is jettisoned. There is no oracle left
> to consult and lecture room open that names the name of Taliesin.
> The learned who write in encyclopaedias are like the bards at the
> Court of Deganwy, who in the presence of Taliesin they become
> mute mutterers of blerwm-blerwm. This is very remarkable when
> we recall the fact that out earlier and better poets esteemed Taliesin

as their "chief," and most assuredly they were right. What, then, is the explanation of the neglect, not to say boycott, of our time?[218]

How times have changed, for just one century later, the name of Taliesin is openly discussed, and there are indeed lecture rooms and oracles that consult with him, and new works are constantly being developed to connect to these ancient wisdoms. In the latest work on the Book of Taliesin, the authors state:

> It is fitting enough that the name of Taliesin should surface again in more recent times as the persona of very diverse poets trying to understand their art, both in Wales and beyond.[219]

This and a plethora of other works reflect the need the world has for Awen—and its mother is alive and well and thriving. Her cauldron is as full as it ever was, if not overflowing.

And now she has found you.

Where there is inspiration, there is magic.

Where there is magic, there is hope.

Where there is hope, there is always a brighter future.

She is muse, she is goddess, she is witch—she is Cerridwen, *Mam yr Awen*.

Y Diwedd / The End

---

218 Evans, *Facsimile and Text of the Book of Taliesin*, i.
219 Lewis and Williams, *The Book of Taliesin*, xxxiv.

A Guide to Welsh Pronunciation

There are no silent letters in the Welsh alphabet, as every letter has a sound and is pronounced phonetically. The stress of any word almost exclusively stands on the penultimate (second to last) syllable. The sound of a vowel is elongated if it appears with a circumflex above it; in Welsh this is referred to as a "to Bach" (a little roof) and appears thus: "ô," e.g., Don without the circumflex would be pronounced as *Donn*. With the addition of a circumflex, Dôn, it would be pronounced in the same manner as the English word *dawn*.

The Modern Welsh Alphabet

a, b, c, ch, d, dd, e, f, ff, g, ng, h, i, l, ll, m, n, o, p, ph, r, rh, s, t, th, u, w, y

Welsh Vowels

A—Short as in *mat*, long as in *farmer*
E—Short as in *let*, long as in *bear*
I—Short as in *pit*, long as in *meet*
O—Short as in *lot*, long as in *lore*

U—Short as in *ill*, long as in *limb*. This is a tricky sound to mimic and sounds different between north and South Wales. In South Wales it is similar to the sound of the letter I, whilst in the north it resembles the French U and is often decribed as a sound one makes to express repulsion. This is perhaps one of the most difficult letters to articulate phonetically in written English.

W—Short as in *look*, long as in *fool*.

Y—Short as in *up*, long as in *under*, or short as the I sound in *hiss*. If present in the final word or syllable, it will sound similar to the letter U. Otherwise, it sounds like "uh."

In some instances, the letters I and W may act as consonants.

Welsh Consonants

Some may be similar in sound to their English counterparts, but with emphasis on heavy aspiration of sound.

B—as in *bin*

C—as in *cat*, never as in *cedar* (the letter K does not appear in modern Welsh but is evident in Middle Welsh; it is pronounced as "C")

Ch—as in *loch*, never as in *chin*

D—as in *dad*

DD—as in *them*, never as in *thick*

E—as in *elephant*

F—as in *van*

FF—as in *off*

G—as in *gate*, never as in *gem*

NG—as in *song*, never as in *linger*

H—as in *hit*; it is never silent

L—as in *lit*

LL—no English equivalent sound. Voice by placing the tip of the tongue in the L position and exhaling voicelessly through the sides of the mouth.

M—as in *mat*

N—as in *nit*

P—as in *part*

PH—as in *phrase*

R—trilled by the tip of the tongue, as *ravioli* in Italian

RH—no counterpart. Voice by placing the tongue in the R position and exhaling quickly and harshly but also voicelessly through the narrow gap that your lips will form.

S—as in *zap*

T—as in *tap*

TH—as in *thick*, never as in *them*

Dipthongs

Diphthongs are two letters that are pronounced as one letter, and they are as follows:

Ae, ai, au, aw, ei, eu, ew, ey, iw, oi, ou, ow, uw, wy, yw

Mutations

Welsh, in common with its other sibling Celtic languages, possesses a phenomenon known as mutations. This changes the initial letter of a word depending on the sentence structure. Spoken Welsh and written Welsh differ in the manner by which they apply mutation rules. Mutations are an intrinsic and essential component of the language and are usually the most difficult aspect to learn. The majority of native Welsh speakers may not necessarily understand the rules for mutations but can instinctively use them. Vowels are never subject to the rules of mutation.

Three different classifications of mutation exist in the Welsh language:

- soft mutation
- aspirate mutation
- nasal mutation

The various sounds can be demonstrated in this list. The presence of an em dash (—) indicates that the consonantal sound does not change.

Consonant	Soft Mutation	Aspirate Mutation	Nasal Mutation
c	g	ch	ngh
p	b	ph	mh
t	d	th	nh
g	disappears	—	ng
b	f	—	m
d	Dd	—	n
ll	l	—	—
m	f	mh	—
rh	r	—	—
n	—	nh	—

Glossary

Note that the Welsh letters ll, ch, dd, and rh remain in their current form, with no phonetic equivalent provided. Please refer to the pronunciation guide.

Adroddol (Add-ROdd-all)—the term for narrative.

Afagddu (Av-AG-thee)—Cerridwen's renamed son, meaning "utter darkness."

Andedion (An-DEAD-yon)—Gaulish term for underworld spirits or gods.

Aneirin (An-AY-reen)—early Welsh bard.

Anian (ANN-yan)—essential nature or quiddity.

Annwfn (Ann-OO-vn) also Annwn (ANN-oon)—Welsh term for the indigenous otherworld of the Welsh Celts.

Aranrhod (Ar-ANN-rhod)—goddess, daughter of the mother goddess Dôn and Beli Mawr.

Armes Prydein (ARR-mess PRUD-ain)—The Prophesy of the Island of Britain, early Welsh prophetic poem.

Awen (Ah-when)—Blessed, holy breath; the spirit of creative transformation and inspiration.

Awenydd (ion) (Ah-WHEN-idd) [yon]—a person(s) who is imbibed with Awen.

Ayrwen (AER-wen)—Celtic goddess of war and battle, tutelary deity of the modern River Dee.

Bard/Bardd (BARRED/BARR-dd)—designation for those who express the Awen by creative means.

Barddoniaeth (Barr-dd-ON-yaeth)—the practise of bardism.

Beirdd (BAY-rr-dd)—the collective noun for bard/bardd

Beli Mawr (BELL-ee MAH-oor)—ancestor deity of the British pantheon. Literally means big fire or light.

Bendigedig (Ben-DEE-ged-eeg)—something that is blessed.

Blodeuedd/Blodeuwedd (Blod-AYE-edd/Blod-AYE-wedd)—woman created from flowers in the fourth branch of the Mabinogi. Her name changes into the second form when she is transformed by magic into an owl.

Bol Croen (BOLL KRR-oyn)—literally translated as "skin belly" and synonymous with the womb, coracle, or vessel into which the newborn potential Taliesin is placed.

Brittonic (BRIT-tonic)—the predecessor to Welsh, also classified as the P Celtic group of languages.

Cadair (KAD-ayr)—A chair. Position within the bardic school and metred poetry.

Cainc (KAIN-ck)—Welsh term for branch.

Calan Gaeaf/Nos Galan Gaeaf (KAL-ann GAY-av/NOSS GAL-ann GAY-av)—The calends of winter, with the second example being the designation for All Hallows Eve.

Celfyddyd (Kel-FUDD-id)—craft.

Cerdd Dafod (KERR-dd DAV-odd)—literally means the music or song of the tongue. It is a style of poetic discipline.

Cerridwen (kerr-ID-when)—the Mother of Awen, goddess of inspiration.

Crochen (CROCH-en)—cauldron.

Cuhelyn Fardd (Kee-HELL-in VARR-dd)—an early Welsh bard.

Culhwch (KILL-who-ch)—protagonist of the Culhwch ac Olwen tale.

Cyfrin (KUV-reen)—Welsh term for mystic or mystical.

Cyfrinach (Kuv-REEN-ach)—Welsh for secret.

Cynfeirdd (KIN-VAIR-dd)—the early bards.

Cynghanedd (Kung-HAN-aedd)—a discipline of Welsh metred poetry.

Cywydd (KOW-widd)—a poem created by strict metrical composition.

Dallmor Dallme (DALL-more DALL-mare)—one of the names attributed to Morda, who also tends to Cerridwen's cauldron.

Doeth (DO-eeth)—wise.

Dofydd (DOV-idd)—a designation for one of the divisions of the divine.

Dôn (DAWN)—Welsh mother goddess.

Duw (Dew)—Welsh for the Christian concept of God.

Dwfn (DOO-vn)—unfathomably deep.

Eisteddfod (ais-TEDD-vod)—a festival of Welsh culture and bardism.

Elffin (ELF-in)—the name of the man who finds Taliesin at the salmon weir.

Englyn (ion) (ENG-lyn) [eeon]—a form of Welsh verse usually in four lines.

Goewin (GO-ween)—a maiden in whose lap the king must maintain his feet.

Gogynfeirdd (go-GEEN-vairdd)—the not-so-early bards.

Gogyrwen—*see* Ogyrfen.

Goidelic (GOY-delik)—the language group of the Q Celts.

Gorsedd (GORE-sedd)—a seat or collective noun for bards.

Govannon (GOVANN-on)—smith god of the fourth branch of the Mabinogi and son of Dôn.

Gwiddon/Widdon (GWEE-ddon/WEE-ddon)—an early designation for a monstrous female and a sorcerer.

Gwion Bach (GWEE-on BA-ch)—the main protagonist and metaphor for the student of the Celtic mysteries.

Gwrach (GOO-rach)—a repulsive and repugnant thing. Later, a common word for witch.

Gwyddoniaeth (gwee-THON-eeayth)—the modern word for science.

Gwydion (GWID-eeon)—magican of the fourth branch of the Mabinogi and frequently named in the Book of Taliesin.

Gwyn ap Nudd (GWIN ap NEE-dd)—a Celtic deity and king of Annwfn.

Hen (HÊN) [with emphasis on the "e" sound]—the Welsh term for old or ancient.

Hendregadredd (henday-GAD-redd)—a collection of manuscripts located at the National Library of Wales.

Hengerdd (hên-GER-dd)—the old songs.

Henwen (HEN-when)—the name of a sacred hwch in the Triads of the Island of Britain.

Hiraeth (HEER-ayth)—a longing for Wales that only a Welsh person can feel.

Hwch (WHO-ch)—a sacred porcine.

Hwch Ddu Gwta (WHO-ch thee GOO-ta)—the tailless black sow of Welsh Hallowe'en customs.

Lleu Llaw Gyffes (LL-ay LL-aw GUFF-ess)—abandoned son of Aranrhod, central figure in the fourth branch of the Mabinogi. His name means "fair-haired one with the skillful hand."

Llyn Tegid (LL-in TEG-id)—the name of the lake reputed to be the legendary home of Cerridwen and her family.

Llŷr (LL-ir)—Welsh god of the sea.

Llywarch Hen (LLOW-arch Hen)—ancient Welsh bard.

Mabinogi (mab-INN-ogee)—small tales or tales of youth. The collective name given to a series of native Welsh myths.

Maelgwn (MAYL-goon)—a North Wales chieftain in the time of the tale of Taliesin.

Mam (MAM)—Welsh word for mother.

Marwnad (marr-OON-ad)—a eulogy death song.

Math (MATH)—Druid king of the fourth branch of the Mabinogi.

Menw (MEN-oo)—from *The Barddas of Iolo Morganwg*, Menw is the first to see the rays of the Awen.

Menwyd (MEN-wid)—the parent of Menw.

Mochyn/Moch (MOCH-in/MO-ch)—Welsh for pig/pigs.

Modron (MOD-ron)—Welsh mother goddess.

Morda (MORE-da)—the usual name for the blind man employed to stoke the fire beneath Cerridwen's cauldron.

Morfran (MORE-vran)—the son of Cerridwen and Tegid Foel.

Nantlleu (NANT-llay)—a region in the Snowdonia National Park famed for its associations with Lleu Llaw Gyffes.

Ogyrfen/gogyrwen (OGR-ven/GOGRE-when)—the personification of the system of bardic sieving and winnowing. When subject to mutation, the initial G is dropped.

Olwen (ALL-when)—the subject of Culhwch's affection in the tale of Culhwch ac Olwen.

Palug (PAL-ig)—a legendary cat that brought about the downfall of the Isle of Anglesey.

Peniarth (PEN-eearth)—a collection of manuscripts held at the National Library of Wales.

Penllyn (PEN-lleen)—a region to the west of Snowdonia.

Pheryllt (FAIR-eelltt)—legendary magicians whom Cerridwen consulted to brew the Awen.

Plant (PLANT)—Welsh word for children.

Preiddeu (PRAY-they)—spoils.

Prifardd (PREE-vardd)—designation for Chief Bard.

Proffwydol (PROFF-wee-dole)—a term meaning prophesy and prophetic.

Pryderi (PRUD-air-ee)—the son of Pwyll and Rhiannon.

Pwyll (PWEE-ll)—the main character of the first branch of the Mabinogi; consort of Rhiannon.

Rhiannon (rhee-ANN-on)—Welsh goddess of sovereignty.

Rhith (RHEE-th)—the ordinary shape and form of something.

Swyn (ZOO-in)—Welsh word for spell, charm, magic, enchantment, witchcraft.

Swyn-Wraig (ZOO-in OO-raig)—the designation for a female practitioner of swyn.

Swyngyfaredd (zooin-GUV-aredd)—the practise of swyn.

Swynol (ZOO-eenall)—pertaining to swyn.

Swynwr (ZOO-in-oorr)—the designation for a male practitioner of swyn.

Talhaearn Tad Awen (tal-HAYAR-nnh TAD AH-when)—one of the earliest named bards of the sixth century and a contemporary of the historical Taliesin.

Taliesin (tal-YES-inn)—a portmanteau meaning one with a radiant brow.

Taw (TAO)—Welsh for peace and silence.

Tegid Foel (TEG-id VO-yal)—Cerridwen's consort.

Twrch Trwyth (TOOR-ch TRUE-ith)—a sacred porcine in the tale of Culhwch ac Olwen.

Uchelwyr (eech-ELL-weer)—the bards of the nobility.

Y Bala (UH BAL-ah)—the town in North Wales that is associated with Cerridwen and her family.

Y Nod Cyfrin (UH NOD KYV-reen)—a term for the symbol of the three rays, meaning the mystic mark.

Resources

Online version of *Geiriadur Prifysgol Cymru* (*Dictionary of the Welsh Language*):

www.welsh-dictionary.ac.uk

Anglesey Druid Order: Rekindling the ancient seat of learning. Welsh Druidry mystery school and initiatory order. Details of in-person and online training can be found at:

www.angleseydruidorder.co.uk

For sound files of rituals and a glossary of words, visit:

www.youtube.com (search for the Kristoffer Hughes channel)

Bibliography

Manuscripts Consulted

All manuscripts, unless noted, are held at the National Library of Wales and can be viewed digitally on their website:

https://www.library.wales/discover/digital-gallery/manuscripts/

NLW MS 5276D. Chronicle of the History of the World. Elis Gruffudd. Circa 1552.

Peniarth Manuscript 111. Hanes Taliesin. John Jones. 1607.

Peniarth Manuscript 2. Designated the title Llyfr Taliesin (Book of Taliesin). First half of the fourteenth century.

Peniarth MS 1. Designated the title Llyfr Du Caerfyrddin (Black Book of Carmarthen). Circa 1250.

NLW MS 6680B. Designated the title Hendregadredd Manuscript. Circa 1282.

Peniarth MS 4. Designated the title Llyfr Gwyn Rhydderch (The White Book of Rhydderch). Circa mid-fourteenth century.

Jesus College MS 111. Designated the title Llyfr Coch Hergest (The Red Book of Hergest). Circa 1382. Held at the Bodleian Library, Oxford. Digital manuscript available at https://medieval.bodleian.ox.ac.uk/catalog /manuscript_10635.

Secondary Sources

Aldhouse-Green, Miranda. *Caesar's Druids: Story of an Ancient Priesthood*. New Haven: Yale University Press, 2010.

Aldhouse-Green, Miranda, and Ray Howell. *Celtic Wales*. Cardiff: University of Wales Press, 2017.

Ap Dafydd, Myrddin. *Clywed* Cynghanedd—*Cwrs Cerdd Dafod*. Llanrwst: Gwasg Carreg Gwalch, 2003.

Bevan, Gareth, and Patrick Donovan, eds. *Geiriadur Prifysgol Cymru (A Dictionary of the Welsh Language)*. Cardiff: University of Wales Press, 2004.

Boyd, Matthieu, ed. and trans. *The Four Branches of the Mabinogi*. Ontario: Broadview Press, 2017.

Bromwich, Rachel, ed. *Culhwch ac Olwen*. Caerdydd: Gwasg Prifysgol Cymru, 1997.

———, ed. *Trioedd Ynys Prydein—The Triads of the Island of Britain*. Cardiff: University of Wales Press, 2006.

Bromwich, Rachel, Idris Foster, and R. Brinley-Jones, eds. *Astudiaethau ar yr Hengerdd*. Cardiff: University of Wales Press, 1978.

Bromwich, Rachel, and Ifor Williams. *The Beginnings of Welsh Poetry*. Cardiff: University of Wales Press, 1980.

Bryant-Quinn, Paul M., ed. *Apocryffa Siôn Cent*. Aberystwyth: Ganolfan Uwchefrydiau Cymreig a Cheltaidd Prifysgol Cymru, 2004.

Caerwyn Williams, J. E. "Gildas, Maelgwn, and the Bards," *Welsh Society and Nationhood: Historical Essays Presented to Glanmor Williams*. Cardiff: University of Wales Press, 1984.

———. *Poets of the Welsh Princes*. Cardiff: University of Wales Press, 1994.

Caerwyn Williams, J. E., and R. Geraint Gruffydd, eds. *Bardos: Penodau ar y Traddodiad Barddol Cymreig a Cheltaidd*. Cardiff: University of Wales Press, 1982.

Caerwyn-Williams, J. E., and Ifor Williams. *The Poems of Taliesin*. Dublin: Dublin Institute for Advanced Studies, 1968.

Cambrensis, Giraldus. *The Journey through Wales and the Description of Wales*. New York: Penguin, 1978.

Charnell-White, Cathryn. *Bardic Circles: National, Regional and Personal Identity in the Bardic Vision of Iolo Morganwg*. Cardiff: University of Wales Press, 2007.

Clancy, Joseph P., ed. *Medieval Welsh Poems*. Dublin: Four Courts, 2003.

Collis, John. "The Origin and Spread of the Celts." *Studia Celtica XXX* (1996):17–34.

Conran, Anthony, trans. *Welsh Verse*. Bridgend: Seren, 2017.

Constantine, Mary-Ann. *The Truth Against the World: Iolo Morganwg and Romantic Forgery*. Cardiff: University of Wales Press, 2007.

Daniel, R. Iestyn, ed. *Gwaith Casnodyn*. Aberystwyth: Ganolfan Uwchefrydiau Cymreig a Cheltaidd Prifysgol Cymru, 1999.

Daniel, R. Iestyn, with Marged Haycock, Dafydd Johnstone, and Jenny Rowland, eds. *Cyfoeth y Testun, Ysgrifau ar lenyddiaeth Gymraeg yr Oesoedd Canol*. Caerdydd: Gwasg Prifysgol Cymru, 2003.

Davies, Edward. *The Mythology and Rites of the British Druids*. London: J. Booth, 1809.

Davies, Janet. *The Welsh Language*. Cardiff: University of Wales Press, 2014.

Davies, Sioned. *The Mabinogion*. Oxford: Oxford University Press, 2007.

Edwards, Hywel Teifi. *The Eisteddfod*. Cardiff: University of Wales Press, 2016.

Edwards, Owen Morgan. *Gwaith Siôn Cent*. Llanuwchllyn: Ab Owen, 1914.

Evans, J. Gwenogvryn, ed. *The Facsimile of the Black Book of Carmarthen*. Oxford: private, 1888.

Evans, J. Gwenogvryn. *The Facsimile and Text of the Book of Taliesin*. Llanbedrog: Evans, 1910.

Farley, Julia, and Fraser Hunter. *Celts: Art and Identity*. London: The British Museum Press, 2015.

Farrar, Janet, and Stewart Farrar. *The Witches' Goddess*. London: Robert Hale, 1987.

Ford, Patrick K. *The Mabinogi and Other Medieval Welsh Tales*. Los Angeles: University of California Press, 1977.

———. "On the Significance of Some Arthurian Names in Welsh." *Bulletin of the Board of Celtic Studies* 30 (1983):268–273.

———. *Ystoria Taliesin*. Cardiff: University of Wales Press, 1992.

Gass, Robert. *Chanting: Discovering Spirit in Sound*. New York: Broadway Books, 1999.

Geoffrey of Monmouth. *The History of the Kings of Britain*. London: Penguin Classics, 1966.

———. *The Life of Merlin: Vita Merlini*. Marston Gate: Forgotten Books, 2008.

Graves, Robert. *The White Goddess: A Historical Grammar of Poetic Myth*. London: Faber & Faber, 1952.

Gruffydd, Geraint R. "A Poem in Praise of Cuhelyn Fardd from the Black Book of Carmarthen." *Studia Celtica X/XI* (1975–76):199.

Gruffydd, William John. *The Mabinogion*. London: Honourable Society of Cymmrodorion, 1913.

Haeussler, Ralph, and Anthony King, eds. *Celtic Religions in the Roman Period: Personal, Local and Global*. Aberystwyth: Celtic Studies Publications, 2017.

Hamp, Eric. "Celtic Banuo." *Bulletin of the Board of Celtic Studies* 27 (1993).

———. *Mabinogi: Transactions of the Honourable Society of Cymmrodorion 1975*. London: Honourable Society of Cymmrodorion, 1975.

———. "Varia II." *Eriu* 29 (1978).

Haycock, Marged. "Preiddeu Annwn and the Figure of Taliesin." *Studia Celtica XVIII/XIX* (1983/84):52–78.

Haycock, Marged, ed. and trans. *Legendary Poems from the Book of Taliesin*. Aberystwyth: CMCS, 2007.

Haycock, Marged, ed. and trans. *Prophecies from the Book of Taliesin*. Aberystwyth: CMCS, 2013.

Hopwood, Mererid. *Singing in Chains: Listening to Welsh Verse*. LLandysyl: Gwasg Gomer, 2016.

Hughes, Ian. *Math Uab Mathonwy*. Dublin: Dublin Institute for Advanced Studies, 2013.

Hughes, Kristoffer. *From the Cauldron Born: Exploring the Magic of Welsh Legend and Lore*. Woodbury: Llewellyn Publications, 2012.

Hutton, Ronald. *Blood and Mistletoe: The History of the Druids in Britain*. New Haven: Yale University Press: 2009.

———. *The Druids*. London: Hambledon Continuum, 2007.

———. *Pagan Britain*. New Haven: Yale University Press, 2013.

————. *The Stations of the Sun: A History of the Ritual Year in Britain.* Oxford: Oxford University Press, 1996.

————. *The Witch: A History of Fear from Ancient Times to the Present.* New Haven: Yale University Press, 2018.

Ifans, Dafydd, and Rhiannon Ifans. *Y Mabinogion.* Llandysul: Gwasg Gomer, 1980.

Jackstone, Hurlston Kenneth. *The International Popular Tale and Early Welsh Tradition.* Cardiff: University of Wales Press, 1961.

James, David Emrys. *Beirdd y Babell/Y Gyfrol Gyntaf.* Wrexham: Hughes a'I Fab, 1939.

Jarman, A. O. H. *The Cynfeirdd: Early Welsh Poets and Poetry.* Cardiff: University of Wales Press, 1981.

Jarman, A. O. H., ed. and trans. *Llyfr Du Caerfyrddin.* Caerdydd: Gwas Prifysgol Cymru, 1982.

Jenkins, Geraint H. *A Rattleskull Genuis: The Many Faces of Iolo Morganwg.* Cardiff: University of Wales Press, 2009.

————. *Y Digymar Iolo Morganwg.* Talybont: Y Lolfa, 2018.

Johnston, D. R., ed. *Gwaith Iolo Goch.* Cardiff: University of Wales Press, 1988.

Jones, Elin M., and Nerys Ann Jones. *Gwaith Llywarch ap Llywelyn "Prydydd y Moch."* Cardiff: University of Wales Press, 1991.

Jones, J. *Llên Gwerin Sir Gaernarfon.* Caernarfon: Cwmni y Cyhoeddwyr Cymreig, 1908.

Jones, Mair. *The Bard Is a Very Singular Character.* Cardiff: University of Wales Press, 2010.

Jones, Nerys Ann, and Ann Parry Owen, eds. *Gwaith Cynddelw Brydydd Mawr.* 2 vols. Cardiff: University of Wales Press, 1991–1995.

Jones, Thomas Gwynn. *Welsh Folklore and Folk-Custom.* Cambridge: Rowman and Littlefield, 1979.

Koch, John T., ed. *Celtic Culture: A Historical Encyclopaedia.* 5 vols. Santa Barbara: ABC-CLIO, 2006.

Koch, John T., ed. *The Celtic Heroic Age: Literary Sources for Ancient Celtic Europe and Early Ireland and Wales.* Aberystwyth: Celtic Studies Publications, 2003.

Lewis, Gwyneth, and Rowan Williams, trans. *The Book of Taliesin: Poems of Warfare and Praise in an Enchanted Britain.* London: Penguin Classics, 2019.

Lloyd, Idwal D. *Celtic Word Craft and Introduction to Welsh Poetic Art*. Redruth: Dyllansow Truran, 1985.

Loffler, Marion. *The Literary and Historical Legacy of Iolo Morganwg 1826–1926*. Cardiff: University of Wales Press, 2007.

Lynch, Frances. *Prehistoric Anglesey*. Llangefni: The Anglesey Antiquarian Society, 1970.

MacCulloch, J. A. *The Religion of the Ancient Celts*. Edinburgh: T&T Clark, 1911.

Matonis, A. T. E., and Daniel F. Melia, eds. *Celtic Language, Celtic Culture: A Festschrift for Eric P. Hamp*. Van Nuys: Ford and Bailie, 1990.

Mees, Bernard, and Nick Nicholas. "Greek Curses and the Celtic Underworld." *Studia Celtica XLVI* (2012):23–38.

Megaw, Ruth, and Vincent Megaw. "Do the Ancient Celts Still Live?" *Studia Celtica XXXI* (1997):107–123.

Middleton, William, and G. J. Williams. *Barddoniaeth neu Brydyddiaeth*. Cardiff: University of Wales Press, 1930.

Miles, Dilwyn. *The Secret of the Bards of the Isle of Britain*. Llandybie: Gwasg Dinefwr Press, 1992.

Môn, Lewys. *Gwaith Lewys Môn*. Cardiff: University of Wales Press, 1975.

Morgan-Edwards, Owen, ed. *Gwaith Siôn Cent*. Llanuwchllyn: Ab Owen, 1914.

Morgan, Morien O. *The Mabin of the Mabinogion*. London: Whittaker & Co., 1900.

Morris-Jones, John. *Cerdd Dafod: Sef Celfyddyd Barddoniaeth Cymru*. Cardiff: University of Wales Press.

———. "Taliesin." *Y Cymmrodor: The Magazine of the Honourable Society of Cymmrodorion* 28 (London, 1918).

Morus-Baird, Gwilym. *Understanding Welsh Myths, Book 1*. Welsh mythology. com. 2016.

Myrddin-Fardd, John Jones. *Llên Gwerin Sir Gaernarfon*. Caernarfon: Cwmni y Cyhoeddwyr Cymreig, 1908.

Nichols, Ross. *The Book of Druidry*. London: Thorsons, 1992.

Owen, Trefor M. *The Customs and Traditions of Wales*. Cardiff: University of Wales Press, 2016.

Parker, Will. *The Four Branches of the Mabinogi*. California: Bardic Press, 2005.

Parry, John Jay. *The Life of Merlin, Vita Merlini*. Marston Gate: Forgotten Books, 2008.

Radin, Dean. *Real Magic*. New York: Harmony Books, 2018.

Roberts, Ellis W. *To the Mystic Mark: Y Nod Cyfrin*. Scranton, PA: Byron Books, 1979.

Sheldrake, Rupert. *Ways to Go Beyond and Why They Work*. London: Coronet, 2019.

———. *Science and Spiritual Practises*. London: Coronet, 2017.

Skene, W. F. *The Four Ancient Books of Wales*. Edinburgh: Edmonston and Douglas, 1869.

Suggett, Richard. *A History of Magic and Witchcraft in Wales*. Stroud: The History Press, 2008.

———. *Welsh Witches: Narratives of Witchcraft and Magic from Sixteenth and Seventeenth Century Wales*. Atramentous Press, 2018.

Sullivan, C. W. III, ed. *The Mabinogi: A Book of Essays*. Abingdon: Garland Publishing, 1996.

Taylor, Timothy. *The Buried Soul: How Humans Invented Death*. London: Fourth Estate, 2003.

Telyndru, Jhenah. *Avalon Within*. Woodbury, Llewellyn Publications, 2005.

———. *Rhiannon: Divine Queen of the Celtic Britons*. Winchester: Moon Books, 2018.

Thomas, Gwyn. *Y Traddodiad Barddol*. Cardiff: University of Wales Press, 2012.

Thompson, Stith. *Motif-Index of Folk Literature: A Classification of Narrative Elements in Folktales, Ballads, Fables, Mediaeval Romances, Exempla, Fabliaux, Jest-Books, and Local Legends*. Copenhagen: Rosenkilde and Bagger, 1955–58.

Turner, Sharon. *A History of the Anglo-Saxons*. Charleston: Nabu Press, 2011.

Valiente, Doreen. *An ABC of Witchcraft*. London: Robert Hale, 1973.

Wall, Martin. *The Magical History of Britain*. Stroud: Amberley, 2019.

Williams, Dafydd Wyn. *Traddodiad Barddol Môn 1400–1724 Braslun*. LLandysyl: Gwasg Gomer, 2017.

Williams, Edward. *Poems Lyric and Pastoral*. 2 vols. London: J. Nichols, 1794.

Williams, Glanmor, ed. *Welsh Society and Nationhood*. Cardiff: University of Wales Press, 1984.

Williams, Gwyn. *An Introduction to Welsh Poetry: From the Beginnings to the Sixteenth Century.* London: Faber & Faber, 1953.

Williams, Ifor. *Armes Prydein o Lyfr Taliesin.* Cardiff: University of Wales Press, 1955.

———. *The Beginnings of Welsh Poetry.* Edited by Rachel Bromwich. Cardiff: University of Wales Press. 1980.

———. *Chwedl Taliesin.* Caerdydd: Gwasg Prifysgol Cymru, 1957.

———. *Pedeir Keinc y Mabinogi.* Caerdydd: Gwasg Prifysgol Cymru, 1978.

Williams, John (Ab Ithel), ed. *The Barddas of Iolo Morganwg.* Boston: Weiser, 2004.

Wohlleben, Peter. *The Hidden Life of Trees.* London: William Collins, 2017.

Zakroff, Laura Tempest. *Sigil Witchery.* Woodbury: Llewellyn Publications, 2018.

Index